MANAGING
AFRICAN
PORTUGAL

MANAGING AFRICAN PORTUGAL

The Citizen-Migrant Distinction

Kesha Fikes

Duke University Press   Durham and London   2009

© 2009 Duke University Press

All rights reserved.

Printed in the United States of America on
acid-free paper ∞

Designed by Heather Hensley

Typeset in Arno Pro by Keystone Typesetting, Inc.

Library of Congress Cataloging-in-Publication
Data appear on the last printed page of this book.

for Brenda

CONTENTS

PREFACE

This book is about the tensions that underscore what are otherwise felt as mundane encounters, looking specifically at experiences of belonging and exclusion in Portugal from the mid-1990s through the early 2000s. I consider why the conditions of Portugal's accession to the European Economic Community (EEC) in 1986 and its economic integration into the European Union (EU) in 1996 fundamentally changed the daily encounter between African migrants and Portuguese citizens. Where this encounter once revolved around the legacy of the colonial past, by the end of the century the organizing tension had shifted to a new concept of citizenship that was associated with requirements for EU membership. Accordingly, the process of accession and economic integration involved new forms of social regulation that mutually altered how citizens and migrants experienced their historic "likeness" and "difference."

Portugal had five colonies in Africa—Angola, Mozambique, São Tomé and Príncipe, Guinea-Bissau, and Cape Verde—that it maintained through the early to mid-1970s. Colonial subjects in the first four were *indígenas*, or indigenous subjects, while Cape Verdeans legally held the status of Portuguese citizen. These legal differences were connected to differing labor regimes: indígenas were required by law to work under contract (through 1959), while Cape Verdeans *in theory* bore the legal right to work for themselves. The focus of this book is on Cape Verdeans, yet in the latter chapters their historic distinctiveness becomes blurry, insignificant even, as they come to occupy the same migrant status as those once legally categorized as indígenas in former Portuguese Africa.

My initial objectives were not to study shifts in perceptions and labels applied to Cape Verdeans, as will soon become clear. But my focus on this community and its legal "losses" became an opportunity to question the shifting contours in the meaning of Portuguese citizenship over the latter half of the twentieth century. Attention to Cape Verdeans and their changing association with Africanity in the Portuguese national imagination—especially when in proximity of the metropole—is an opportunity to question not only ideas about the occupation of migrant status, but also what it means to already be a citizen.

Beginning in the late 1950s, men from Cape Verde were recruited for work in Portugal in the areas of mining, public works, carpentry, and hotel service. At the time, Cape Verdean workers were supposedly selected because they were the only citizens in the Portuguese African colonies and because they were typed as racially and culturally closer to the Portuguese than workers from the other colonies, (things rendering them the better choice for work in the metropole). Yet Cape Verdeans had already been emigrating before this period (see Carreira 1977a; Meintel 1984; Halter 1993; dos Anjos 2002; Fernandes 2002). Cape Verde receives little to no rainfall and was plagued by cyclic famines throughout the first half of the twentieth century. The colonial administration managed drought and starvation through regulated emigrations to locations across the globe, locations that also received working-poor Portuguese nationals from continental Portugal, the Azores, and Madeira. These destinations included Africa (namely Portuguese Africa and South Africa, the latter for white citizens), Asia (Macau, East Timor, and Goa), the Americas, and northwestern Europe.

Although Cape Verdeans in theory possessed Portuguese citizenship, in practice not all were able to exercise the rights associated with it. Only select Cape Verdeans emigrated to Portuguese Africa under the status of Portuguese citizen. In such cases, they worked as colonial administrators or as entrepreneurs who generally sold Portuguese products. More commonly, large portions of the Cape Verdean population were exported as indentured labor to Portuguese Africa, to São Tomé in particular. Planters in São Tomé throughout the early to mid-twentieth century referred to Cape Verdeans as non-citizens, specifically as indígenas and *cabo-indígenas*. Thus the colonial administration's response to environmental crisis positioned Cape Verdean status as tenuous; the possession of Portuguese citizenship or indígena status *in practice* was determined by the empire's labor and administrative needs at any given moment.

Cape Verdean political identity, then, would take on its legal qualities as Cape Verdeans were distributed in space as they emigrated, as travel to each destination required different forms of documentation (see Fikes 2007). Those emigrating to Portuguese African colonies received documentation that combined the terms of their labor worth with their colonial designation—as a native of colonial Cape Verde or a citizen-administrator. And those traveling to Europe and the Americas received Portuguese passports. These migrants were no different on paper from Portuguese emigrants who also traveled west, including the continental Portuguese, Azoreans, and Madeirans; they each received the same Portuguese passport, largely a response to a 1922 immigration law in the United States that prevented nonliterate Africans from entry. The economic necessity for emigration from both Portugal and its islands generated a heterogeneous community of Portuguese nationals *outside* of Portuguese space, composed of metropolitans and colonials alike.

Cape Verdean emigration to Portugal would escalate by the late 1960s; and this pool of workers would gradually include larger numbers of women by the early 1970s. It would not take long before residence in the metropole amplified the awareness that Cape Verdeans were not in fact recognized as Portuguese, most especially not in Portugal (see also Silverstein 2004 on France). In Lisbon the fallacy of Lusotropicalism (see chapter 1)—dictator António Salazar's assertion that the empire was a pluri-racial union of Portuguese nationals—was laid bare by the normativity of everyday enactments of racism. Other conditions, tied to the lives of white Portuguese citizens in the metropole, also brought these tensions to the surface: the war against what were called terrorist forces in Portuguese Africa rerouted Portuguese men—men who otherwise would have traveled to France as economic migrants—to Africa for military service. Those who stayed behind labored alongside the new Cape Verdean male workforce as they listened to news about Portugal's antiterrorist war in Africa, watching family and neighbors returned maimed or deceased. Tensions, as suspected, were high.

An early morning coup for democracy on April 25, 1974 further complicated the situation. The new democratic administration associated the humiliation of late colonialism with the former fascist regime, hence disassociating the new government from the nation's colonial past. This disassociative process—where there was never discussion concerning the implications of late colonialism—would be accompanied by the new administration's efforts to maintain a continuous flow of Cape Verdean labor after 1975, the year of Cape Verdean independence. Through bilateral accords that were extended to the other colonies through the late 1970s, a familiar diplomatic exchange occurred: Portugal provided technological assistance to former Portuguese Africa, and former Portuguese Africa provided Portugal with workers. All the while, there was no public format for discussing how either party had been affected by a violent war that ended so abruptly. Democracy in Portugal brought the four remaining colonial wars to a halt—Guinea-Bissau achieved independence first in 1973—as the new government quickly entered into negotiations for African sovereignty. Portugal, and Lisbon in particular—with the largest immigrant base in the country—became a stage for discordant outbursts among those identified as Portuguese and African. People were left to work out the tensions themselves, leaving the African experience of racism and the Portuguese experience of war trauma as personal matters in which neither state nor society would intervene. An otherwise benign mistake such as stepping on another's toe could trigger unguarded recollections of things that Portuguese democracy was supposed to have dissolved.

It would be easy to move to the conclusion that the simultaneity of decolonization in Africa and democratization in Portugal was the primary cause of the continuing social tensions that plagued the Portuguese-African relationship in Portugal in the 1980s and 1990s. Yet when one begins to consider the new roles that each of these parties would assume during preparations for accession in the 1980s, the stakes of integration into the EEC highlight the magnitude of this process. Mutually coordinated changes in nationality and immigrations laws were made in the early 1980s; they restricted Portuguese citizenship to descendents abroad (excluding Cape Verdeans), while proposing new obstacles to Africans seeking naturalization in Portugal (see chapter 1). As working and working-poor Portuguese citizens (Portugal's majority) and Cape Verdeans labored in similar capacities in the metropole—albeit at different wages—it is important to address the process that would progressively hierarchize these groups through paired labor encounters, thus dissolving the roughly even worker positions from which tensions were previously expressed. It was the road to accession that created the conditions for such changes in policy and in thought. And this means that accession accomplished far more *socially* than the shift to democracy in altering how people were made to connect with each other in the course of their daily lives. I argue that there was something particular to Portugal's accession that shaped how people experienced it as a socially definitive moment. In essence, it was not the aftermath of decolonization and democracy, as significant as these moments were, that ultimately transformed everyday practices of Portuguese-African sociality in Portugal. Rather, it was the process of accession to the EEC that remapped their social trajectories along a gradated labor continuum.

I probe the impact of these shifts in labor-centered activities that involved Portuguese citizens and African immigrants between the mid-1990s and the early 2000s. In contrast to scholarship that focuses on encounters in institutionalized settings, I attend to mundane interactions between diverse individuals at work, and I observe how the tensions that emerge within these hierarchized labor settings articulate with the meaning of Portugal's economic incorporation into the EU in 1996. Here, as labor positions shifted, Portuguese references to racial distinction and the colonial past began to change from popular "working-class" outbursts of rage and discontent to a disciplined middle-class commitment to tolerance and diversity. I trace these discursive transformations to examine the enactment of new ideals of Portuguese-African difference. *Managing African Portugal* details how people lived these shifts through immediate engagements with their other, for citizen and migrant alike.

Everyone felt the effects of integration. For instance, entering a grocery store and finding countless varieties of apples that grow perfectly well in Portugal, but which are imported from Spain—hence disrupting local patterns of agricultural production and distribution—were signs that drastic changes had already taken place. So too were responses to the economic transition that included the growing popularity of the Popular Party (Partido Popular, or PP), a far right–wing political party with a working-class base and a vocal anti-immigrant agenda (see also Holmes 2000). But the relationships that parenthetically crystallized these shifts—like the domestically-situated citizen-migrant labor encounter between *women*— were not necessarily felt in these obvious ways. These changes felt more personal; they were experienced as choices concerning the kind of person that an individual wanted to be in relation to one's regard for others—

whether citizen or migrant—as opposed to simply being intangible and impersonal effects of market influences (see also Povinelli 2006).

Disparate procedures and events in direct dialogue with Portugal's accession process—policies for the advancement of Portuguese women, new immigration and nationalities laws, and state-sponsored anti-discrimination campaigns—culminated in effects that transformed citizens into migrants' managers and migrants into citizen-dependents. The ways people processed these initiatives had an impact on Portuguese-African sociality, whether in state-intervened labor encounters or not. The practice of citizenship by citizens increasingly involved new, distanced, and yet polished ways of engaging difference at work, at that same time that African labor was rendered increasingly vulnerable in relation to citizen's labor needs or managerial roles at work. Thus, similar to the colonizer-colonized dichotomy that Fanon (1967) and Memmi (1965) spoke of, where the effects of this asymmetrical connection are tied to political administration, labor, and quotidian sociality, I discuss how the citizen-migrant distinction surfaces as a meaningful, available construct that is the product of the obscured character of local government after accession (see also Holmes 2000).

Scholars focusing on migration in the context of nationalism argue that migrants have long played representational roles that shape state policy (Honig 2001; Ngai 2004) and everyday practice (Ong 2003): migrants are used to index what a nation is and is not, imaginatively-speaking. I add to this argument a different focus on daily practice, one where migrant status is regulated through enactments that teach "citizens" how to be citizens in the most ordinary or passing moments, and where the inhabitance or embodiment of citizenship is accomplished through practices that teach "migrants" how to be migrants. Taking a cue from Jacques Rancière (1999, 2004), I treat citizenship as a tenuous potential that belongs to no one, but that instead surfaces in association with the appearance of select subjects whose actions happen to reproduce the status quo. My task, therefore, is to describe how the ethnographer comes to observe the inhabitance of citizenship and the resultant pairings of citizen-migrant actors when both parties are empirically treated as if they possess the same social potential. In this book I detail how the concept of EU citizenship is solidified in the popular imagination as people are mutually made to meet each other from new included and excluded locations.

I describe what it is that "citizens" and "migrants" do in the course of daily activities that involve both for extended periods of time and whose repeated effect manifests and fixes the appearance of one's paired other. I work hard not to privilege either citizen or migrant (though I work through the lens of Cape Verdean experience), but to understand how one's essence is constituted in dialogue with its other. Therefore I do not treat citizenship as the universal category for determining the possession of rights, where migrant status operates as the default condition of rightlessness. Instead I think about the quotidian, taken-for-granted practice of citizenship as a biopolitical process, lived through the necessity of a particular encounter with the migrant to reproduce the idea of citizenship status. It is thus not something that can be observed in relation to what one group does or does not possess in an abstract legal sense, as noted by Ong (2003) and Holston (2008); citizenship needs to be observed through the encounters that yield its qualities. Because my objective is to develop an analysis that can account for the totality of actors within a given social context—or at least in the ways that totality is felt on the ground, as there are always other actors on the fringes who go unnoticed—I treat the citizen-migrant distinction as a capacity that comes to life through interaction.

The proposed citizen-migrant framework has its limitations: it does not adequately capture how many people live these categories. For instance, some citizens are married to migrants, as De Genova (2002) notes, and many citizens in Portugal are African nationals by birth. But the representational power of absolute distinctions is at the heart of my concern (cf. Gilroy 1987). I focus on how people come to feel, sense, and see these divisions as normative and continuous, independent of the infinite relationships in their lives that beg otherwise. My interest is how a citizen-migrant distinction is rendered public information, as something that consensually shapes (in a Gramscian sense) how people justify what they have to do to get by under circumstances experienced as uneventful but also highly contentious.

The ethnographic focus of this book is a fish market that at one time employed both Portuguese and Cape Verdean women. The Portuguese women began leaving their jobs at the market in the 1980s while Cape Verdeans continued on through the early 2000s. Both groups left the fish market to seek work in low-wage professions as maids, nannies, kitchen help, and factory workers, but their respective occupation of these new roles generated strikingly different results. Poor Portuguese women had no publicly defined place in Portuguese society as waged domestics; by contrast, poor Cape Verdean women were understood to have taken up their rightful, definitive role—as employees of Portuguese citizens, women in particular. By following the trajectories of the Cape Verdean women I encountered in the fish market, and observing their growing distance from working-poor Portuguese women, I demonstrate how citizens and migrants collectively came to know what to do to inhabit, slip into, or evade these relationally regulative positions. Moreover, these trajectories disclose the way ideals of Portugal's modernity becomes visible through everyday practices associated with what was *seen* as one's national status. The positions that poor Portuguese and Cape Verdean women took up manifested understandings about moving forward or backward along a path of EU modernization, respectively.

The ideal qualities of Portuguese citizenship continued to change through the late-twentieth century, and I detail when and how the practice of citizenship instantiated what ambiguously stood-in for EU modernity. However, this labeling of an ordinary or taken-for-granted practice as an instantiation of such a modernity is difficult to convey ethnographically. In his assessment of the reality of transnational citizenship in Europe, that is, EU citizenship, Étienne Balibar (2004: viii) notes the rise of disconnected phenomena usually treated by social scientists as a unified instrument— "*supranational structures* (above all in the form of administrations and representative bodies)," on the one hand, and "*postnational cosmopolitan anticipations,* (in particular, the attempt to create a political identity that is open to continuous admission of new peoples and cultures) in the construction of Europe," on the other. The intangible space between these separate realities is left to the imagination. In southern and eastern Europe, where geopolitical marginality transforms the experience of this gap into anxiety, and where its closure is taken on as the nation's responsibility, the reality of the space between administration and political identity remains awkwardly vague. Yet the demand for good performance is met by practices that are indeed concrete and tangible. For instance, the desire to homogenize regionally diverse communities with different life trajectories (i.e., of urban and agrarian backgrounds) entails constructing a nation that looks and feels socially uniform through media and commodity consumption, educational reform, etc. My concern are those subjects and subject relationships that concretize the idea of uniformity, and this is what I mean by the enactment of EU modernity through a new practice of Portuguese citizenship. I address how individuals recognized as citizens and migrants are positioned in the market in ways that reflect a meeting between administration and political identity. In particular, I consider how this meeting constitutively de-historicizes the terms of the Portuguese-African relationship by privileging accession over democracy/decolonization as Portugal's definitive modernizing moment. Ethnographically I observe how a labor-mediated boundary between these groups would eventually harden. In the process a perception of uniformity and normalcy was vocally challenged less and less by contentious references to the colonial past. *Managing African Portugal* considers how the different activities in which these groups participated would bring this boundary to life, making it sensical irrespective of the past or of the magnitude of an economic crisis that negatively affected all.

My work ends in the early 2000s. The timing marks the moment when the boundary in question did in fact represent what it projected—a definitive and ahistorical citizen-migrant distinction. Today, in the late 2000s, communities from eastern Europe (the Ukraine, Moldavia, and Russia), Brazil, and non-Portuguese-speaking China are the largest migrant groups coming to Portugal. The recent circumstances surrounding their presence likewise dispel reflection on the colonial past (irrespective of Brazil's history) thus contributing to the understanding of Portugal within the European present (see Trioullot 1995). Interestingly, state representatives' references to race in the media further disassociate Portugal's cultural and even "biological" association with the colonies. Daily commentary on the significance of Barack Obama's presidential campaign in the United States became the first stage on which officials made regular reference to race as an object of politics since the colonial wars in the 1960s and early 1970s and select skinhead activities in the 1990s that I address in chapter 1. Significantly, it was not former colonial Africa that instigated this dialogue about race, hence further disassociating the colonial past from the present. This book documents a period in time when references to difference still communicated with the colonial past, and where the space between expectation and lived experience had yet to be concealed. Therefore, normalcy is defined by the moment when people cease to draw on the contentious past to establish truth claims in the present. It is the moment when turning to the past is awkward, provincial even, and when people work through explanations of social division that resonate with interpretations of the EU present.

Managing African Portugal is an ethnography of the fabrication of social cohesion and civility, where different categories of personhood become increasingly fixated at the same moment that inter- and multi-cultural practices paradoxically take center stage. It is about how former colonizers and the colonized come to mutually enact normalcy, banality even, in the "consensual" investment in letting things slide for the sake of getting by, at least until the next eruption (see Mbembe 2001). The labor encounter is the place where quotidian enactments of division are commonplace and trite because of the legitimacy of unevenness in these daily routines. Of course, these encounters are densely textured by acts of resistance, the things we anthropologists generally focus on. But even as people resist in work encounters, they also become concerned, over time, with job security, competitive incomes, and sometimes a compromised sense of tranquility in their lives (see Sacks 1988). This book tells the story of how people in Portugal—"citizens" and "migrants" alike—got to that place, when the neoliberal underpinnings of the accession process made income security a new kind of personal responsibility and necessity. I thus describe what happened in the encounter between the migrant preoccupied with income and residency in new ways and the citizen caught-up in and interpellated by expectations of national uniformity that were tied to EU modernity.

ACKNOWLEDGMENTS

This work is the product of encounters I have had with numerous friends and colleagues. I am indebted to the members of my doctoral committee—Marcyliena Morgan, Sondra Hale, Karen Brodkin, and Valerie Smith—for their generous and supportive mentorship. I am also honored to have been a member of DIRE (Discourse, Identity, Representation, Ethics—or Ethnicity; we never resolved what the *E* stood for). DIRE was a collective at UCLA composed of the following graduate students in the mid-1990s: Patricia Baquedano-Lopes, Lanita Jacobs Huey, Soyoun Kim, Dionne Bennet, Adrienne Lo, Sepa Sete, and me.

In Portugal I worked with two research assistants whose support and brilliance facilitated my time in the archives and in the field. Carlos Alberto de Jesus Alvês has been working with me in Lisbon for over seven years. Carlos is a historian of Angola with an incredibly sharp eye for the small details. I am indebted to his commitment to my research. I also want to thank my dear friend and genius assistant, Antonio Tomás. His talent and unconditional support have been a real gift.

My colleagues in Lisbon—Cristiana Bastos, João Vasconcelos, João de Pina Cabral, Jorge Varanda, and especially Miguel Vale de Almeida—make me believe that business should be mixed with pleasure. A wonderful blend of friendship and rigorous intellectual support define my relationship with each of these individuals. Thank you. I also want to send a special thanks to Marilia Santos, Annabelle Barnes, Mickey Traneaus, Howard Sonenklar, Catarina Brandão, Marc Humpich, Vera Melo, Maria Leão, Nathalie Decrette, and Danis Bois. And I am extremely grateful to my dear friends Linda da Costa and Miguel Varela who have stopped at nothing to make Lisbon a home for me.

In Cape Verde I had the good fortune of meeting individuals and families who are inspiring, bighearted, and oh-so-well informed—about everything. Over the past ten years I have grown with the Moreira dos Santos family, the Brito family, and the Mascarenhas family. Having these home bases made all the difference during my trips to Cape Verde, and I am especially appreciative of my dear friend Vladimir Monteiro, whose unconditional support and comradeship were inspiring. I am also grateful for my friendship with Adlisa Delgado and her family and the Santos Silva family; I cherish their guidance during and beyond my time in Cape Verde. And there are two really sharp women who work at the Arquivo Histórico Nacional (AHN) in Praia—Fátima (Fatinha) Amado and Maria José Almeida. They helped me track down nonarchived materials that have made all the difference in my research. Our working relationship grew into warm friendship over the years.

I have benefited from interactions with many other teachers and supporters as well. In Boston, several yeas ago, Manuel Gonçalves taught me Cape Verdean Kriolu. Without him there is absolutely no way that I would have been able to capture the details of the interactions that I examine in this book. Brackette Williams's and Beth Povinelli's encouragement and feedback have made me value and problematize that which makes us uncomfortable and transform this disquiet into inquiry. Their brilliance never ceases to amaze me.

And I learned so much everyday from exchanges with colleagues at the University of Chicago, especially Joe Masco, William Mazzarella, François Richard, Ray Fogelman, Michael Silverstein, Jessica Cattelino, Danilyn Rutherford, John Kelly, Hussein Agrama, Jennifer Cole, Manuela Carneiro da Cunha, and Shannon Dawdy. I want to send a special note of thanks to Michel-Rolph Trouillot, Sue Gal, Stephan Palmié, Judy Farquhar, and Jean and John Comaroff for their commitment to my growth.

I have also benefited from my participation in the Anthropology of Europe Workshop and the African Studies Workshop, both at the University of Chicago. Earlier versions of chapters that I presented in these workshops were developed into some of the text in this book. I am grateful for the exchanges I have had with Rosa Williams, Filipe Gonçalves, and Jonathan Rosa, and I am indebted to Andrea Muelebach and Anwen Tormey for generously close readings of the final drafts of this book. I also want to thank the students in my Spring 2008 and Winter 2009 Travel and Migration graduate seminars for providing insightful commentaries that helped me further address the implications of this book in ways I had not anticipated. Finally, I want to send a special thanks to Philip Mcabee and David Forero, both dear friends and technical masters whose computer genius has helped me out on seemingly infinite occasions.

I had wonderful colleagues at the University of Florida. I appreciate my encounters with Luise White, Brenda Chalfin, and Irma McClaurin, and I feel honored to have worked with Dawn Fischer, Lonn Monroe, and William Schumann. Other great, supportive colleagues whose influence is felt in this book include Deborah Tomas, Asale Ajani, and Maude Hines.

In addition, I want to thank the two anonymous reviewers of an article I wrote in *Feminist Review* who gave the most eye-opening feedback; they suggested exactly what I needed to hear to begin thinking about things more broadly but with greater precision at the same time. The three anonymous readers of this book at Duke University Press also provided sharp feedback; the detail they put into their readings proved extremely helpful and in many instances went beyond the call of duty.

This book has been supported by multiple grants and fellowships: Wenner-Gren's Doctoral Fieldwork and Hunt Post-doctoral Fellowship; the Social Science Research Council's International and Area Studies Post-doctoral Fellowship; the Ford Foundation's Minority Postdoctoral Fellowship; the University of Chicago's Franke Institute's in-residence fellowship; the Social Sciences Divisional Research Grant at the University of Chicago; and travel grants from the Center for the Study of Race, Politics, and Culture and the Center for Latin American Studies, both also at Chicago. I also thank George Dussaud for allowing the use of his photographs and the Arquivo Municipal de Lisboa's Arquivo Fotográfico, which granted generous permission to use as many photographs as I wanted.

Ken Wissoker, my editor, has been a patient and enthusiastic supporter of this book project for some time now, as has Tim Elfenbein, who walked me through the end of the production process. Their investment means a lot to me. And Laura Helper-Ferris, who helped me edit earlier versions, aided in shaping this document into the current product.

My biggest debt is to the women who formerly worked as peixeiras for allowing me to observe their lives up close and to learn from them, often under the most physically and emotionally demanding circumstances. Thank you for your kindness, flexibility, and friendship.

How to thank my family? My great-grandmother, Maudella Ball, my parents, Brenda and Charles Fikes, my godmother, Jackie Garner, and my remarkable sister, Krysten Fikes, have helped me so much from the beginning, never questioning my decisions and always supporting my aspirations. None of what is now this book would have happened without them.

INTRODUCTION

I took my first trip to Lisbon by train, via Spain; it was the summer of 1988. I arrived at an international station called Santa Apolónia. Within minutes of departing the station, which was adjacent to the Tagus River, I ran into a row of hardy-looking, no-nonsense women fishmongers, or peixeiras.[1] Peixeiras sold many varieties of fish from vats atop stationary tables. At first "glance,"[2] most of them were white, Portuguese, and perhaps middle-aged and above; a smaller percentage were black and around the same ages. It was clear to me on hearing them advertise their fish, in a hoarse but siren-like sound from the gut—"Ssardiiiiiiiiiiiiiinha!" (sardines) and "E CARAPAUUUUUUUUUU" (mackerel)—that they all meant serious business.

What struck me most about this bustling scenario was the sea of male and female customers of every age and color. They stood in close proximity as they haggled with peixeiras, stepping on each other's toes, bumping elbows, and clumsily reaching across each other. As I made my way through the crowd, the scene made an impression on me. I was familiar with Lusotropicalist ideology, a Brazilian narrative celebrating the practice of racial-cultural intimacy among the Portuguese and those they colonized. Multiple sources further claimed that the Portuguese believed themselves incapable of racism because of this ideology. But I had also read the works of Charles Boxer and Gerald Bender who, each in his own way, argued that this ideology was in fact a myth never actually deployed in practice. Bender tells the story of an indigenous woman in southern Angola who was legally married to a Portuguese army officer. He left his post after they married.

Though they had been together for several years, had five sons, and both spoke each other's native tongue—Ovambo and Portuguese—they refused to communicate in the other's language. When Bender asked the indigenous women why her husband never spoke to her in Ovambo, she replied that he said he "would never speak the language of dogs" (1978: 218–19). This kind of information—with an emphasis on conflict—textured my thoughts as I mulled over an interpretation of what I had observed near the riverbank.

Within a day I noted racist skinhead graffiti on public surfaces—trains, buses, bathrooms, billboards, and even on the walls of apartment complexes. And I soon heard about activist groups like the Guinean Association for Social Solidarity (Associação Guineense de Solidariedade Social) that were struggling to help immigrant workers find homes. They reported that many Portuguese property owners were not shy about their aversion to renting to African immigrants. Africans made up some 70 percent of Portugal's immigrant pool at the time (Serviço de Estraneiros e Fronteiras 1988). There was real tension in the air. In 1986 Portugal entered the European Economic Community (EEC) and people felt tremendous anxiety around what Portugal stood to lose and gain from this process. Also by the mid-1980s, immigration from former Portuguese Africa (Cape Verde, Angola, Mozambique, Guinea-Bissau, and São Tomé and Príncipe) had accelerated to an unprecedented pace. Unemployment was high, wages were low, and EEC export restrictions in areas like agriculture seemed, to the majority working-poor, to have further jeopardized Portugal's marginal economy. Many believed that the only winner in the accession process was "Brussels," a word that often stands in for decision-making western Europe. And indeed the founding EEC member-states imagined Spain and Portugal as a fortress protecting Europe from Africa, and as places where service and industry markets could expand using cheap labor.

As I learned about these issues I kept running into peixeiras on a daily basis in different areas of the city. I saw white peixeiras selling fish door to door in the early morning hours in old neighborhoods, such as the Alfâma, the Bairro Alto, and Madragôa. I also observed black and white women (though more of the former) in front of train stations with considerable morning traffic, like Carcavelos, Algés, Cascais, and Cais do Sodré. Again, the customers at each of the stations were diverse and customer sociability was intense, energetic, and familiar. I watched how food circulated across

Peixeiras and customers along the *zona ribeirinha*, Lisbon, 1966. PHOTOGRAPH BY
ARMANDO SERÓDIO. COURTESY OF THE LISBON MUNICIPAL ARCHIVES

communities. These non- and semi-regulated networks, which bound the
campo (countryside) and the *cidade* (city) to each other, generated steady
income for some while providing a means of exchange without money for
others (see Sousa Santos 1986). The vendors I saw along the Tagus, in the
zona ribeirinha, participated in this economy; the black women, who I later
learned were Cape Verdean, entered the market alongside white women in
the late 1960s. Both communities of women were making ends meet by
supplying inexpensive food to the needy, both citizens and migrants alike,
in an economy with well over a century of market history in this area of
the city.

Entry into the EEC marked something new for Portugal. Accession
occurred just a little over ten years after the country's 1974 coup for
democracy against the Salazar-Caetano dictatorship. Between 1973 and
1975 independence movements in the Portuguese African colonies had
further lead to large-scale African migrations to Portugal. As a result, a new
democracy was dealing with the nation's sudden demographic shift at the
same time that it worked to adapt to EEC political, commercial, and technological standards. In fact, during deliberations on Portugal's entry into
the community, the EEC critiqued the market conditions in which peixeiras
had thrived. European officials feared an employment crisis in Portugal, an
issue previously addressed through Portuguese emigrations to European

countries farther north (France, Germany, and Luxembourg, for instance), the Americas (mainly Canada, the United States, and Brazil), or to Africa (namely Angola, Mozambique, and South Africa) during the colonial period. To complicate matters, Portugal's *retornado* phenomenon—the nearly 1 million Portuguese nationals who returned to a Portugal of 8.5 million during and after the colonial wars (see Pires 1984; Baganha 1998)—added a further burden to the pre-existent market crisis. Though the European Commission was clearly more concerned with defense-related issues, it would be most vocal (in print) about the economic feasibility of Portugal's integration (CES 1977: 15; 1979). I arrived some years after these debates began, and the Lisbon with which I became acquainted had already changed. Talk of retornados was slipping out of everyday parlance; national attention had now turned to the country's shift from an *e*migrant to an *im*migrant country.

Several trips later it was very clear that Lisbon was on a different course. The city was preparing in earnest for its debut as the City of European Culture in 1994 when I began fieldwork (see Dacosta-Holton 1998); it used EEC structural funds for diverse infrastructural projects and market-related investments. Massive projects like the CCB (the Centro Cultural de Belém) were under construction to host official EEC business, world-renowned artists, and other events of national and international importance. I also witnessed the building of new factories, pharmaceutical plants, and new and technologically upgraded hospitals throughout Lisbon's new suburbs. These suburbs had resulted from new highways; they condensed the time-space between an increasingly expensive Lisbon and an emergent housing market in rural *aldeias* (villages) and other smaller urban centers. Highways expanded the outer limits of the Lisbon metropolitan area, transforming aldeias at the edges of the city into soon-to-be suburbs, as opposed to campo. All this construction made Lisbon's developers the first professional community of wealthy entrepreneurs in newly democratic Portugal.

Though massive highway construction most clearly signaled changes to come, so too did the policing of the peixeira market that seemed to be thriving during my first trip. The shift was marked by the presence of baton-waving municipal police at train hubs, the absence of stationary tables for displaying fish near and around the zona ribeirinha and Cais do Sodré, and the demographic predominance of Cape Verdean women in public spaces previously dominated by Portuguese peixeiras. An anti-clandestine vending law created in 1979 (*Decreto-lei* 122) seemed to have been enforced with a vengeance. The law had been observed in less central areas of the city and had largely targeted Portuguese Roma and Hindu Indian entrepreneurs (see Lopes 2006), in addition to Portuguese vendors of various products and Cape Verdean peixeiras. Yet then policing was less extreme.

Beginning in the early 1990s, Cape Verdean women without long-standing connections to neighborhoods, in which middle-aged to elderly Portuguese women continued to sell fish, had to rely on busy, centrally located areas to stay in business. They had to operate under difficult conditions, transporting heavy buckets of ice and fish between covert locations. When police were absent peixeiras could be found at the entryways of train stations. When police were present they could generally be found behind the stations or along secluded side entrances. Though the overall number of Cape Verdean peixeiras was dwindling from a community of roughly five hundred down to one hundred—as older women started to drop out due to the physical demands of running—women in their late twenties and their thirties who had just arrived in Portugal steadily entered this economy. Some worked everyday while others relied on one day of income to make ends meet. By the late 1990s the public face of the unlicensed peixeira market in Lisbon was that of the Cape Verdean women. And this new demography transformed this market's purpose and its appearance.

The city's visible regulation of Cape Verdean peixeira activity, beginning between 1989 and 1990, involved violent physical and vocal confrontations, including racial slurs audible to the public, like "Sua preta!" (Your ugly blackness/niggerness), "Volta para a tua terra!" (Go back to your country), "Matei pretos como vocês!" (I killed blacks/niggers like you), or "Fora das ruas! Portugal já faz parte da Europa!" (Get off the streets! Portugal is now a part of Europe). These daily theatrics felt surreal because most pedestrians just walked by, seemingly involved in their own thoughts, without missing a step. The year before such scenarios would have seemed unimaginable, at least in central and densely populated settings. But just as curious was the contradiction that this form of policing posed to the popular idea that the Portuguese were characteristically anti-racist. At the time, some city representatives swore to ignore racist skinhead graffiti because "there was no place for racial hatred in Portugal" (see chapter 1).

Thus the regularity of racist police violence and the banal responses to it from pedestrians generated questions about the drama on display, in which peixeiras starred as criminals, passersby as law-abiding civilians, and where police orchestrated the distinction (Comaroff and Comaroff 2004). Why and how had public race-oriented aggressions—the very thing that the nation understood itself to be incapable of—become benign performances in this context? And what was meaningful about the types of activities that seemed to justify the routine staging of such intervention? These were the questions that began to pique my curiosity.

Fast-forward thirteen years, to 2003. Cape Verdean peixeiras have disappeared from public view in open urban spaces. This is largely because the port facility where they purchased fish in Lisbon—where the Tagus meets the Atlantic Ocean—was relocated to the suburbs, reportedly for public health reasons. The new inland location in the county of Loures, some fifty miles east of the previous facility, was ranked as the most technologically advanced wholesale market in the European Community (EC). As of the mid-2000s it was the only wholesale fish facility up to code according to EC regulations on conservation and climate control. And by the early 2000s it had become increasingly unconscionable to purchase fish on the street. People in Lisbon now rely more and more on various large-scale grocery stores, often regardless of their budgets, while once a week licensed markets are sites for finding specialized organic food or for family leisure; some tourist guidebooks even recommend these markets as wholesome excursions.

The build-up to the shift in consumer practice is telling. Between the 1990s and the early 2000s, as they decreasingly shopped in markets, people also began to participate in the retail consumption of nonsubsistence items like high-end appliances and furniture, luxury cars, and vacation packages outside of Portugal. While these things were purchased at costs paralleling those in other western European cities, incomes in Portugal on average were over 30 percent less than those earned among northern EC member-states. Still, such purchases could be made through the extension of credit cards to the masses by the mid-1990s, right as Portugal's economy was fully integrated into the EU structure in 1996, and thus around the time that Portugal adopted the Euro as its monetary unit in 1998. In essence, credit transformed people's relationships to capital through new and quicker means of access to it. In theory, civilians were now accountable for their own behaviors through their relationship to the market, as opposed to their civic responsiveness to centralized state policies under fascism. Modernity was tied to one's potential to consume, and a new consumer profile became associated with the meaning of civic practice and citizenship. Ideally this profile was of a diligent, educated, nonmigrant worker who participated in leisure consumption.

While poor Portuguese women would be included in the new, upgraded nation, they did not quite feature as real participants. The ten hours per day that many of them labored as low-wage workers had little productive role in the nation's modernizing agenda, one that celebrated the image of a newly feminized white-collar sector of EU *citizens* (see V. Ferreira 1998). Poor and especially elderly Portuguese women had an odd relationship to the benefits of EU citizenship: they did not have the steady incomes or resources enabling them to take advantage of access to credit or stable work opportunities in other member-states. The fact that poor Portuguese women "wasted" these privileges perhaps explains why they came to stand in for provincialism and the "underdeveloped" past. By contrast, poor Cape Verdean women, like other African women, had assumed a "rightful," socially productive role as appendages to Portuguese civilians and thus as catalysts for appearances of European modernity. Though Cape Verdean women labored for the same ten hours as did their working-poor Portuguese peers, their work *as migrants for citizens* signified something else, something tied to the practice and meaning of a new kind of citizenship. Just as the consumption of high-end commodities through various means of credit became the norm for those with access to it, modern citizenship existed as a qualitative potential—one that required concrete agents such as objects and bodies to materialize it.

The African immigrant woman thus became, among other things, one of the properties giving clarity to the idea of Portugal's revised proximity to Europe. As this association came into focus, historic narratives of Cape Verdean particularity—in its proximity to Portugueseness—were blurred. Cape Vedeans became indistinguishable in popular representations from other African national groups. At the same time, the ideal of the Portuguese citizen became synonymous with a picture of middle-classness. The mutual effect of these perceptions—where the enactment of particular kinds of labor came to mediate the modernization trajectory—crystallized blackness and whiteness as separate social entities. In the process, Luso-tropical imaginaries of racial "in-betweenness" or miscegenation were effectively dispelled, losing coherence and social value.³ An African woman's labor (in its low-wage context) became a site where Portugal's shift from an emigrant to an *im*migrant nation could be visibly confirmed, thus partially instantiating evidence of the country's newly attained status.

The new labor encounter that bound citizen and migrant to each other—whether in homes, on construction sites, or in restaurants—thus happened as the immigrant became more visible. This visibility was not only tied to local tensions around employment and job scarcity for the working-poor with citizenship, but also, in a celebratory sense, to a new antiracist and multicultural movement that emerged in the mid-1990s, largely by the hand of the Portuguese state. State-supported programs celebrating Portugal's diversity targeted black migrants. Accordingly, anti-racism as a campaign was about circumventing blackness in ways that newly distinguished it from the real national body. In practice, the campaign did more than blur the presence of thousands of blacks with Por-tuguese citizenship. By associating the cultivation of antiracism with the domestic management of foreignness, the state's antiracism campaign ne-gated itself as an *internal* civil process and instead imagined a means of defense for the nation where the migrant existed as outsider.

State-supported diversity programs and new labor encounters hap-pened concurrently and fostered something begging further study: state-recognized employment arrangements became impromptu spaces where expressions of racism were openly recognized as a Portuguese possibility. The former belief that Portuguese individuals could not be racist was fading among the general public. Inventive color-blind rituals, akin to the routines of political correctness practiced in other liberal settings, soon took hold in the hierarchized labor encounter. Somehow, in just over a decade, "racism" had evolved from something effaceable and even nego-tiable to something incriminating.

In considering the role that changes in consumer habits have played in the articulation of Portuguese modernity, I explore the connection be-tween the consumption of objects and persons, on the one hand, and the new visibility of racism, on the other. These simultaneously occurring phenomena share a point of connection that demands exploration; they both play a part in Portugal's modernization. I question the importance of the dissolution of miscegenation rhetoric in the moment that one can be held accountable for racist expression. How and why does this process of racial polarization trigger the nation's "conversion" to EU modernity?

Managing African Portugal attends to the shifting lives of Cape Verdean peixeiras through a focus on Portuguese national engagements with ideals of EU modernity. I consider how the inhabitance of European citizenship, conceived as a tangible modernizing agent, is manifested through practices that produce, name, or reference a new, dehistoricized other. While there are substantial numbers of black Portuguese citizens and white African nationals in Portugal, I treat the concepts "Portuguese" and "African" as synonyms for "whiteness" and "blackness," respectively, to illustrate how these ideas were popularly recognized in accordance with legal ideals circulating across institutions and communities from the 1990s through the early 2000s. I treat citizenship specifically in this setting—for the dominant majority who possess it—as an agentive property that comes to life through the possession and consumption of objects and others. I thus examine Portuguese citizenship, in its manifestation of EU modernity, as an interactive dynamic and qualitative potential.

If we are to develop an account of the social prowess in market forces, of the ways regulatory strategies are exercised through these forces, and of the means through which the neoliberal state recognizes autonomy in select individuals through their market behaviors, it is paramount that we develop accounts of the mechanisms by which citizens feel the state's presence-at-a-distance in their daily lives. Such an account is essential when persons occupying the status of citizen can experience their alignment with the law by enacting particular roles with migrants: here the definitive barrier between themselves and the foreigner is the difference in their proximity to the state. In the case of Portugal, there is thus something incredibly meaningful about *the relationship between citizens' increasing sense of limited accountability to the state, on the one hand, and migrants' increased experiences of being vulnerable to it, on the other.* The events and conditions surrounding the dismantling of Cape Verdean peixeiras' street sales, coupled with EU and local government strategies for stimulating the market, are among the many processes through which citizen and migrant emerged as distinctive, disconnected figures in the experience of their different relationships to the Portuguese state, *and thus to each other.* I am interested in the relationship between these two figures, specifically in how this relationship can be examined as an example of governmentality, or where the mutual inhabitance of these roles takes on a social life of its own, expanding and complicating its regulatory potential through a relationship that normalizes its boundary. When the state manages citizens through consumption, in an environment where hierarchically connected subjects not only consume differently, but in which one actually "consumes" the other, society is regulated not simply through the consumption of objects and services, but also through the consumption of people. Therefore, critiques of neo-liberal reasoning that attend to the ambiguous presence of the state cannot grasp the totality of a scenario if they are ethnographically limited to one of the following: 1) how citizens are desensitized to the state's presence through consumption; or 2) how the vulnerable are victim to state scrutiny in the same moment that they reside beyond the state's care. A more productive critique would consider how the terms of the relationship between the two subject categories that bear these different orientations (or whichever juxtaposed categories are relevant) mutually constitute the nature of the state in this relational sense, in any given moment. In other words an assessment of neoliberal forms of regulation requires attention to social relationships and not specific subjects as a starting point for analysis.

This focus on relationships leads us to ask how the contemporary moral underpinnings of difference—as something that now requires delicate handling in Portugal—are unwittingly brokered in ways that shape practices of sociality in the labor market or in income-earning settings. In this book I focus on a series of sites where migrants and citizens were mutually interpellated into relational roles, often against their will, and where new models of respectable social distance curiously took shape as these sites were dispelled or upgraded. My goal is not to argue that Lusotropicalism and the racial continuum that it espoused did in fact exist at one point, or to lament the dissolution of the rhetoric surrounding these ideas. Rather, I illustrate how the state's presence was felt differently by citizens and migrants in semiregulated economic practices that were becoming obsolete in much of urban Lisbon. By focusing on Cape Verdean peixeiras and the means through which they were routed into waged full-time work, I explore what their changing relationships to Portuguese nationals tell us about state intervention, in addition to the practice of Portuguese citizenship in relation to the EU.

The exclusionary status of the immigrant and/or the formerly colonized subject in western Europe, and now in the context of an expanding EU, is not a new topic. Interdisciplinary scholarship has rigorously observed how the democratic idealism of EU citizenship camouflages what this idea comes to mean and do to people on the ground (see Shore 2004; Balibar 2004; Holmes 2000). What is more, scholars focusing specifically on migrant marginalization in Europe have pinpointed sites at which citizenship comes to legally and socially mediate exclusion. In general, studies either focus on the subjects and communities for whom citizenship, as a possession, is alien, or they attend to those domains, such as education, health care, housing, and labor markets, that enforce or magnify a person's non-inclusive status and thus perpetuate the lived experience of vulnerability. The suffering of those who are variably recognized by the state but deemed unworthy of the basic political protections enjoyed by other citizens is identified in these studies with a fundamental fallacy in contemporary democracies.

In thinking about what it means that poor white and black women's political locations add or subtract value from the renewed concept of Portuguese citizenship, it is clear that we need to reframe this approach to citizenship. Studies too often exclude the dominant nationals' lived experience of citizenship from research on migrants' daily reality (see Holmes 2000 for a noteworthy exception). Analyses of the migrant crisis commonly rely on what is seen or felt—the victim/migrant and his or her relation to a violent, neglectful, or non-compassionate state or set of institutions. But this treatment obscures a range of less obvious factors, such as the place of citizens in establishing the perception of a migrant-state divide. That said, an important body of work in anthropology is attending to the different ways citizens participate in migrant vulnerability.[4] Miriam Ticktin (2007) emphasizes the discretionary power in citizenship, noting how citizens in their roles as both state officials and humanitarian workers are caught up in the determination of migrants' fates. We not only get a vivid picture of the ways migrant vulnerability surfaces at the intersection of humanitarian ethics and state politics, but also of the ways citizenship is constituted in the option to evade a condition of recognition in which one exists between ethics and politics. Here, the essence of citizenship is *not* caught between ethics and politics, and the enactment of this allowance establishes this trap as the migrants'. Aihwa Ong (2003), in a different direction and geographic location, addresses how citizens regulate appropriate models of behavior in the migrants' integrative experience. Here, encounters with bureaucracy are never simply about attending to legal matters, but always also about being informed of ways of being "American." In this sense, importantly, citizens stand-in as teachers. In yet another vein, Nicholas De Genova (2002) problematizes how citizens and migrants are extracted from each other in ways that blur relationships that span both categories, such as kinship. He draws our attention to the reality that citizens and migrants often live in the same household, suggesting that citizens' personal alliances and interests may lie with the migrants' as opposed to the state for which they pertain. This observation is significant because it also speaks to the centrality of citizens' compliance with state operations. If the absence of compliance can get citizens into trouble, the *reach* of the governing power in citizenship is revealed: it is thus something that necessarily governs and is governing all at once.

Managing African Portugal draws attention to a critical element of this recent research on citizenship—the sociality of the citizen-migrant connection—and it suggests what such attention can teach us about the mechanics of governance across a range of settings. This book adds to these ongoing discussions by introducing two temporal dimensions to the equation. The first is repetition. I focus on everyday labor encounters to address how the governing potential in citizenship is wielded through repetitive observation and instruction, the constant management of the migrant's hours, and the labor conditions that even physiologically shape migrants' bodies. Migrants' encounters with citizen-officials play a pervasive role in the migrant experience. These moments are often episodic, lasting anywhere between 30 minutes to 10 hours in a day, for instance, and are set within encounters that are grounded in different social expectations and interactive requirements. Therefore, I want to think about the instructional and governing potential in citizenship under work-related conditions of surveillance, where disciplinary practice organizes the power in citizenship through different temporal scales.

The second and related temporal dimension is the experience of normalcy and continuity in asymmetry. Many accounts of migratory experience focus on extreme examples of vulnerability, particularly of the nationless refugee or the undocumented migrant. But I am also interested in understanding the kinds of sociality that are produced between the law-abiding citizen and the documented migrant. These encounters are curious because the mutual adherence to the law of both citizen and migrant can frame their encounter as void of conflict. Yet adherence to legal guidelines does not create equality or evenness; it only recognizes the terms under which both parties have variably chosen to enter into a given encounter. My concern is the condition of sociality that is produced through such meetings, particularly in the neoliberal setting. I discuss the nature of the governing role taken up by citizens in what appear to be smooth, cohesive, and nonconflictual encounters with migrants.

When thinking through the managerial capacity in citizenship, it is important to note distinctions between encounters that appear conflictual and those that are perceived as normative. The distinction speaks to different conditions of migrant visibility, and thus teaches us something about the mechanics of government and power in a given setting. Jacques Rancière (1999, 2004, 2006) suggests that close attention to these differences in visibility is essential not only to understanding how democracies operate in practice, but also in identifying a broader conceptual crisis in philosophical approaches to the project of equality. He argues that social equality is treated in political philosophy as a goal rather than recognizing it, in a radical turn, as the only thing that already exists. Rancière is positing that the political domain is the field that is inherently neutral because it only comes to life through the process by which subjects are recognized as citizens, or not. Accordingly, the site we need to attend to is not the political or juridicial realm but instead the *social* (a suggestion similar to that of Marx), or the space where asymmetry is justified because the political realm is reserved as the location for correcting inequalities. In short, Rancière observes an error in logic: on the one hand, the political realm is conventionally critiqued as biased in its given orientation and thus the cause of inequality; on the other, the social domain is imagined as a neutral field of *hierarchized* actors that requires political correcting. He resolves this error in reasoning by claiming that rights do not belong to any individual, and above all not to the citizen. Rather consent—for the elite and the abject alike—is the condition by which people come to exhibit the qualities that we type as those of the citizen and the Other. Time, here, is a sensitive element; people do not simply enact and thus materialize the roles they would like to inhabit or experience beyond institutional scrutiny. History, in the Marxist sense, suggests that people are already positioned; therefore, in the process of producing norms, consent is about engaging in activities that reproduce the social place from which one is already standing. The crisis is thus the neutral status given to a reproductive social cycle (like Foucauldian governmentality) that is treated as depoliticized asymmetry.

My inquiry begins by asking what consent looks like, or what happens to it when social categories and the conditions of their existence change. If rights—whether pertaining to Portugal or the EU—are never a given, and hence are not automatically possessed by persons categorized as Portuguese citizens, what practices render the possession of EU citizenship the neutrally positioned right or privilege of the Portuguese national, particularly under shifting political conditions? Rancière's argument yields an analytic imaginary that challenges the exclusive ethnographic focus on the migrant-state relationship. By not privileging the tensions between the vulnerable and the state—which would neutralize the social realm—other actors *imagined* to be in sync with or beyond the law can be figured into the social equation of migrant living. This analytic imaginary questions that of theorists who place power solely in the hands of the state. Whereas Giorgio Agamben in *Homo Sacer* (1998:6), for instance, skeptically asks, "What is the point at which the voluntary servitude of individuals comes into contact with objective power?" hence suggesting that the two do not meet, I point to the various faces of objective power that are not officially bound to the political realm. They exist in a dynamic produced through asymmetries, modes of sociality that can be observed through the banality of the hierarchical encounter.

Rancière's radical privileging of the social realm helps us think through the ways black women's relationships to middle-income Portuguese nationals communicate a smooth linkage between Portuguese citizenship and EU modernity. I consider what ethnographic scrutiny of the changing meaning of citizenship in the mid- to late 1990s might convey about new practices of sociality and their governing effects in Portugal. Further, I ask what the new ideologies that hierarchically pair persons identified as citizens and migrants can teach us about EU member-states attempts to reconcile the gap between the local practice of national identity and the structural limitations imposed by EC guidelines.

In my analysis I maintain a dichotomous framework to emphasize the role of relativity in the dynamic of subjectivization.[5] However, in the context of migrant focused studies, I change the general ethnographic components of this dichotomy from state-citizen or state-migrant to citizen-migrant to reflect the role that citizenship plays in the regulation of society where citizens both govern and *are* governed through their relationships with migrants. Methodologically, this distinction allows us to consider when and how migrant status is necessary for the management of society, for instance, the role played by black women's low-waged labor in Portugal. The process by which "the black domestic" adds value to Portuguese citizenship is an instantiation of a norm and thus a reflection of the effective regulation of government. Ann Laura Stoler (1995b, 2002) has strongly advocated for this type of approach in a different fashion through her work on colonial Indonesia. She emphasizes the penalties suffered by European colonists who acted in ways suggesting their equality, rather than superiority, to "natives." Her point is to question how particular patterns of relationality between the colonizer and the colonized stood in for order, and how the impossibility of creating the ideal formula or mode of sociality for that order dictated the nature of political rule in the colonies. Stoler's observations push us to address not just how marginality exposes the realities of citizenship but also how citizenship as an ideal is a never-ending process, a regulatory potential with meaningful effects.

We therefore need to rethink the presumption of belonging when confronting the paradoxical nature of democracy. The abject do not lack rights in relation to the state because rights are experiences exercised through *appropriate* relationships (see Stoler 1995b, 2002). Thus if individuals can enact modes of being with others, modes that trigger citizenship, then we need to probe those relative terms of possession while reassessing how we have equated rights, or rather power, with citizenship (see Rancière 1999, 2004, 2006). The aim here—if we want to treat the exclusionary status of the migrant as a social problem while capturing the work of citizenship in the process—is to develop analyses that can account for the totality of actors that pertain to a given social context. This involves theorizing citizenship not only as a site where subjects are constituted, but also as a potentially agentive force and practice—something acted on—in the configuration of exclusionary living. In places like southern and eastern Europe, where accession to the EU positions citizenship as a target, or rather as something achieved through the mastery of particular behaviors and the exhibition of particular values, it is important to inquire into the *regulatory* character of citizenship for its possessor and its other alike: its inhabitance enables far-reaching strategies for governance.

The question is not only, How is power bottled in or emanating from the ambiguous confines of citizenship? but also, How are people informed about the supposed powers held within it? With this in mind, at which sites do Portuguese nationals gather their understanding of the powers thought to be invested in EU citizenship? How is this understanding rendered legible through designated relationships? And how do EU member-states intervene in their societies in ways that enable or enforce the encounters that happen to establish the citizen-migrant distinction?

In *The Empire of Love*, Elizabeth Povinelli (2006) emphasizes the continuum that exists between asymmetrically juxtaposed communities. She suggests that life and death are not absolute spheres of determination; there is a space inbetween where life is conditioned by a widened spatiotemporal dimension—whether imaginary or transnationally realized— that mediates existence along a valuable-dispensable continuum. The experience of distance enabled by such scattering—whether subjective or geographic—is tied to a logic where liberal individuality easily reduces the recognition of the Other to sentiment: the redistribution of material resources, for instance, would violate principles of equality that ride on the individual, not the masses. Distance is inherently paradoxical, and hence infinitely productive: it divides people at the same time that division is the condition upon which sentiment becomes a response and a possibility. I want to apply this treatment of distance to the citizen-migrant relationship —one where migrant vulnerability is usually figured in association with the uncaring state—to give more attention to the biting regulatory actions of ordinary practice between ordinary people. In *Managing African Portugal* I examine labor encounters where acts of respect and tolerance toward the migrant (see esp. chapter 4) are imagined in ways that profess the virtues of contemporary civility—hence the power thought to be in citizenship. Such beliefs are a condition of a citizen-migrant labor agreement that operates through the logic of a valuable-dispensable continuum.

People generally imagine labor, public health, education, and housing as rewards or opportunities bestowed upon deserving individuals, attributes imagined to have nothing to do with positionality. I am thus interested in those sites that intimately involve model citizens and lesser documented others in encounters popularly identified as expressions of responsible civic practice, as opposed to the consumption of others. This book considers the role that ethnography can play in unearthing the meaning and practice of Portuguese citizenship—in its relation to EU modernity—as it is constituted through the relationship between the rational, civic-minded citizen and the obedient migrant. I want to understand how this distinction takes shape on the ground, how people come to stand in, by force or desire, for categorical possessions that ride on the legibility of legitimate relative difference.

EU PORTUGAL AND CONSUMPTION

Since the mid-1990s, people living in Portugal have referred to the new liberal era through past-present comparisons. The media addresses socially relevant statistical shifts on a daily basis, following trends in consumption habits such as new home and automobile ownership patterns, of both the nation and other EU member-states. The nation's progress is measured by evaluating Portugal's status in relation to other states. Often the comparisons are restricted to those southern states that entered the EEC at around the same period, Greece and Spain. Occupying the first or the last of these three places can prove meaningful.

These comparative European statistics do more than simply portray ideals of national progress through changing social habits. As soon as they include so-called modernizing criteria—the number of women in the white-collar workforce, overseas vacations, annual increases in postgraduate education, celebrated nonmarried civil unions with children, increased divorce rates, and pro-abortion surveys—the comparisons also speak to the categorical creation of new subjects in a newly imagined space where Europe begins south of Portugal and not at the Pyrenees. These social habits and the circulation of information about them are essential to the new profile of the Portuguese national as an EU citizen. And yet, like elsewhere, debt is mounting; skilled and educated individuals experience extended periods of unemployment or continue to live in extended families, not necessarily by choice. It is important to consider the economic limitations that are real to Portugal and to address the resourceful social arrangements and routines that produce an experience conceived of as EU modernity.

The normativity of the middle-class imaginary is relatively new, the country now having moved, according to consumer habit-based statistics, beyond a demography composed of working-poor masses and a small elite. Economists saw the retail market in the mid-1990s as one of the primary sites that confirmed the rise of middle-class communities. While few Portuguese households, at least through the early 2000s, lived outside of working class conditions without extensive financial debt, middle-classness existed as a tangible ideal, particularly in Lisbon. Banks instantiated this ideal in their advertisements for mortgages with depictions of fair-skinned Portuguese nuclear families starring the protective father, the modern but domestically oriented mother, the older athletic brother, his younger fair-haired and light-eyed sister, and sometimes the family dog. While the realities of an increasingly over-extended financial market meant that few could comfortably live this ideal, the ads suggested that one could live it through relationships.

In the mid-1990s the introduction of credit and bankcards extended to just about any citizen and documented migrant who could prove regular employment, regardless of income, would prove essential to these appearances. It meant that a particular relationship to spending would no longer be exclusive to the elite; low- and semi-skilled workers now had buying power. In a move that virtually revolutionized people's relationships to cash and spending, individuals could now consume with credit cards rather than having to rely on a layaway system, a practice previously limited to stores selling furniture, appliances, and the like. EU citizenship quickly became associated with legible "middle-class" practices and hence with an expanding economy. And middle-classness explained why fewer people in the northern regions had to emigrate to places like France, England, or Germany for economic reasons, thus revealing that Portugal really had changed: it was no longer just an economic emigrant country.

Significantly, Portugal's newfound economic mobility would in many ways enhance the lives of Portuguese nationals abroad. In 1996 Portugal became one of Europe's Schengen states, meaning that Portuguese workers no longer needed work visas to seek employment in northwestern Europe (though one should note that this does not exclude them from labor recruitment shams in places like England or France, as countless news reports highlight). Likewise, in 1999 the United States removed visa restrictions from Portugal, thus in practice recognizing the country as a member of

Europe as opposed to the "South." In effect, the Portuguese national ceased to be exclusively imagined by northwestern Europe and the United States alike as a sojourning economic figure; in theory, the national was a new kind of worker, as well as a potential cash-spending tourist. Regardless of the realities of the market, the Portuguese national had acquired some degree of status as a leisure consumer, the antithesis of the migrant-peasant.

So when the national talk show celebrity Hérman, an actor with brilliant comedic timing, impersonates a Portuguese woman from the Alentejo (a peasant and communist-identified region in southern central Portugal)— portraying her as rugged, backward, illiterate, and non-feminine—he dialogues with the new modern figure by pointing to the problematic gap between the *Alentejana* and the *Lisboeta* (someone from Lisbon). The slippage is referenced again through the everyday "folk" that he invites to participate in the show, such as Lisbon-based traditional song and dance troops that perform *marchas populares* (popular or folk marches) during holiday and saints festivals. Importantly, the "authentic" participants in these events have historically included urban working-poor entrepreneurs like peixeiras. Here, Hérman manipulates the cultural gap for additional laughs by situating these groups within the comedic space of the talk show. By showcasing them in ways that suggest they take themselves too seriously—through subtle and explicit forms of mocking—the format of the show turns their performance into a national joke. No one told them that the dedication with which they commit themselves to the performance of folk song and dance is something of the past. These dances are supposed to be respected as tradition, not embraced as an instantiation of the present. The joke, in effect, is on them. The television audience, instructed through the comedic set-up, laughs *at* them, not *with* them.

By the mid- to late 1990s the former colonial migrant, that is, the "immigrant," had assumed the rightful and nonlaughable role as the living exemplar of tradition. This occurred through the city's sponsorship of African cultural events that also stood in for Portuguese respect for diversity. Through local festivals that showcase PALOP (Países Africanos de Língua Oficial Portuguesa, African Countries Whose Official Language is Portuguese) cuisine and dance events, present-day displays of tradition are tied to the subject of diversity (not of the nation) while simultaneously portraying a progressive national agenda. Although these ideas might appear benign, they produce a noteworthy effect: they liken race-identified social strife in Portugal with conflicts ongoing in other wealthy EU member-states, positing the existence of racism as a *local* sign for Portuguese modernity. Where racial conflict—in the sense of something requiring attention and management—and marginalized ethnic minorities might signify the end of civility or fascism in one context, its presence can also signify something else in Portugal because of racial conflict's imaginary links to urbanity, liberal state intervention, and thus modernity and development.

COLONIAL AND POST-INDEPENDENCE
CAPE VERDEAN LABOR RECRUITMENT

Africans—elites, clergy, and slaves—have lived in Portugal for centuries. After the abolition of slavery in Portugal in the early nineteenth century, former slaves—persons categorized by the state as *negros* and *mestiços*—disappeared from statistics as they were absorbed into the national population.[6] Simultaneously, freed negros and mestiços regularly emigrated to Portugal from Africa where they continued to be popularly and legally identified in these racialized terms because of their non-natal status, as evidenced in eighteenth and nineteenth century theater and poetry that refers to blackness and Africanity, as well as the varieties of nineteenth and early to mid-twentieth century kitsch artifacts that circulate widely today as antique collectibles in Portugal.

It was not until about the late 1950s that the African presence began to look like it does today with large settlements of African-identified individuals cohabitating. With some two-thirds of the Portuguese national population overseas by the 1960s (Baganha 1998)—in Portuguese Africa, the Americas, or northward western Europe—the state began to recruit Cape Verdean male workers for foreign-owned mining projects, and domestic construction and public works jobs, all in Portugal (see Batalha 2004; Fikes 2005b). Part of the logic behind recruiting Cape Verdeans was tied to the belief that they shared racial-cultural affinities with the Portuguese. Yet while Cape Verdean elites educated in Portugal in the early and mid-twentieth century attest to unequal treatment, any ideas about their so-called likeness to the Portuguese would be utterly dispelled once their impoverished compatriots—former indentured Cape Verdean migrants—arrived in Portugal. Specifically, popular anxieties by nationals that pertained to new migrant recruits were applied to all blacks, thus transforming the character of the discrimination that the elite had long experienced.

The majority of Cape Verdeans who voluntarily migrated to Portugal prior to the 1960s were educated elites hailing primarily from the islands in the archipelago whose inhabitants were authorized to partake in voluntary emigrations outside of Portuguese space. Though all Cape Verdeans were citizens, in theory, residents of these islands were legally exempt from forced labor (see Meintel 1984). Such communities, primarily from the northern islands of São Vicente, Santo Antão, and São Nicolau, migrated to Portugal as Portuguese nationals from the early twentieth century through independence. However, thousands of people from these three islands—those from Santo Antão in particular—became contract workers in São Tomé and Angola, a consequence of drought and famine. Although legally they were not obliged to emigrate to Portuguese Africa, these emigrations were administered inconsistently. By the mid-1960s, the Portuguese state's organized recruitment of Cape Verdeans paid little attention to islands of origin, something that had long dictated its Cape Verdean migration routes (Meintel 1984; Fikes 2007). Instead, the state recruited workers from all of the archipelago's islands—including those workers who had previously circulated almost exclusively within "native" African labor networks—in a move that would begin to shift how migration mediated conceptions of Cape Verdean racial and national identity in the metropole. As I have argued elsewhere (Fikes 2007), this move contributed to the definitive identification of all Cape Verdeans in Portugal as black, regardless of an individual's island affiliation and hence degree of so-called civility, in the period after independence.

Between 1955 and 1973 some eighty-seven thousand documented Cape Verdeans migrated to Lisbon (Batalha 2004: 134; Carreira 1983), a number that does not include those elites with a long history of moving back and forth for educational or nonmanual labor related reasons.[7] Recruitments continued after Portuguese democracy (1974) and the African independence movements (1973–75) through bilateral agreements that recognized the newly independent Lusophone African countries. Men from Guinea-Bissau and later São Tomé would be added to the recruitment pool by the late 1970s as these countries signed diplomatic accords with Portugal. Angolans and a much smaller percentage of Mozambicans (many of whom migrated to South Africa to work in the mines) likewise joined the work force, as economic migrants and sometimes as refugees, by the early 1980s.

The initial recruitment of Cape Verdean male workers to the metropole coincided with drastic shifts in Portugal's domestic economy. The economy at the time of its entrance into the EFTA (European Free Trade Association) in 1960 was based primarily on labor exports, remittances, tourism, and colonial balances (from imports to the colonies) (Eisfeld 1986: 41). The remainder of the state's income came from so-called fragile exports produced by low-skilled, low-wage metropolitan labor. Member states of EFTA instituted nonreciprocal trade advantages for Portugal through 1980; the advantage for Portugal was the slow elimination of import duties (Eisfeld: 29). The disadvantage, however, would be the nineteen-year period between Portugal's first request for entry into the EEC and its eventual entrée in 1986. During these years Portugal did apply for, and received, a series of grants from the EFTA and the EEC. The country invested the bulk of this aid, particularly in the 1960s and 1970s, in the development of infrastructure. However, problems with agrarian production led to a rural exodus, primarily to France, that limited the potential pool of workers available for industrial growth and public works projects. Cape Verdean men filled a large percentage of these vacancies between the mid-1960s and the early 1970s (see Batalha 2004; Esteves 1991). As both citizens *and* subjects of the empire they had low and non-negotiable wages seen as ideal for industrial development.

Cape Verdeans could travel to the metropole as migrant laborers after petitioning to the Cabinet of Economics (Direcção-Geral de Economia) in the Overseas Ministry (Ministério do Ultramar). These petitions were made from the archipelago through a public labor institute called the Instituto do Trabalho, Previdência e Acção Social (Institute for Labor, Support, and Social Action; ITPAS). In 1971, in an effort to manage the large numbers of workers who increasingly chose the metropole for work over plantations in Portuguese Africa, the Overseas Ministry mandated that ITPAS form an agency to monitor migrant settlement in Portugal. At the time, many workers holding contracts in isolated northern and southern areas of Portugal were leaving their jobs (without notice or on being fired) and relocating to Lisbon. That same year ITPAS created an internal agency called the Nucleo de Apoio aos Trabalhadores Migrantes Caboverdianos (Nucleus of Support for the Cape Verdean Migrant Worker; NA) to manage the trajectories of Cape Verdeans in Portugal.

The NA's tasks included monitoring all logistics pertaining to migration to Portugal, with an emphasis on risk management. The agency employed social scientists and bilingual Cape Verdean mediators in Portugal and Cape Verde to respond to complaints from Portuguese co-workers and employers and to handle any grievances channeled through Lisbon's municipal office. As experts on Cape Verdean "nature," these mediators were responsible for designing plans that would improve the terms of migrants' integration, and thus generate productive communication between labor and migration-related officials in Portugal and Cape Verde. ITPAS administrators also compiled a list of everything a respectable worker would need once he arrived in the metropole, including two week start-up income and the number of pants or underwear required.

These risk management objectives were not limited to what happened to workers once they resided in the metropole. The administration had always intended for recruited workers to send remittances back to Cape Verde to subsidize household expenses. ITPAS social experts therefore examined the relationship between steady work in the metropole and the maintenance of family back home. The Overseas Ministry worried about a connection between the unemployed male migrant and his remittance-dependent family in Cape Verde. In essence, male unemployment in Portugal was feared as a sign of neglected family obligations back home. To remedy the perceived crisis, ITPAS in 1973 recommended enforcing measures that strictly limited emigration to precontracted individuals. The screened, precontracted male worker formed a part of this risk management strategy; his traceability enabled ITPAS to ensure that he remained financially accountable to family at home and socially accountable for his temporary stay in Portugal.

The strategy failed to work due to increased labor demands. As civilians continued to complain about Cape Verdean male vagrancy, ITPAS envisioned family-reunification policies—*agrupamento familiar*—as an answer to these concerns. These policies drew on strategies that national ministry officials had used in the 1950s to encourage Portuguese wives to join their husbands in Portuguese Africa (see Castelo 2007). Then the aim had been to prevent lone Portuguese men from engaging in deviant activities with African women. Similarly, to maintain the integrity of society in the metropole, Cape Verdean men were allowed to petition for their spouses and families. To do so they had to prove their job security as well as access to adequate housing and income for persons presumed to be nonworking dependents. The documentation required for individuals emigrating through family reunification did not include proof of precontracted work; rather, everything depended on the resident male migrant's economic and material security. Moreover, because men were the only workers who could legitimately prove their income and housing security—the recruitment market primarily targeted men—petitions were implicitly gendered as male. By contrast, the beneficiaries of these requests were children and females who were assumed to be inactive or nonworking. Men sending for their partners were also supposed to be legally married to them. Hence these policies were meant to select and maintain particular moral subjects through the very practice and observance of reunification guidelines. In short, families reconstituted in Portugal were supposed to comprise an employed male head of the family and his nonworking dependents. As António Carreira (1983) has noted, few of these policies actually succeeded because the agents involved in the recruitment process were rarely able to effectively communicate with each other to maintain these standards, presumably because of the demand for labor and the infinite recruitment networks responding to them.

While ITPAS' anti-vagrancy strategies incorporated Cape Verdean women into their labor-management vision, Cape Verdean women were apparently not initially imagined as part of the actual labor scene in Portugal. Considering that Cape Verdean women from all islands had a substantial history of labor migration—to western Europe, the Americas, and especially to São Tomé and Príncipe—this exclusion is meaningful because it suggests an attempt to transform Cape Verdean women into new subjects, subjects whose "femininity" could be brokered for disciplinary purposes.

In Cape Verde the inhabitants of the island of Santiago—making up the largest percentage of Portugal's migratory workforce by the 1970s—were historically figured as a masculine, single-gender or gender-neutral community of workers (see Meintel 1984; Fikes 2007). Santiaguense men and women, different from the residents of the northern islands mentioned earlier, had been the main targets of contracted emigrations to the cacao plantations of São Tomé as mandated by early 1860s post-abolition laws and practiced through the early 1970s (see Meintel 1984; Fikes forthcoming). Significantly, narratives of Santiaguense appropriateness for such labor did not generally distinguish workers by gender (Fikes 2007, forthcoming). Because the NA in the 1970s contracted working-poor individuals from every island in the archipelago, at a time when forced labor had already been outlawed for some ten years, NA operations in the metropole had another effect: the introduction of Santiaguense women as pacifying agents into Portuguese society would aid in the changed perception of the racial-cultural composition of the Cape Verdean subject in Cape Verde proper. Cape Verdean migrations to Portugal worked against previous colonial images of gender-neutral or savage Santiaguense qualities because movement to Portugal ceased to be tied to elite social practices. Male-targeted migrations to the metropole effectively "Africanized" *all* Cape Verdean subjects from the perspective of the colonial administration (Fikes 2007). By rendering historic island distinctions of civility and savagery obsolete, family reunification guidelines effectively *gendered* the working-poor Santiaguense through ideas binding labor diligence to family unity. By 1973, *in* Portugal, working-poor Cape Verdean men and women were understood to have distinctive roles, with their own supposedly natural duties.

The presence of Cape Verdean women in Portugal also generated unforeseeable consequences. The NA, renamed CATU (Centro de Apoio do Trabalhador do Ultramar, Support Center for the Overseas Worker), did not realize that the women they had typed as dependents associated work outside the home with a woman's moral and social respectability; self-earned money had always been tied to ideals of responsible selfhood and mothering in Cape Verde (Fikes 2000, 2005b).[8] On their arrival in Portugal, spouses, mothers, and sisters routinely sought opportunities to generate their own income. Some women chose not to work, but many made money cooking for men in dormitories and hostels, in and outside Lisbon. Other women, particularly those in Lisbon and Setúbal (a city south of Lisbon, across the Tagus), integrated themselves into fishmonger economies, alongside urban-poor Portuguese women. As Luís Batalha (2004) has documented, some transported wooden crates of fish that they purchased wholesale for retailers and individual buyers. Interestingly, this job had previously been reserved for poor retired Portuguese men, called *arrastas*. Thus Cape Verdean women began to assume these roles reserved for Portuguese men. Other Cape Verdean women sold their own fish on the streets alongside female Portuguese fishmongers, the market that is the focus of this ethnography. Their insertion into an already stigmatized economy had yet to mean anything to the authorities. It would be after Portugal's accession to the EEC that their activities would be targeted for disbandment.

Cape Verdean women thus entered a peculiar economic scene: they inserted themselves into a market that the state monitored with a distant eye. Moreover, Portuguese peixeira work is very heavily stigmatized, largely because it involves women handling fish and carrying sharp utensils that are used to quickly gut fish. Because of this they were both looked down upon and oddly respected, even fetishized.[9] Cape Verdean peixeiras initially got some mileage from this historic identity as "folks not to be messed with." As João Lopes Filho (2007) has documented, the Portuguese media already associated Cape Verdeanness with brutal knifings by the 1980s, which emphasized that this tool was commonly used to settle disputes between individuals. Yet this view would change again in the 1990s as policing transformed unlicensed peixeira work in urban and tourist designated places into a disdainful and intolerable market practice. In light of this history it appears especially important to carefully analyze the different representational values associated with Cape Verdean women's new lives as domestics vis-à-vis emergent understandings of Portuguese citizenship and EU modernity.

TWENTY-FOUR HOURS, THREE FIELD SITES

In addition to thinking through how to capture citizenship as a potential, in its relation to the migrant, and vice-versa, the present work is also about the methodological process of documenting potentiality. The time constraints of fieldwork complicate what it means to document change, particularly when observing ordinary phenomena. So one searches for other ways of measuring change in the ethnography. I documented three separate labor activities that occurred over the course of a twenty-four hour period. These include 1) video-recorded encounters between working class and working-poor Portuguese men and the Cape Verdean migrant women to whom they sold fish, 2) video-recorded interactions among this same group of women as they sold their fish to civilians, under policed conditions, and 3) exchanges I witnessed as a participant observer of Cape Verdean domestics and janitors and the working-poor and middle-class Portuguese women who managed or employed them, respectively. Notably, these activities occurred at different hours during the same work day, but they each had a different place in the trajectory of Portuguese modernity. The first is the product of the poor's historic experience of urban living in Lisbon, the second is tied to the municipal efforts to clean-up Lisbon after accession, and the third is the only scenario that remains today and thus reflects the kinds of work that are acceptable in the current era. When I first starting documenting these encounters in the mid-1990s, I knew that these different scenarios were connected because I followed the same women in and out of them. But it would not be until the early 2000s, when the first two had dissolved, that I began to see the fuller picture, to question the role of accession, and especially to consider how Portugal's economic integration in 1996 played a role in these dramatic shifts. When I documented these scenarios between 1994 and 2003 they co-existed. Accordingly, they are the product of a historical circumstance that enabled the simultaneity of their existence. This is how I think about the meaning of accession and its impact in Portugal; I address it as the condition that would move and shift the composition of the relationships in these three scenarios. My role as ethnographer is to determine the terms of their co-existence, such that the tensions between the scenarios generate meaningful information about the accession process.

This analysis is further complicated by my initial perceptions of Cape Verdean women's roles as peixeiras. At first I thought that the women primarily understood themselves to be "peixeiras" and that they worked as domestics for the purpose of establishing residency, to collect medical and social security benefits, or to fulfill other bureaucratic needs like opening bank accounts. While doing doctoral fieldwork between 1994 and 1998, my sole aim was to document the peixeira economy that seemed to thrive independent of violent city and state-backed police aggressions. Yet within the period between 2002 and 2003, as I witnessed their public activities come to a halt, I realized that they were no longer "peixeiras." Their relationships to their own bodies, their use of their daily hours, and the different Portuguese women who would become their new interlocutors at work, all emphasized drastic transformations: they had shifted to the labor status of "domestic."

These are the circumstances that have shaped my reading of the relationship between the three scenarios as indicative of modernizing change. It is precisely retrospect—the privilege of thinking through these events in the present—that contours the sense I make of their connection. The point is not to assume that these events were independently moving along a determined path; what matters is how former Cape Verdean peixeiras pull seemingly disparate events into dialogue with each other and which converge into a narrative about Portugal's EU modernity. What counts, then, is what the new terms of Cape Verdean women's relationships to Portuguese women conveyed about the emergent character of the Portuguese state and thus about the very process of accession and economic integration.

THE CHAPTERS

The first ethnographic scenario, described in chapter 2, occurs at a location called Docapesca, situated along a port area of the Tagus River, that was inaugurated by the Portuguese state in the 1950s with the hope of centralizing the wide distribution of fish to the general public. Docapesca was open to buyers between the hours of roughly 11 p.m. to 7 a.m. There, Cape Verdean peixeiras purchased fish primarily from wholesale vendors, Portuguese men who were also fishmongers. I conducted my fieldwork just as the city of Lisbon and the Ministry of Agriculture and Fisheries were beginning to rigorously regulate food conservation practices, an effort leading to the closure of this facility in 2003. At the time, developers had also expressed an interest in luxury urbanization projects along Lisbon's riverbank areas, including the area around Docapesca. The data in this scenario exemplifies a period when external pressures had yet to shut down this facility. Here, encounters between Portuguese men and Cape Verdean women exemplify anxieties about staying in business as the pressures related to infrastructure development mounted.

The second scenario, described in chapter 3, occurs on the streets of Lisbon in front of a train station—Cais do Sodré—in an area undergoing development for commercial expansion. Here, Cape Verdean peixerias sold fish right after having purchased it at Docapesca, roughly between 7 a.m. and 11 a.m. The area saw heavy policing throughout the 1990s in the effort to enforce semi-monitored vending laws. I focus on three types of interactions in this scenario, those between peixeiras and police, between peixeiras and their customers, and between peixeiras and various noncustomers with whom they crossed paths daily. I show how the element of policing in each of these interactions calls on people to assert themselves as particular types of law-abiding or law-defying subjects, a process staged through a black-white tension. Specifically, I detail how ideas concerning a leisure as opposed to a subsistence relationship with the urban landscape are made to polarize pedestrians into "black migrants" and "white citizens" in the spatial confines of Cais do Sodré. Importantly, this chapter must be read in conversation with the previous one. Each ethnographic chapter reveals how new forms of regulation emerged in tandem with the kinds of subjects and activities that contextualized a given setting. It is thus essential to note that sales activity at Cais do Sodré is at least a century old, but that the policing of this area coincides with the efforts to close Docapesca. By tracing the same groups of women through different settings, I illustrate how seemingly separate regulatory practices are unified through particular kinds of subjects, in my case the Cape Verdean peixeira. Her ultimate transition to low-waged women's work highlights the connections among these ostensibly disjointed interventions.

The third scenario, described in chapter 4, observes Portuguese and Cape Verdean women's relationships at work. I focus on one encounter in a household, between employee and employer, and two encounters in janitorial work, between employees and supervisors. This chapter includes three of the four women that appear in chapters 2 and 3. These scenarios occurred right after peixeiras left Cais do Sodré, signaling a transition in their public visibility as they earned wages between the approximate hours of noon and 7 pm. This would be the only scenario where state intervention was about shaping this work for Cape Verdean women, and African women more generally, as opposed to collaborating with the claims to income that Cape Verdean women previously made for themselves by playing a less scrutinizing role in their work lives. While the other scenarios were dissolved by the state in the early 2000s, waged domestic work—which emerged as a niche for African women at the onset of preparations for accession—is the only income practice that remains today. Moreover, while encounters in the other scenarios are characterized by flippant references and responses to raced information and colonial tensions, interaction in domestic encounters is riddled with respectful, instruction-driven exchanges, thus departing from the confrontational exchanges that characterized the previous interactions.

Methodologically, the transcripts roughly follow Emmanuel Schegloff's (2007) conversational analysis format, although I interpret the data in relation to both the setting in which they are embedded and the broader moralizing discourse around which notions of civility are realized through encounters with difference. I thus observe adherence to and the manipulation of social norms in ritualized interaction, in a Goffmanian sense. The ways people index difference through words or affective stances can signal the moral-political climate in a particular space. The degree to which individuals choose to align themselves with the norms of such settings says something about both those individuals and the terms of their relationship to institutional power. I thus consider how people manage these interventions, noting when and how they take them up, refuse them, or trivialize them. Attention to language in this work is not about creating a linguistic analysis of these scenarios, but about drawing the readers' attention to taken for granted rituals in everyday communication that systematically dialogue with or against moralized norms with institutionally relevant implications. The transcripts provide opportunities to observe how people come to participate in or reject normative ideology, the consequences of which say something about how individuals variably choose to align themselves with Portugal's modernizing project, or not.

I began documenting the peixeira scene in late December 1994 when I worked primarily with four Cape Verdean women for whom I have chosen the pseudonyms Bia, Djina, Patrícia, and Manuela. I describe them in more detail in chapter 2 when I begin to discuss their daily activities. I had originally intended to focus only on the meaning of events related to the actual economy: the Docapesca scene and the street sales scene. But because they worked in waged jobs every afternoon I could never arrange to interview them. So I accompanied them to their waged jobs. Because waged, feminized labor—be it as janitors, domestics—is generally isolated, it proved quite easy to follow the women around and help out as I asked questions and reflected on the events of the morning. Although I did not originally imagine this final work scenario as being so central to my study, by 2005 all four women were working in multiple part-time jobs or in one full-time position as household workers, nannies, kitchen assistants, and janitors—as were the majority of their former peixeira colleagues. This was when I understood that the women before me were no longer peixeiras— they had all become "domestics."

one

MISCEGENATION INTERRUPTED

In the introductory chapter I established that Lusotropicalism was an ideology about Portugal's experience of racial fraternity with those whom they colonized. This narrative was used to justify the maintenance of the colonial empire through the mid-1970s when most non-Portuguese colonies in Africa had been liberated by the 1960s. Lusotropical ideology would later be challenged by large-scale African labor migrations to Portugal beginning in the late 1950s. Because Lusotropical sentiment worked from a distance to justify events in the colonies, its irrelevance in the metropole, as experienced by African migrants, drew increased attention to its questionable status. But such scrutiny in Portugal, beginning in the 1980s, did not come from international social scientists as occurred previously. Instead, Portuguese leftists, activists, and resident African communities questioned the Lusotropicalist ideal in relation to the actual experience of African immigrants in Portugal. For African immigrants, specifically persons identified under colonialism as *asimilados* (the assimilated), *civilizados* (the civilized), *mulatos*, or mestiços, the dissolving importance of the ideology affected how they were seen and heard in relation to the supposed in-betweenness of their social status. These privileged colonial identities were variably recognized and valued in Portugal, namely in immediate social exchanges, through the mid-1990s. But something happened between 1974 and the mid-1990s, particularly to the "biological" categories mulato and mestiço— which I use interchangeably—that unsettled them as valuable descriptions of personhood.

In this chapter I describe the dual roles that multiculturalism and the state's interpretation of EEC/EU membership played in dismantling the visibility and thus the viability of the mestiço figure. This category stands apart from that of asimilado or civilizado—synonymous legal designations tied to Portuguese indigeneity policies—because mestiço identity, though often tied to these statuses, was both a social and a biological category that referenced miscegenation. I draw on the history of representations of race and racism in Portugal to outline the various social and institutional strategies that enabled diverse uses of Lusotropical ideology and provide a genealogy of events in which Portuguese-African sociality is reconfigured for diverse ends, such as securing Portugal's accession and economic integration processes.

COMPULSORY AFRICANITY

In 2002 I witnessed something I could never have anticipated at a Lisbon theater during a public debate on the status of black representation. The objective of the debate, with five invited commentators and less than fifteen audience participants, was to generate a dialogue on race relations in contemporary Portugal. The commentators, who identified themselves to the audience either as white Portuguese professionals with Portuguese citizenship or as African professionals with either Portuguese citizenship or immigrant status, worked in the humanities, performing arts, and the social sciences. Everyone on stage understood him or herself as a leftist in the sense that their work aimed to lay bare racism and social marginalization to the general public. The commentators shared the belief that it was nearly impossible for black-identified Portuguese or African nationals to partake in artistic expressions recognized as modern or Western. In fact, they went so far as to argue that non-African-identified expressions were considered inappropriate for the black subject. One of the white commentators corroborated this claim by juxtaposing her experiences as an artist with those Africans. She noted that she too faced obstacles in terms of financial support, but never in terms of the content or message of her work. Next the speakers discussed the crisis of African authenticity or what I like to call, borrowing from Adrienne Rich, "compulsory" Africanity (Rich 1986). As the conversation developed, they linked different requirements for authenticity to different subjects: Portuguese-identified artists possessed the authority to define the narrative, while African-identified artists were supposed to simply receive this information, given their inherent Africanity instinctively guided their gestures. The African commentators then gave evidence of this claim noting how their prose, art, and performances were deemed inauthentic when private and state sponsors of multicultural venues complained that their productions were "not African enough." The white commentators nodded aggressively in agreement.

The first audience respondent, a white-identified Portuguese male who described himself as living and working in former Portuguese Africa, attempted to contribute to the panelists' discussion by problematizing the idea of authenticity. Focusing on dance and theater, he outlined why authenticity created a double bind for blacks. He addressed the ironies of African-inspired dance in Portugal, noting how Portuguese dance professionals were being supported through professional exchanges in Africa, their funding proposals generally including their intention to help sharpen and strengthen African dance techniques. He then added that funding for performers to travel to Portugal to receive training in Western dance genres was limited. African performers did seem to find ample support when they were on tour, he said, especially to African cultural events and to European multicultural venues, but the possibilities for mutual cultural exchanges between performers remained small. He concluded his commentary by stating that the very set-up of exchanges relied on a primitive Africa and a modern Portugal, with subjects from each of these locations staged in relationships that sustained a perverse dynamic. Dangerous imaginaries of African authenticity, he held, could be dismantled and transformed if black-identified performers were not blocked by what was popularly perceived as the limit of their "native potential."

What I found interesting about this person's commentary was not what I thought to be the productive argument; rather, more telling were the audience responses that followed from self-identified mulata artists, each with Portuguese citizenship. Several women responded, immediately challenging the analysis. The first began by stating that her father was white and Portuguese, while her mother was black and African, and that she was born in her mother's homeland in Lusophone Africa. Later in her adolescence she moved back and forth between Portugal and a country situated in northwestern Europe, where her family eventually relocated. Today, as a modern artist working and living between two different European countries, she was dismayed by the complete lack of interest in her work in Portugal, given that it was celebrated in her other home. She argued that in

Portugal her work was perceived as having no specificity. Then, marking herself again as mulata, she said that she defined her work (in a market sense) as the conflation of African and European gestures and that Portuguese audiences found this description unpalatable. She then raised a poignant question: Why was this so, if to be mulata was *to be* Portuguese? She could understand this situation if it were happening in her other place of residence, but the very circumstance that united her parents was definitively Portuguese. She continued by asserting that her presentation of herself as mixed, or mestiça, was not questioned in her other place of residence.

I was puzzled by her juxtaposition of the cultural dynamics of race in these two European countries, as the citizenship and identity practices of her other place of residence, where bi-racial identity has no place in the popular or legal categories that recognize social difference—that is, where people are either white or non-white. It then occurred to me that her point, perhaps, was to emphasize history. For what did she mean by equating "mixed" status with things "Portuguese"? What was the root and goal of her critique? With intense and growing frustration in her voice, she continued by arguing that her identity as mixed was not appreciated in Portugal and that the celebration of discoveries and colonial benevolence—references that seemed to come from nowhere—were hypocritical because she herself was not really visible in Portugal inasmuch as her art no longer had a place in Portuguese society.

This woman's testimony rested on the idea that Portugal was supposed to recognize her and her art as distinctively mestiça, thus qualifying her for inclusion in the nation. This expectation was tied to her claim that to be mulato means to be Portuguese, a claim relying on the particular historical circumstance that brought her parents together in a former Portuguese African colony. In this sense, she used colonial history—and the way it resonates with a particular culturalist narrative—and her increasingly adverse relationship to it as the ground for her critique. By addressing the irony of benevolent depictions of colonization she seemed to be arguing that if she could not publicly embody this benevolence—through herself and the mixed essence of her art—then any insinuation of racial progress or equality in Portugal proves deceptive, fraudulent even, as is any contemporary notion that her identity has immediate value. Importantly, her argument depends on the idea that, at some point, mestiço identity was recognized and valued in Portuguese society: she presented her parent's marital union, marking a moment in the past, to establish a critique of postcolonial reality.

This person's nostalgia for tropicalist intimacy is essentialist, to be sure. However, if we reflect upon the ways EU Portugal continues to represent a version of this myth—for example, through references to "discoveries" that celebrate the colonial past without invoking the former colonial subject or the mixed body—then contemporary nationalist rhetoric is also a select version of the colonial past. The question, then, should not be one that problematizes essentialization; rather, and in consideration of the power differential between the interests of the Portuguese state and the mestiço subject, it should concern the political stakes involved in laying claims to a past already accepted as fictitious or obsolete. In other words, how can the same narratives of intimacy and familiarity once used by the state be invoked by the very subjects who wrote themselves as the victims of such fictions during the colonial wars (see also Scott 1999, 2004)?

The first woman's response was immediately followed by testimonies of other artists who positioned themselves similarly in racial terms. Amongst a seemingly mulato, black, and white crowd, as small as it was, there were no objections. The white Portuguese man, dismayed, walked out of the small auditorium before the testimonies ended. The panelists began to whisper among themselves in bewilderment, concerned about the unpopular political stance taken up by some in the audience. Twenty minutes later I learned of the panelists' frustration; they felt that no one got their collective point on the need to place equal value on the work of black and white artists. As for the audience members, everyone just looked ahead, in isolation. When the debate came to an end people left one by one, or in their respective cliques, in relative silence.

Thinking back to the Portuguese man's comment, I wondered what had inspired this new wave of authenticity in the first place, an authenticity where the performance of a concrete distinction between African and Portuguese identities was mediated through the state enforced dynamic he described. It seemed to have something to do with state-sponsored discourses that now equated diversity with multicultural projects in Portugal, not with former colonial discourses concerning Africa or Africans. But then I started to question the logic of the first audience respondent and the panelists: In what argument did they ground their position? Or rather, what was the moral-political claim that I at first assumed to be the "right" answer and later saw as just as ideologically grounded as other audience members' criticisms?

The arguments from the panelists and the first audience respondent supported the very binary that the state now supports and that bothered the other respondents. So while I originally believed that the first gentleman and the other respondents were not reaching each other, or rather, had not established common ground from which to debate, it later occurred to me that they had indeed been talking about the same thing and that the resulting silence marked a deep disagreement, not a misunderstanding. The comments of the mestiço audience members, because they were not usually voiced in public, could be taken as more radical in this context than those of the panelists or the Portuguese man. They are more radical in that the multiracial schema they support had become obsolete, while the rationale behind the Portuguese man's comment—though grounded in a leftist critique well beyond government policy—replicated the racial schema now considered normative and supported by the state. My point is not to advocate what the mulata respondents lamented or what the panelists pushed. Rather, I want to call attention to the fact that even the most liberal of critiques beg scrutiny, especially when the radical left and the neoliberal state are in agreement with each other: binarism—and hence the disappearance of the mulata figure—is now interpreted as the best method for guaranteeing equal recognition by opposing parties. The normalization of this binary is thus an important site for examining changes in the Portuguese national imaginary concerning social conduct, appropriate forms of recognition, and the management of the self in the presence of difference. The simultaneity of these events and Portugal's public commitment to a modern course of action generates questions about the role of difference in the country's interpretation of its new national status.

Accordingly, the remainder of this chapter discusses Portuguese engagements with difference through ideas about race and racism over time. My aim, however, is not to trace these reflections as representative of an absolute reality. Instead, I attend to the shifts to provide insight into the relationship between racial knowledge and social morality in Portugal. I am more concerned with the depth with which racial knowledge has differently permeated a public and private sense of selfhood, as opposed to questioning or confirming the mythic status of Lusotropicalism.[1]

In the 1930s, the new Salazarian government commissioned colonial eth-nologists to scientifically confirm the purity of Portuguese blood (Castelo 1998; Almeida 2000; Thomaz 2002). Arguably, this was a response to British critiques that drew racialized connections between Portuguese identity and the Portuguese state's "backward" forms of colonial governance (see note 1, this chapter). Physical anthropologists, including Mendes Corrêa (1943) and Eusebio Tamagnini (1934), were assigned to do comparative blood work on Portuguese populations. They compared the blood of those from the metropole to that of nationals in Madeira and the blood of indigenous subjects in Portuguese colonial Africa and India (see Bastos 1998, 2001, 2003; Almeida 2000; Roque 2001). These experiments had important im-plications for white Portuguese emigration to the colonies, specifically to Angola and Mozambique, which had the largest Portuguese settler popula-tions. The studies emphasized that geographic and environmental setting had no impact on blood purity, as British critiques had insinuated in relation to the Portuguese in the eighteenth through the early twentieth centuries. The sojourning Portuguese subject, wherever placed in space, would remain racially pure so long as it did not mix with the natives.

Gilberto Freyre's *Masters and Slaves* (*Casa Grande e Senzala*), which celebrated rather than refuted the ideas insinuated by the British, was not initially accepted by the Portuguese state. Freyre's work challenged how António de Oliveira Salazar's regime had hoped to racially frame Por-tuguese national identity. As Cláudia Castelo (1998) notes in her social history of the Portuguese colonial state's engagement with Portuguese antiracism, the colonial administration was quite bothered by Freyre's miscegenation thesis. *Masters and Slaves* argues that the Portuguese quest for discovery is unique and that the willingness to engage in cultural and biological exchange signals a Portuguese aptitude for colonizing and trans-forming others' civilizations. Freyre further asserts that the Portuguese man's tendency to mate with the Other (when in the tropics) and his physiological capacity to withstand tropical conditions are both factors defining Portuguese prowess. While Freyre's vision does not actually type the Portuguese as non-European, the idea of their tendency to mix pre-sumed as much.

After the tightening of immigration laws in the United States in the 1920s, the Portuguese colonial administration began experimental settlement programs for working-poor and rural families under a family-reunification scheme (see Castelo 2007). By the 1950s, at the height of this program, most non-Portuguese colonies in Africa were beginning to negotiate the end of colonial rule. To an international community now focused on the importance of national sovereignty, Portugal began to appear as politically backward because of its continued investment in its colonial mission. This led to threats of a suspension of Portugal's UN membership in the late 1950s. In the effort to safeguard its membership, and to protect a new industrial boom just taking shape in Portugal, the Salazar regime decided to take up Freyre's rhetoric. By that time Freyre (1958, 1961) had developed a name for his descriptions of hybridity—Lusotropicalism. Henceforth, Lusotropicalism would become Portugal's ideological justification for maintaining and continuing to enforce its colonial mission (Castelo 1998).

In a broadcast to the international community in 1963, Salazar went as far as to state that Portugal and its colonies formed one "pluri-racial," spatial entity. In this context, Salazar promoted and fostered the myth of racial democracy that Freyre had coined, and which was also understood to be in progress in Brazil. Lusotropicalism thus served to sustain what could be called a deterritorialized nationalities policy so that territorial possession would not resemble colonialism (Castelo 1998: 96–100). In essence, Portugal adopted this strategy in an attempt to defuse the charge of racism. Four years prior to this broadcast, Salazar had even renamed the overseas colonies as provinces.

Freyre's ideology was grounded in a narrative of the historic union between the colored or native woman and the white man, with biological reproduction and sexual intimacy treated as evidence of racial democracy. Thus Salazar's administration had to figure out a way to embrace the democratic core of this narrative in a fashion that could maintain and secure white family values and their reproductive capacity in the colonies, particularly given the ongoing project of white family reunifications. Compassion at home would prove key to the state's policy: the administration emphasized the inherent affective qualities of Portugueseness through Catholic discourses emphasizing charity. School children in Portugal developed pen-pal relationships with children throughout Portuguese Africa, while bourgeois church women organized charity drives that likewise stressed the importance of compassion, in ways that never actually dialogued with ideals of fraternity tied to miscegenation. In the metropole, race would thus continue to be imagined as a finite, blood determined state of being; its recognition had no connection to discrimination or to nationals residing in the metropole. Racism, by contrast, was popularly defined as the colonizer's absence of human compassion toward differently raced others *abroad*. Significantly, racism was not tied to ideals of material possession or to an individual's access to rights and freedoms, in an Anglo sense. It was simply about the colonizer's display or absence of affect. Compassion or "empathy without touching" was thus fused with the ideals of multiracial fraternity that derived from the celebration of miscegenation. And so the antiracist myth was a late colonial production, assuming coherence through the everyday practices of schoolchildren and devout church ladies, for instance.

African elites and clergy who traveled to Portugal for educational purposes, as well as Cape Verdean migrant workers, readily attest to the intense racial hostilities they experienced in the 1960s and early 1970s. A young recruited worker told me that he was constantly harassed and accosted by military personnel returning from Guinea, Angola, and Mozambique. One soldier told him to watch out because he himself was not beyond butchering little African boys' penises. Something enabled a comfortable disconnect between how blacks were treated in Portugal and the idea that the Portuguese were not racist.

In Portugal the idea that the Portuguese could not be racist persisted well after democratization in 1974 and through the 1980s. Before the passing of the first antidiscrimination law in 1999 (discussed later), cases of racism were ascribed to the ignorance of the individual person committing the assault, as the myth of antiracism mediated when and how racism could be recognized. Individuals could be typed as racists, but their ignorance disassociated them from the social whole, thus containing racism within the ignorant subject. Systemic forms of discrimination were also strategically mediated. For instance, when Cape Verdeans started migrating in larger numbers to Portugal as temporary workers in the early 1970s, state-influenced newspapers were quick to report on the discrimination the workers experienced (see Sousa 2003). But here, the nature of the argument made all the difference: it was the victims' inferior identities that constitutively made them the subjects of discrimination, or rather drew discrimination to them. As such, no aggressor or culprit was implicated in the act—if you were black you were simply discriminated against. Journalists most likely wrote in this way to send a message to the international community about labor injustices in Portugal, as coverage of Portuguese labor practices from outside had a long and effective history of getting Portugal into trouble. For instance, the International Labor Organization (ILO) had reported unfair labor practices in Portuguese Africa to the international community in the 1940s and 1950s, leading to changes in labor policies applied to indentured workers (Fikes forthcoming). What is meaningful here is that an acceptable method of internal communication was available because the form the reporting on discrimination took did not implicate (from the state's perspective) Portugal or the Portuguese national community in the racism reported.

These observations tell us something about the experience of absent institutional mediation in the ways people recognized and engaged racial difference at this time. The concept of the ignorant individual—the figure capable of committing racist offenses—was strategically useful in normalizing Portuguese national authority, as it was constituted in relation to the Other, while at the same time protecting the state's antiracist image of itself. It is thus important to attend to the productivity of antiracism as a belief endowing national civilians with a particular kind of authority under fascism, especially since this is the very freedom that begins to recede after Portugal's accession.

Below I address those practices that are transforming the encounter between state and society within the context of Portugal's adhesion to the EEC. Under these shifting conditions I describe how racist practice is rendered a social possibility, one that transforms antiracism into the normative target (and thus not just a floating ideology), and one in which racist expression reflects on the social whole, not just on the ignorant individual. I describe how and why it is that EEC and later EU related social changes beginning in the mid-1990s enabled and even required that racism be regarded as a Portuguese possibility. This involves a discussion of a market run for nonsubsistence consumption, and where prescriptions for "fixing" the market resulted in new practices of relationality with others that altered how people previously connected with each other. My objective is to describe how antiracism—now a state-espoused objective manifest through displays of self-control—is one of the forms through which rational behavior is taken to be something manageable through particular kinds of labor encounters.

THE PORTUGUESE MARKET

The national population in Portugal had risen from 8.43 million in 1973 to 9.09 million in 1975 (Baganha 1998). This increase was due in large part to the retornado phenomena; over 800,000 Portuguese nationals (originally from the metropole) had returned from Africa by 1976, and thousands more who had not returned would do so by the early 1980s in response to Angola's civil war (see Pires 1984). In addition, a growing African work-force was recruited for major construction projects in Lisbon and the Algarve as many Portuguese retornados quickly emigrated northward to western Europe or the Americas for higher-paying jobs. Between 1975 and 1977—after the 1974 coup for democracy and the end of the colonial wars in 1975—commercial entrepreneurs began reflecting on how to capitalize on the nation's resources, given that export earnings from the former colonies had ceased as a guaranteed source of income, particularly with postindependence civil wars in Angola and in Mozambique.

Simultaneously, the new socialist government of the Partido Socialista (PS) contemplated how to best employ its non- and semi-skilled workforce in a way that would both use the domestic market and rid it of the commercial monopolies protected under the fascist government. Count-less legal and market-related changes were made to prevent the monopoli-zation of capital. Low-key export firms whose workers were tied to strong trade unions were targeted as essential to Portugal's postfascist develop-ment phase, both economically and psychologically. Here, the govern-ment's objective was to build the confidence and gain the trust of the population through labor unions that would guard against monopolistic practices and fascist forms of state regulation.

In 1977 representatives of Portugal's national commercial association applied for entry to what was then the EEC. Considering the application a long shot, the country had hoped to be accepted in 1979. One reason for the delay to accession, as Daniel Nataf (1995) stresses, was that the postfas-cist Portuguese economic plan supported small-scale companies that fol-lowed labor protectionist measures. These measures included laws restrict-ing forms of production, such as the production of highly valued commodities, that could easily create corporate monopolies. Companies under PS leadership had thus established a relatively even-leveled market that paired production with wage distribution, rather than with demands from the international market.

But from the European Commission's perspective this strategy prevented Portugal from competing effectively on the international market. Uncompetitive wages propelled emigration, draining the nation of skilled professionals. One of the EC's primary prescriptions was the creation of higher-waged markets that could produce internationally competitive goods and services, hence enabling more domestically derived capital to circulate in the local market. But this process demanded state interventions that would not only shift the market, but also generate a primary workforce positioned to labor under such terms.

FIXING THE MARKET

With a social structure composed primarily of a small elite and a majority, working-poor population—composed of rural agrarian workers and an urban working class—one can understand why the socialist leadership adopted the strategy mentioned above. But as Portugal's entry into the EEC became a real possibility, ideas for balancing the market-state encounter generated tense debate. Should Portugal continue to protect the worker as before, thus risking further economic isolation from the west? Or should the country risk inevitable economic struggles to catch up with the rest of the west?

These debates in the media were represented as falling along party lines. The right-to-center Partido Social Democrata (Social Democratic Party, PSD), which assumed office in 1979, the year Portugal was accepted for EEC candidacy, supported what it understood as short-term losses with indispensable long-term gains. For some, the end of reliance on the agrarian sector and its informal divisions signified progress in itself. The Portuguese Communist Party (Partido Comunista Português, PCP), and many in the left-to-center PS, by contrast, feared not only the impact of integration on the worker—as trade and domestic production restrictions would affect the subsistence lifestyles of the majority agrarian work force— but also a situation that would make Portugal newly dependent on other western European countries, in ways beyond migrations. What would a larger European presence in Portugal do to or for Portugal? Under the guidelines of integration, for instance, nationals from wealthier countries in the community had the right to set up cheap wage-labor companies that would make Portuguese workers dependent on non-national European business. National autonomy proved a big concern.

These debates on Portugal's financial destiny and the role of local government continued well after Portugal's actual accession date in 1986. But the PSD did not focus its line of argument on local structural management. The new market the party envisioned was narrated instead in terms of the potential of an economy stimulated by consumption and thus the consumer. Government was imagined as a manager of Portugal's extension of itself outward through individual consumers, in its connection with transnational markets, as opposed to inward and thus dealing with local economic structures. The working-poor did question the role of Portuguese government after accession in relation to the consumer argument. Their conversations responded to a fear of government's absence and the weight of economic expectations that did not seem to connect with working people (see also Holmes 2000). The rise in food and pharmaceutical prices, in addition to property values that made it near impossible to reside in Lisbon proper, emphasized to the working-poor that the state would neglect its previous responsibilities.

The state had been doing some internal tinkering, however, as evidenced by a surge of new laws and policies in the areas of immigration, gender advancement, urban development, and multiculturalism. In essence, the concept of government had changed, becoming more focused on its populations and thus social management (Foucault 2003, 2008). The consequences of this shift in governance not only produced new communities, but it also had an effect that morally hierarchized them as good and bad, distinctions brought to life through versions of civic participation that mirrored the state's new social projects. Four types of state actions can be identified that enabled new forms of social engineering and the visibility of new communities: immigration and nationality laws; state-sponsored multiculturalism; gender advocacy; and urban hygiene management in Lisbon.

Immigration and Nationality Laws

Immigration and nationality laws most explicitly pointed to the existence of new communities and the new social categories to which they pertained. These laws would effectively limit claims to Portuguese citizenship by former-colonial African nationals, while safeguarding the extension of Portuguese nationality and thus citizenship to Portuguese immigrants and their third-generation descendents in diaspora. The process of limiting Africans' claims to Portuguese citizenship proved significant because it was among the first legal processes after democracy and decolonization to close off the possibilities of Portuguese nationality to non-Portuguese descendants of the empire in Africa.

To relay a sense of the impact of this shift, and of the ways immigration and nationality laws were previously intertwined, consider this example: The new democratic Constitution of 1975 preserved a 1959 law stipulating that anyone born in Portugal proper was automatically a Portuguese citizen. The new 1981 law on nationality, by contrast, stated that persons born in Portugal would not be recognized as citizens unless their parents had been legally working and residing in Portugal for a minimum of six consecutive, documented years. With new deportation, residency, and work visa laws that were also passed in 1981 and 1982, laws that jeopardized the rights and political claims of undocumented workers, many migrants either did not meet or could not prove their employment or residency status for six consecutive years (see SOS Racismo 2002). Such a lapse in one's legal record threatened the citizenship potential of migrants' children who were born in Portugal. Meanwhile the grandchildren of Portuguese nationals residing beyond Portuguese space—regardless of any immediate tie to Portugal—could claim Portuguese nationality and thus Portuguese citizenship.

The 1981 nationality law (Lei 37/81) also included a special statute for Portuguese women. Previously, women who married non-Portuguese nationals outside Portugal risked losing their citizenship and well as the ability to pass on their natal citizenship to their children. The risk was especially acute if they were not married to the fathers of their children. The new law preserved women's citizenship, as well as the Portuguese citizenship rights of their children, independent of their place of residence or of the terms of their domestic arrangement.

When reading the immigration and nationality laws together it seems that the 1975 citizenship law (Decreto-lei 305A/1975) that revoked Portuguese nationality status from former Portuguese Africans did not in fact concern defining the terms of nationality by any subject-specific criteria; the 1975 law determined which Africans would remain Portuguese nationals and which Africans would become nationals of their new nation-states, independent of where they were positioned geographically. The nationality and immigration laws of 1981—which outlined who was *not* entitled to Portuguese nationality—*racially* defined the limits of the Portuguese national as a subject. This further suggests that the previous 1975 laws specifically attempted to define the limits of Portuguese national territory—independent of the subjects pertaining to it. As the new 1981 laws coincide with the year in which Portugal negotiated its criteria of accession in 1980, it is clear that it was aimed at resolving any pre-existing confusions concerning who was and was not Portuguese. This would prove especially important since claims could previously be made if one could prove their support of Portuguese patrimony under colonialism through civil service, for instance.

The new immigration and nationality laws would further limit claims to citizenship after two amnesty periods for the legalization of undocumented migrants in 1992 and in 1996. While the laws mentioned above effectively terminated any legal privileges allotted to Lusophone Africans, the amnesty periods dealt with the postcolonial present: they aimed to count the undocumented migrant labor force that was estimated to far exceed the legal resident population (see SOS Racismo 2002). The amnesty periods did not offer legalized status to anyone who applied, and the previous laws closed loopholes that those denied could have used. Importantly, labor quotas drove immigration policy during these periods; the quotas were established to predetermine the number of workers to be legalized in accordance with construction and public works labor demands. In effect, each legalization period generated huge pools of traceable, deportable workers. It enabled closer estimates of the undocumented resident migrant population while enforcing transparent and legitimate avenues for penalizing the evasion of deportation, and thus criminalizing nondocumented residency more broadly than before. As SOS Racismo (2002) has argued, the two amnesties demarcated distinctions between legal and illegal subjects in ways that symbolically criminalized the figure of the migrant, independent of his or her legal status. Whereas in the recent past Portuguese-African differences were blurred by the retornado phenomenon (see Pires 1984), or by the fact that a substantial percentage of Cape Verdeans were able to retroactively claim Portuguese citizenship before 1981—regardless of whether they had lived in Portugal or not—the new laws seemed to put uncertainties to rest at the same moment when the state began to participate more deeply in the creation of disposable labor. The effect of these shifts would be the visibility of definite Portuguese and African communities that were legally categorized as either citizens or migrants, respectively.

Multiculturalism

One can trace the emergent social impact of this citizen-migrant distinction to the early 1990s. It was at this time that Lisbon began to sponsor its first multicultural events that showcased African immigrant communities. In one sense, these municipal celebrations signified modernity because they marked Portugal's transition from an emigrant to an immigrant nation. In another, they figured skewed narratives of tropicalism that promoted an ideal of Portuguese tolerance for difference (having discarded references to miscegenation), narratives mirroring Europe's commitment to antiracism. In 1995, a state commission was established to monitor ethnic minority issues to both celebrate and protect the virtues of tolerance. Named the Alto Commissário das Minorias Étnicas (High Commission for Ethnic Minorities, ACIME), it rubberstamped the planning of all public diversity events. The commission's presence in local lives expanded as it hired social workers—black and white citizens alike—to deal with first- and second-generation immigrant youth issues in the areas of education, public outreach, and public health.

The mid-1990s can be characterized as the birth of diversity. 1995 saw the launch of a satellite radio program, RDP Africa, a subsidiary of Radiodifusão Portuguesa, a public service broadcasting organization. The program transmitted from Lisbon but was broadcast throughout Portugal, in each of the country's former African colonies, and in Brazil. The original objective was to showcase music from PALOP musicians. However Cape Verdeans soon started advertising social events on the station. They turned RDP Africa into an important vehicle for circulating information on immigrant legal counsel, announcements on the deceased, and news about CD launches (see Maciel 2005). On Wednesdays there were free concerts, book signings, and other art events in the RDP auditorium in the center of Lisbon, at Amoreiras. This venue would become the first official space in which Africans, specifically African youths, from diverse backgrounds could congregate during the day on a regular basis under planned circumstances. This proved incredibly significant because most Africans lived in

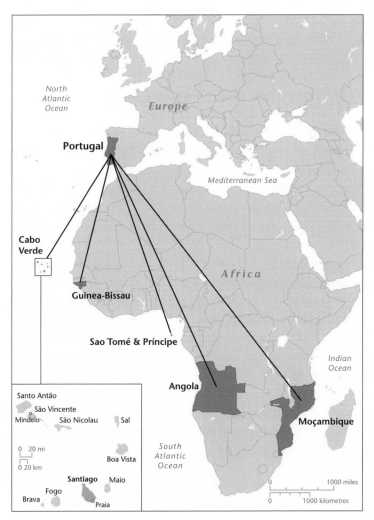

PALOP map: Lusophone African migrations to Portugal

nation-based shanty communities or were dispersed throughout working-poor Portuguese neighborhoods on the outskirts of Lisbon. In addition, when I was in the field in mid-1998, a civil war broke out in Guinea-Bissau that destroyed most of the capital city of Bissau's infrastructure. RDP Africa kept family in Lisbon informed about the whereabouts of family dispersed from Guinea into neighboring counties like Senegal and Gambia. Similar information circulated toward the end of Angola's civil war. RDP Africa thus connected diverse African nationals who listened to this radio programming. Not only had a common condition of exclusion linked them to each other in Portugal, but they also became the daily recipients of information from different locations. Moreover, the terms under which they took in this information in Portugal also tied them to each other. It created some of the conditions under which communities would come to inscribe and recognize themselves as diasporic or "migrant," in juxtaposition to Portuguese citizens, whether these individuals were citizens or not.

As the project developing out of RDP Africa became more popular, people felt the need to define it; everyone recognized that the conditions giving birth to it were indeed a departure from the recent past. So while there had been no official civil rights movement with a designated set of demands, a black cultural movement had curiously taken shape through the support and recognition of the community by city and state government. The terminology used to describe this new cultural movement was *lusofonia*, a term that uniquely characterized the shared characteristics of persons from the Portuguese-speaking world. In practice, it worked as a code word in Portugal for migrant experience. As the word began to circulate in the media, becoming popularized, intellectuals became suspicious of it. Angolan novelist and poet Ondjaki, who resides in Portugal and Angola, critiqued it for being a convenient Portuguese descriptor of Lusophone experience that included Africans, for instance, but not the Portuguese (see Maciel 2005: 38). The critique also hinted at the fact that the term was not self-ascribing, particularly because black youths often refer to themselves with the English term "black."

Indeed, in contrast to Lusotropicalism, Lusofonia did not recall narratives of inter-racial mixing. Instead it identified the common *cultural* thread of Portugueseness in African (and Brazilian) experience in relation to history, language, food, and music. As noted by Ondjaki, Portugal itself was excluded from the description. The consequence was an evasion of talk of blood or race. Alfredo Margarido (2000) traces the origins of this word to post-1974 events as the Portuguese version of francophonie, where it is used to describe the linguistic specificity of Portuguese-speaking or *Lusophone space* (espaço lusofono). Its popularity would expand in 1996 with the establishment of the Community of Portuguese Language Countries (Comunidade dos Países de Língua Portuguesa, CPLP) with members from Lusophone Africa and Brazil (with East Timor later joining in 2002). 1996 also coincides with the year of Portugal's economic integration into the EU when Portugal began abiding by trade restrictions that did not necessarily honor its historic commercial networks. Because the CPLP's primary functions have been in the areas of trade and the movement of people among these specific countries, it can be understood as a legal structure that guarantees a continuity of export profits for Portugal through the CPLP arrangement.

Another institutional effect, this time through the use of social workers, was the transformation of "troubled" youth into participants in city-sponsored projects. In a strange way, disenfranchised youth became a sign of Lisbon's urban development: racial crises and troubles with assimilation signaled modern problems of the sort that supposedly advanced capitalist nations have to manage and incorporate into their rehabilitative agendas. Yet what the state read as a sign of urban development, activist organizations, such as SOS Racismo, the Guinean Association for Social Solidarity, and the Associação Cultural Moinho da Juventude (the Youth's Cultural Windmill Association), interpreted as signs of misguided government and lost opportunity (Lieve Meersschaert, pers. comm.). The 1990s saw dozens of cases where developers and labor contractors would disappear without paying workers once a construction project was finished. Activists wanted the city to focus on migrant vulnerability in a market where more money meant more exploitation. Organizations were also worried about the integration crises experienced by first- and second-generation youths who were either repeating primary school grades or dropping out of high school. They wanted the city to be more active in promoting retention and after-school activities, particularly since parents often worked well over ten hours per day and therefore were not present in households. Moreover, activists associated migrant vulnerability to labor exploitation with state tolerance for racism. Many believed the state was guilty of not monitoring situations that enabled exploitation.

SOS Racismo had been documenting the activities of skinhead groups tied to the Movement for National Action (Movimento de Acção Nacional, MAN), an extreme right-wing group with connections to similar organizations in other European countries. These groups were known for starting fights with African immigrants in places like Lisbon's famous Bairro Alto neighborhood. But city officials publicly refused to hear the voices of hatred, emphasizing that to be attentive to these groups was to validate their presence and thus contradict the tolerant atmosphere that was characteristic of Portuguese society. On May 26, 1993, the state secretary for youth stated, in an article titled "Em Portugal não há perigo da xenophobia" (Xenophobia Poses No Threat in Portugal), "In Portugal this problem of intolerance, xenophobia, and racism is fortunately less prevalent than in other countries. First of all, as everyone knows this is because ever since the time of Afonos de Albuquerque—*a naval officer who established the first Portuguese Empire in Asia*—there has been a politics of proximity between races and cultures" ("Devo dizer, contudo, que em Portugal este problema da intolerância, da xenofonia e do racismo felizmente tem uma expressão menos grave do que noutros países. Em primeiro lugar, porque todos sabemos que desde o tempo de Afonso de Albuquerque houve uma política muito clara de aproxiimação de raças e culturas"). The newspaper citing this statement, *Correio de Manhã*, had access to another unquoted claim from this government official: "Portuguese youths are porters of an attitude of tolerance in relation to other races." Here, the secretary enters into a dialogue with Lusotropicalist logic by binding antiracist practice to Portuguese qualities that are the product of the colonial encounter. The ideology would thus surface in institutional contexts through explanations that selectively chose the moments when the myth was taken at face value. The secretary for youth then specified where and how the state would take action against counterproductive groups and activities: through intercultural dialogue among diverse groups and through the dissemination of information in schools.

On June 10, 1995, in the early hours of the morning, this dismissiveness would be challenged. A Portuguese citizen of Cape Verdean parentage named Alcino Monteiro was brutally stabbed to death by a group of skinheads in the Bairro Alto. Skinheads had attacked blacks in this neighborhood before, but this was the first time someone was killed. African-immigrant and Portuguese-national-community activists finally had a concrete example to draw from: skinheads had brutally murdered a man in the name of the white race. It took four years for activists' pleas to be partially heard. Portugal put into effect its first antidiscrimination law in 1999.[2]

The nature of the debate that followed proved telling. In the media, many conversations were about acknowledging the existence of racism in Portugal. Dozens of articles were written with titles such as "Are the Portuguese Racist?" "Is There Racism in Portugal?" or "I Killed a Negro" (the latter referring to a confession from the colonial wars). The tropicalist myth that associated sex and biology with antiracism no longer held. But another theme brought out by the debate, circulating largely outside the mainstream press in blogs and conversations in African neighborhoods, turned on how Monteiro was identified in the media. It seemed that journalists did not know how to peg him, clumsily referring to him as "Cape Verdean," rather than a Portuguese citizen. But Monteiro had been naturalized at a young age and had even served in the Portuguese military. The criticism, in effect, was about the media's refusal to include him in the nation, a refusal tied to the circumstances of his death in the first place. So as one line of debate generated anxieties about the implications of the Portuguese individual being "a racist," a less circulated narrative questioned how one of the nation's own could be killed.

Monteiro's death illuminates that the admittance of racism and the crisis of inclusion not only play out as incommensurate realities, but represent discourses that never have to meet or be reconciled (see Povinelli 2002, 2006). How can an object of political discourse such as racism assume such disparate trajectories? And how is it that these different narratives— antiracism and exclusion—could develop separate relationships to a concept and a practice that both logics repudiated? In a country where race ceased to be a domestic legal category after slavery, where the state trivialized racism until recently, and where acts of intolerance were effaceable misdemeanors, Monteiro's death triggered something new. It transformed interactions involving others into moments that needed to be approached with great caution, and approached through the use of new categories for publicly naming Otherness. Yet even cautious action, as illustrated below, did not end up being about the promotion of equal recognition; instead, it was about the *social management of Portuguese behavior toward others*.

By spring of 1998, some time after the first multicultural projects, I realized that *preto*, a word that can be used pejoratively to refer to a black person, had been tagged as politically incorrect in what felt like a very short period of time. Similar shifts were happening elsewhere, such as in Brazil, but the terms and stakes were quite different in Portugal. In Portugal there was no organized grassroots social movement publicly challenging the state's engagement with racialized discourse or that tried to politicize the masses through designated racial terminologies. Politicized racial discourse, particularly in Lisbon, had a very clear link to the city's multicultural affairs; political correctness in effect was sanctioned and disseminated from the top from the very beginning. It circulated through state-sponsored antidiscrimination television ads, city-sponsored multicultural and antiracist events—including a marathon against racism in Lisbon in 1998—and upgraded school curriculum on Portugal's African immigrant presence in civics and history courses. There were, however, no institutional reflections concerning the official dismissal of racism in the past.

Still, people worked to reconcile this omission through underground movements ranging from community hip-hop groups to radical and leftist Portuguese artists and activists. Concerning the latter, I saw a play in 1997 entitled "Neves mil em abril" (It Rains a lot in April). In the play, the unspoken consequences of racism are worked out through a group of young working-class Portuguese men—one whose father had fought in Angola—who gang rape a working-class mulata in their neighborhood. The moral of the story is the need to reconcile old colonial tensions under difficult socioeconomic conditions. Aside from these marginal commentaries in out of the way playhouses, and in out of the way *bairros*, the state was involved in campaigns that lumped the crisis of racism in with other practices marginalizing groups like the disabled and those who were HIV positive. So in the same moment that the state assumed the responsibility for (re)educating the public, antidiscrimination was not exclusively tied to antiracism. Accordingly, being antiracist was not about reconciliation, in practice, but about normative practices of civility in relation to all differences in an era of broad social change.

As *preto* became unacceptable replacement words like *negro, minoria étnica*, and *pessoa de côr* (person of color, which had existed before) surfaced as the politically appropriate labels for people of African descent. Interestingly, *preto* would just as quickly be put back into use; by 2006, uttering this word reflected the speaker's commitment and knowledge of social reality. Important here is not that the word had for a brief period become unacceptable, but that its new use signals a commitment to "keeping it real," or naming the situation for what it is, however discomforting. Yet prior to this, in the mid-1990s, the shift was hugely significant, and not just because this kind of linguistic knowledge seemed to circulate very quickly and across diverse communities. During this period, as evidenced by a rise in media reports entitled, "Is There Racism in Portugal" and "Are

We Racists," Portuguese society began to assume what neither it nor the state would previously admit: that racism *might* exist in the country. Notably, Wendy Brown (2006) has shown that, while tolerance discourse circulates in the domain of the law, it is not in fact codified by law. Tolerance only exists as a personal virtue, a sentiment. Brown considers this paradox an example of governmentality because of the ways civilians assume responsibility for *attitudes* that the state endorses but can never enforce. This is precisely what has happened in Portugal. The Portuguese national's accountability for the public expression of his or her *feelings* about difference defined the terms under which racism would be taken up as a Portuguese possibility.

Preto has always been considered potentially pejorative; its meaning is defined by the intentionality of the speaker, which slides along a spectrum whose poles would be *black* and *nigger* in English. Intentionality is tied to a speaker's known social face or to the terms of familiarity between the speaker, the audience, and the black person in question. In the past, word choice in Lisbon had little lasting effect on the social face of a speaker; *preto*, for instance, was used in public on a regular basis. But by the mid-1990s I noticed that commercial employees and bureaucrats would hypercorrect their speech if they began a description of a person with *preto*: "Pre . . . ou quer dizer um *negro*" ("Nig . . . I mean, *black*"). When someone did say *preto* it was often understood to be by accident, as empathetic apologies that usually followed suggest. In other cases a speaker might not make reference to race at all, preferring instead to inconsistently use what were considered politically correct references such as *etnicidade*, *minoria étnica, pessoa de côr*, or national descriptives like *angolano* or *cabo-verdiano*. These displays only magnified the idea of difference through the dance of trying to avoid the existence of real social divisions.

For the mass media in Portugal *negro* had always been an option, even during the colonial period. This term has been available in Portugal since at least the sixteenth century when it was used in slave registries or for places such as neighborhoods or streets historically associated with blacks, both enslaved and free, such as Rua do Poço dos Negros (Street of the Negro's Drinking Well), a small street in the old neighborhood of São Bento not far from the city center (see also Tinhorão 1988). What is important about the avoidances, hypercorrections, and apologies I observed was that they often occurred between individuals, whether an audience was present or not. This suggested not only an emergent consensus concerning the norms for the recognition of difference, but also that word choices for difference reflected self-regulated choices where individuals increasingly fashioned their personal ethics according to social politics that recognized racism as a possibility. On a deeper level, this heightened awareness about the performative work of word choice—in its capacity to establish or prevent a temporary state of equality between speakers— changed how people joked or got angry with each other in designated settings, thereby altering the very terms of sociality among people categorized as black and white.

Portugal, and Lisbon in particular, also has large Indian (from India, Pakistan, and Mozambique) and Chinese (from Macau) communities that predate accession. From the late 1990s through early 2000s Brazilian and Eastern European emigration increased as well; today they far outnumber incoming African immigrants. But in the mid-1990s these communities did not range among those for whom appropriate recognition mattered, as this was strictly a black-white or African-Portuguese issue. Thus at the same moment when civilized forms of recognition were reserved for persons understood to be of African descent, "the Chinese" ("o chino") would be the nonpoliticized target of jokes that explicitly conveyed messages of cultural unintelligibility. Through television and theater performances that treated all East Asian identities, Chinese, Japanese, and so on, as characters to be worn and performed—such as manipulating the slant of one's eyes— "the Chinese" became a site of comic relief; they became a safe haven where the presumption of racism could not penetrate or trigger guilt. Antiracism, in practice, translated into tolerance for blackness.

The shift therefore seemed to turn on a distinction between race and racism. These terms are now recognized as pertaining to separate domains of knowledge, one being a neutral descriptor and the other an inherently problematic practice (see Seshadri-Cooks 2000). This distinction does not just protect the potential (black) subject from racist practice, but more importantly, preserves the social face of the potential (white) offender.

As being Portuguese no longer justified the absence of racism, people began participating in public rituals that expressed one's antiracist stance. Not everyone chose to adhere to the new rules, but their use, refusal, or avoidance politically located the speaker, regardless, in ways not previously meaningful. The antiracist game proves complex because as a moral-political principle it effectively blurs distinctions between the political left and right, hence making it impossible to establish an approach to race or racism as a specific political claim or ideology.

Middle Class White Woman

While immigration laws and political correctness had the effect of defining the limits of migrant inclusivity in Portugal, other changes simultaneously established who would be newly recognized as visible political participants in the nation, such as Portuguese women. Nearly every year between 1977 and 1986, laws were passed that protected Portuguese women in the areas of employment and promotion, maternity leave, spousal abuse, and family planning. In theory these policies protected all citizens and documented migrants, but in practice their rhetoric dialogued with ideas about white-collar advancement and thus with the figure of the white subject. In 1986 a four-year affirmative action law passed that promoted the presence of Portuguese women in the skilled workforce; it has been renewed every four years since. While poor Portuguese women have always worked, the introduction of women into the skilled and semi-skilled work force required the abolition of laws that previously positioned women as the responsibility of their husbands, fathers, and male guardians. In 1977, as João de Pina Cabral (2003: 92–98) notes, the PS government changed a 1967 civil code on marriage. Among other things the new law prevented husbands from determining family residence for women (article 1672); it authorized women to choose work outside the home without written permission from their husbands (article 1686); and it protected women from having their labor contracts canceled by their husbands (article 1676). These changes were important because the first modifications undertaken to recognize women's equality to men—the constitutional modifications made in 1975—did not establish the terms under which women would become socially autonomous in practice (Ferreira 1994, 1995, 1998). These changes not only began the process of legally protecting women in the workplace, but they also identified women as active, decision-making participants, independent of how this played out through their relationships with Portuguese men.

As the politics of domestic responsibility were not influenced by these legal changes, working women, not surprisingly, continued to experience the social pressures of maintaining the home. Elite families had always hired domestics, but for new middle-class families and single women hiring a domestic became a new option as a form of consumption. The hiring of African women, however, was a gradual process, and therefore it is important to remark on the simultaneity of middle-class incomes for some women and the rise in the hiring of African domestics. It was not until the early to mid-1980s that African women came into great demand as household and janitorial workers. Before this poor urban and rural Portuguese women had done this work; African women—the vast majority of them being Cape Verdean until the early 1980s—were involved in informal market practices or did not work at all.

A number of reasons explain the new desirability of black women as domestics, and the logic behind them requires attention to a relationship between the visibility of white Portuguese women, on the one hand, and the dissolution of mestiça imagery, on the other. Here one can trace the co-emergence of the homogeneous concept of desexualized black womanhood and the idea of the independent, middle-class white woman figure to the normalization of the latter. While there is of course nothing natural about the inverse relationship between these two constructs, they became tied to each other over time as ideals of national inclusivity shifted from Lusotropicalism to modernized enactments of Lusofonia. I started to make this connection for myself after two random conversations I had in 1989, one with a South African woman married to an elite Portuguese man, and another with a Portuguese woman who was also from an elite family. Both told me that they preferred black women as domestics because they took orders from them instead of from their husbands. And both noted that Portuguese domestics tended to subvert their domestic authority by not recognizing them as their real supervisors. I heard four other versions of this same narrative during early 1990s—after that, oddly, I never heard them again. What struck me about the comments was that they did not emphasize that black women's labor was cheaper, or even that their migrant status may have facilitated the labor arrangement. Instead what mattered to the women was that which was socially enabled by their relationship: it cut out a previous mediating factor, the Portuguese husband/patriarch. The immediacy of this encounter, between middle class and elite Portuguese women and working-poor African women, later got me thinking about several issues: first, how the appearance of women's advancements is relationally constituted; and second, what the absence of a patriarch does to the miscegenation narrative—indirectly, the same-sex labor arrangement interrupts the tropicalist idea.

Regarding the first issue, Virgínia Ferreira (1994, 1995, 1998) speaks of the paradoxical nature of Portuguese women's advancements. She notes the types of social entanglements women are caught in because of Portugal's geopolitical position: Portuguese women earn less than other women in the EU, as well as Portuguese men; they work longer waged hours than female counterparts in the EU; and they are often not taken seriously as workers because of a political culture common to most corporate spaces. In effect, the very condition supposedly instantiating their modernity—their active participation in the workforce—also emphasizes their local and transnational vulnerability to the changes from which they are *expected* to benefit. Portuguese women, thus, find themselves in a triple-bind: Portugal's placement in the EU further complicates their management of home and family.

While white Portuguese women certainly feel the weight of these expectations in their material or financial relationship to the market, there is also another indirect social realm that emphasizes these demands—the media. Here, images showcase Portuguese women managing hectic work schedules, such as in advertisements for new household appliances. The ability to balance numerous responsibilities becomes definitive of modern womanhood. But there are other related images that speak to Portuguese women but which do not feature them at all. Take for instance the popular asexual or mammified images of the dark-skinned black woman—smiling and dancing agreeably. These images can be found throughout the national landscape in coffee advertisements—and the accompanying espresso cups and sugar packages that Portugal's innumerable cafés use, servicing millions daily—on billboards, in magazines, and especially in popular Brazilian *telenovelas*. Because these images engage ideas about servitude—a form of domesticity—they constitutively dialogue with Portuguese women as well. As the waged domestic labor market was synonymous with black womanhood by the 1980s, these images figure a Portuguese woman—the domestic's employer—in the background. In this sense, expectations of modernity for Portuguese women work in insidious ways. Whether she can afford to or actually does hire a black domestic or not, the two have already been paired through the relational reality of modern domesticity, one of many sites where Portuguese women practice European modernity (see also Grewal 1996).

The second issue, miscegenation, is again related to the issue of reconfigured femininity. In 1998, for instance, I read a feature article in a magazine insert of the left-to-center newspaper *O público*. Titled "Cinco retratos dos manequins" ("Profiles of Five Models"), it caught my attention because one of the models who identified herself as mestiça—hence continuing to refer to *herself* in this way—lamented the fact that her look had gone out of style. She was experiencing difficulty finding work because she was not negra or "black enough." She went on to stress that successfully working models tended to be either "really" black or "really" white. Interestingly, of the five models featured, two were mestiço and one was black. The other mestiço (male) model did not report any trouble finding work, or at least none relative to his racial visibility.

Reading this had me wondering whether something was happening with the multiracial schema and with the specific location of the female mestiça within it. It was difficult to discern whether this model's employment troubles were tied specifically to Portugal or to other fashion capitals, as the top modeling agencies send their models out for assignments all over the world. Regardless, internationally standardized trends of racial desirability resonate with Portugal's modernized story of itself. In one sense, the dismantlement of mestiça imagery in Portugal cannot be neatly unpacked from broader globalized trends. In another, the very terms under which such imagery is dissolved remains linked to a colonial history that has positioned and configured racial referents for diverse ends.

In "Facts of Blackness," Denise Ferreira da Silva (1998) focuses our attention on the centrality of the female figure in the configuration of *mestiçagem*, or miscegenation discourse in Brazil. She argues that mestiçagem is inherently gendered, relying on the presumed docility of femininity in the colonial encounter. While the concept is popularly conceived as cutting across genders (of African women and men), the mechanics of the idea rest on the tropicalist sentiment of the narrative: the original moment of miscegenation, the sexual encounter, is embodied by the mestiça figure. In this sense, the eroticized "mixed" female figure is a metaphor for continuity between Portugueseness and Otherness.

In thinking about the productivity of the citizen-migrant distinction, where distinctions are created out of singularity (Gal 2002, 2005), the dissolution of the mestiça figure seems paramount to severing or dichotomizing racial continuities. How the mestiça figure becomes socially irrelevant to the contemporary Portuguese national imaginary is thus the question that needs to be answered. The consequence of this process—a new black-white binary—resonates with the citizen-migrant logic instigated through nationality and immigration laws. If previous popular discourses substantiated the impossibility of racist practice due to miscegenation, what is the character of racialized sociality in Portugal without the mestiça? And more importantly, what are the social arrangements that erase the mestiça's visibility?

There is certainly no fixed number of practices that accomplish the work of the racial binary. But same-sex labor relationships between Portuguese and African women is certainly one of them. From the empire's perspective, the proof of Lusotropicalism is the mestiça—a product of the encounter between the Portuguese man and the colonized woman. My concern is what happens when this encounter is no longer viable in the imagination and where the practice of intimacy is reduced, legitimately, to the waged household setting, one where the epitomized encounter is between "different" women.

Urban Hygiene, Modernization, and Accountability

Upgraded domesticity was not the only modernizing shift that involved social appearances. The city of Lisbon has a department of urban hygiene, the Departamento de Higiene Urbana, formed in 1998. Its publicity asserts that the department's aim is to hold the *individual* accountable for Lisbon's urban development. This includes, for example, individual participation in maintaining the cleanliness of the city, the appropriate pedestrian usage of urban space, and a commitment to recycling. Attention to the Department of Urban Hygiene is important because the department emphasizes a practice of personal accountability that does not directly concern the creation of separate populations. The effects of regulating urban space under this department's guidelines, however, produced the visibility of distinctions across communities. As the city policed the upkeep of the department's objectives, those whose work patterns "defiled" the urban landscape became noticeable to the law-abiding pedestrian and the city in new ways.

In the mid- to late 1990s the working-poor continued to rely on unlicensed sales to make ends meet. Citizens were, however, increasingly leaving these markets for other working-poor jobs while migrants and national Roma communities continued to thrive on them. The Department of Urban Hygiene, reinforcing the public complaints of police officers, disparaged unlicensed activities in urbanized spaces. The department specifically concerned itself with the interests of the civilian with a particular relationship to the urban landscape—one who used it responsibly for leisure and passage. In this way, its policies not only demoralized those who used urban space for work, but it also created a distinction between different types of production—"real" work and "play" work, the latter tied to subsistence related activities.

This work distinction and its ties to urban civic practice also combined with new notions about product distribution and public health. The department understood itself as a teacher, informing the public about the importance of food conservation and thus why civilians should purchase perishables from licensed vendors and established retailers. Its participation in the management of distribution also meant controlling *who* was involved in this process (see chapter 2). By limiting the actors involved in distributive networks to licensed vendors with capital, the department helped to sustain the figure of the law-abiding wholesaler. This figure had existed for some time in city-sponsored markets inaugurated in the 1960s; but its counterpart, the street vendor, had been able to make a living, or at least to make ends meet, for many years. The aggressive enforcement of street sales in the mid- to late 1990s disrupted a variety of social networks that had historically mediated commercial practices: the unlicensed vendor, once an important participant in the distribution of licensed wholesale vendors' products, lost his or her place in this chain of distribution.

The cumulative effect of police enforcement of vending laws and the new policies of the hygiene department did something else as well: in addition to drawing a line between "play" and "work," it also promoted a type of distanced sociality in the marketplace as familiarity, the basis upon which food items were commonly purchased beforehand, slowly came to an end. The physical positioning of select workers in state-regulated spaces further transformed the types of social networks that markets produced and relied on, hence producing new kinds of consumers. In the process, the figure of the peixeira in Lisbon transitioned from a politically irrelevant, urban-poor

The inauguration of a new market, Mercado de Alvalade-Norte, Lisbon, 1964.
PHOTOGRAPH BY ARMANDO SERÔDIO. COURTESY OF THE LISBON
MUNICIPAL ARCHIVES

Venda ambulante: an unlicensed fish sale in the Alfâma, Lisbon, 1966. PHOTOGRAPH
BY ARMANDO SERÔDIO. COURTESY OF THE LISBON MUNICIPAL ARCHIVES

worker to a site upon which people could fashion themselves as for or against ongoing changes. This transition brings up questions about the translatability of the black peixeira as a recognizable cultural sign, particularly given that she had not been criminalized before and, in fact, had previously been portrayed as a pacifying agent to unruly Cape Verdean men.

As a researcher working in Lisbon, I have found it difficult to find competing views on the impact of integration on the city. Debates about accession usually centered on the changing conditions of agrarian workers and the agrarian industry. Vagueness surrounded the question of what would become of the urban poor, or what would become of the environments that generated low but steady income for those people of a certain age who often also had limited literacy. They worked in jobs considered typical of Lisbon, such as the informal sale of various goods and services (such as ironing), or in civil service capacities that did not require high-level literacy (such as street sweeping or monitoring the entrances of government buildings). The new situation proved especially difficult because the urban poor was now also comprised of substantial numbers of rural migrants (see Cordeiro 2001).[3] To this end, perhaps the greatest complication involved the presumption that Lisbon's position as the urban center required marginal management in comparison to other less developed cities. While projects concerning urban appearances were well underway in Lisbon, policies attentive to the afterlife of the urban poor were ill-defined, thus explaining why the informal sector was largely dismantled without attention to the countless lives that would be affected.

The idea of a modern Lisbon, as such, was reduced in practice to the immediate interests of a few elites and developers (see Dacosta-Holton 1998). With the social critique of economic changes focused on the rural areas, the changes to Lisbon would only be reflected on after the fact, as the hotly contested municipal elections spanning the spring and summer of 2007 attest. Sometime during that spring everyone woke up to the realization that Lisbon's urban development had been improperly managed, making only some folks rich to the detriment of the city. While rural areas were the targets of official discourse, Lisbon was the site where modernity presumably was evolving on its own.

AFTER THOUGHTS

In this chapter I have tried to establish how a particular configuration of the citizen-migrant distinction can variably stand in as the picture of social order across social realms ranging from immigration policies to urban hygiene projects. It is no coincidence that the "middle woman," the mestiça/mulata figure—at least in her capacity to call on the Portuguese colonial past—has been expelled from the everyday imaginary. The binarized racial dichotomy that severed continuities believed to exist between Portugueseness and blackness parallels the citizen-migrant dichotomy that is legitimately engaged in daily practice. This suggests new ways of treating Lusotropicalism as an object of study. Rather that questioning whether this ideology existed at one time in practice, it is crucial to ask what its presence and absence have enabled and disabled over time. By positioning tropicalism as an authorial allowance for the white Portuguese citizen under Salazarian fascism, we can focus not only on the practices of social relationality it informed but also on the ways in which these practices effectively negated the possibility of publicly conceiving of racist practice in the metropole.

What we are observing in the events spanning the mid- to late 1990s is the changing manifestation of the state's face and the ways it has connected the virtues of the antiracist commitment to one's behavior as a participant in a new labor environment. That the left's identity politics has now become indistinguishable from that promoted by the liberal state—where respect for Africanity is tied, for different reasons, to each group's agenda—reveals a tension between an ethics of recognition and legitimate labor practice that has been concealed by the new citizen-migrant encounter (see Ticktin 2007). Today there is consensus across the political spectrum about the utility of Africanity: the citizen-migrant dichotomy has become a stabilized point of reference that generates uncomfortable silences, as observed in a Lisbon theater, when it is questioned.

In what follows I describe how discourses tied to the realms of influence described above—market practices, changes in immigration law, gender politics, and urban hygiene policies—began to effect how people typed as African and Portuguese would work out new imaginaries of this division through their encounters with each other. The background information in this chapter provides the basis for interpreting the decisions that Cape Verdean peixeiras and their interlocutors made as they mutually dealt with how they were being repositioned in relation to each other in Lisbon's new modernizing trajectory. It helps to connect the anxieties surrounding the fish market at Docapesca, the policing of peixeira activity on the street, and the banality of the gendered and politely enacted labor encounter that occurs in the waged, domestic-related work setting. Although spontaneous dialogue is context specific, it is also in conversation with nonvisible, external events that shape how people interpret their immediate context (see Duranti and Goodwin 1992). In this sense, the details above help shape an account of the diverse social worlds out of which a new citizen-migrant distinction would become standardized by the early 2000s.

two

RI(GH)TES OF INTIMACY AT DOCAPESCA

On December 29, 1994, I visited Docapesca (lit., fishing dock) de Lisboa, in the town of Pedrouços, for the first time. I wanted to see where peixeiras bought their fish to complement my planned study on their street activities. There was minimum, unarmed security outside of the facility, meaning that anyone could enter through either an official, attended gate or through an unattended western entrance, as most peixeiras did. The facility was open for business to the general public between the approximate hours of 11 p.m. and 7 a.m., Tuesday through Saturday. Fresh and frozen local fish, as well as fish from various areas in North and West Africa, was resold here to diverse businesses seated in Greater Metropolitan Lisbon and to those located in other regions of Portugal. Among the twenty Docapesca facilities in Portugal, this Lisbon station was by far the largest, and it sold the widest variety of fish in the country.

Docapesca was situated at a port near the intersection of the River Tagus and the Atlantic Ocean. The Pedrouços facility was organized into two connected and brightly lit arenas. The inside was sectioned into two hundred–plus stalls. These stalls lined the walls of the facility, and they also stood back to back in the area's interior. Local boats and merchant sea ships docked directly at the facility, where fish was swiftly auctioned to wholesale vendors. The establishments at Docapesca ranged from the small-scale family business that serviced cafés, neighborhood restaurants, and *peixarias* (small, licensed, peixeira-run fish shops) to the large-scale distributor catering to popular restaurants, megagroceries, and hotels. Pedrouços also serviced a group of entrepreneurs—

licensed and unlicensed Portuguese and Cape Verdean peixeiras—who sold fish to the public.

The Portuguese men who made up the majority in this space largely came from working-class and working-poor backgrounds. Lisbon locals here mixed with people from other regions of the country who relied on the Pedrouços station for larger quantities of fish, or for fish varieties nonindigenous to their regions. Company owners, mostly of middle age and beyond, had often inherited their businesses. The teen to middle-aged sons of these owners often served as employees, but spouses and adult daughters were also present, though in far smaller numbers. Their visibility was generally limited by their bookkeeping and cashier work, activities positioning them at the back of a stall or in a small cashier's booth. Interactions with peixeiras were usually limited to financial transactions in these less focal spaces. It was also common to see nonfamily employees, in which case these workers were generally young men. In addition, there were non-Portuguese company owners, from Spain and Ireland, for instance. Some worked both in their home countries and in Lisbon, while other non-Portuguese nationals had married into Portuguese families.

Cape Verdean peixeiras were drawn to their work and this market because no one would hire them when they first arrived in Portugal. But even when waged work, paying a meager $200 to $400 per month, became an option for Cape Verdean women in the early 1980s, fish sales brought in up to four times that amount, depending on the volume of fish sold and the peixeiras' client base. They generally made at least $25 per day, sometimes up to $100, five days a week.

Guinean (from Guinea-Bissau) and Cape Verdean men were also present around the facility, though they rarely entered it. These men worked as peixeiras' drivers. They picked them up from their homes, helped them load fish into their vans or covered pickup trucks, and then dropped them off at their sales destinations throughout the city. The Guinean and Cape Verdean communities speak a mutually intelligible Portuguese-based Creole. Furthermore, Cape Verde and Guinea-Bissau fought a joint revolution against the Portuguese on Guinean soil, making for connections that helped cultivate mutual relationships in this setting. Guinean and Cape Verdean men generally kept to themselves, talking up everything from soccer to romantic relationships.

Cape Verdean peixeiras had their own stories in this facility. For one, they represented a particular type of market: they primarily bought low volumes of fish that drew from stocks not already purchased by restaurateurs or hotel owners and personnel. This is not to say that the quality of the fish they purchased was bad; all fresh fish entered Portugal on ice by 10 p.m. or 11 p.m. Most licensed business owners (or their agents) purchased in high volumes between midnight and 2 a.m. While some peixeiras did arrive by midnight—either to purchase at higher volumes or for transportation-related purposes —low-volume purchases, generally no more than four or five boxes per person, enabled those that sold on the street to manage their supply and to maneuver quickly when confronted by police.

Between 1995 and 1998 Cape Verdean peixeiras' purchases made up between 5 and 7 percent of small vendors' daily wholesale profits. But there were certainly days on which their purchases accounted for over 50 percent of sales, generally when a vendor offered a high volume of a variety of fish that was in demand by peixeiras' customers. Peixeiras purchased their daily supply from companies of various sizes, but they primarily targeted mid-level and small vendors that tended to sell cheaper varieties of fish or varieties consumed by households on a daily basis. Peixeira activity, then, supported the facility as a whole, buying fresh stock that otherwise would not have been sold, thus prevented losses for small family businesses. Vendors and peixeiras, however, did not narrate their survival as dependent on one another; peixeiras had multiple vendors from which to choose, and vendors had multiple clients.

I regularly followed four women during their rounds at Docapesca: Patrícia, Bia, Djina, and Manuela. Patrícia and Bia were both in their early forties in the late 1990s. Patrícia had emigrated to Portugal in 1971 (as a Portuguese national and a colonial subject), and she had been purchasing and reselling fish in the Cais do Sodré and Santos areas of Lisbon since the mid-1970s. Bia emigrated to Portugal in 1985; she started purchasing and reselling fish a month after her arrival. Djina emigrated to Portugal in 1994 and began peixeira work about six months into her stay; she was thirty at the time of my study. Manuela emigrated to Portugal in 1998; she was twenty-seven and Patrícia's sister-in-law. She began peixeira work some six months after arriving and after having observed Patrícia's economic independence: Patrícia sent money home to Cape Verde on a monthly basis while simultaneously maintaining a family of six in a shanty community on the outskirts of Lisbon. In addition, Manuela liked the idea of a daily income. It meant that she never had to worry about miscellaneous daily expenses (e.g., food, medicine, international phone calls, public transportation).

What happened inside the facility, roughly between the hours of midnight and 7 a.m., were negotiations among individuals who understood themselves to be there of their own will. Here, no labor contracts bound the individuals to each other; the quantity and quality of fish largely determined who interacted with whom, as well as the character of the negotiations. One extant set of rules, however, dealt with one's conduct during business interactions. In general, these exchanges involved displays of familiarity and intimacy between wholesale vendors and their clients. Their transactions became opportunities for soliciting intimate details, such as on the interlocutor's wellness or things particular to their life. What caught my attention, however, was the commercial value embedded in references to race in these exchanges: vendors were using raced information—information just beginning to be avoided beyond this market space—to communicate their interest or disinterest in peixeiras as customers, and at times as sexual objects or as "abject" outsiders. Importantly, this raced information not only cut across time and space—as it could be used to rationalize the present through the colonial past, for instance—but also grounded itself in a moral sensibility that valued the profitable, and thus the successful, transaction.

I stress the contextual importance of this space to establish the logic that would propel people to engage with references to race that were in dialogue with a tropicalist imaginary. I want to emphasize that these actors were not in fact living out a tropical legacy, but rather participating in a form of discourse that had been normative to the context. While each actor present was privy to the tropicalist narrative, there were practices in play that brokered racial information for immediate, profitable ends. These games rode on the exchange of money for fish, as opposed to wages for labor, for example. In this sense, there was an element in this economic exchange that was experienced as equitable and that mirrors what can stand in as evidence for the application of Lusotropicalism to daily living. Peixeiras' ability to spontaneously participate in the creation of commercial value from raced information also sustains this perception. The remainder of this chapter works through ways of interpreting the persistence of

Docapesca—a vendor
assists a peixeira with
a box of frozen fish,
1995. VIDEO STILL BY
THE AUTHOR

Docapesca—
negotiating fish
purchasing options,
1995. VIDEO STILL
BY THE AUTHOR

Docapesca—
purchases of the day,
1995. VIDEO STILL
BY THE AUTHOR

explicit racial discourse at Docapesca. In the process I tie these exchanges to working-poor income strategies that would soon be rendered obsolete, hence regulating the kinds of subjects, and thus subject encounters, enabled to partake in state monitored labor scenarios.

MARKET ETHICS AT DOCAPESCA

On their arrival, peixeiras circled the facility as they inspected the daily supply and inquired about prices. Their actions involved picking up the fish, poking for firmness, and inspecting the gills, eye quality, and odor. Peixeiras requested prices per kilo before haggling. If a vendor accepted her first offer, the peixeira often purchased the fish on the spot. If the vendor was annoyed by the offer, the client generally put the fish down and walked away with noticeable nonchalance, taking away her gaze as if the interaction had never happened. If a peixeira believed that a vendor would change his price, she would generally return a second, third, or even fourth time to attempt renegotiation. The inspection-haggling routine was then repeated. Once a deal was made, the vendor generally placed a small square of paper with the peixeira's first name (generally her birth name and not the one used by her peers and family) on the open crate of fish. When a peixeira had completed all her purchases, she would pay another Cape Verdean woman—generally a peixeira's daughter or an elderly woman who had retired from selling fish—to collect her crates throughout the facility. Peixeiras, as well as other customers, purchased the fish either after the verbal agreement was made or once they were ready to have the fish retrieved as they prepared to leave the facility. A reciprocal honor system was in place here: vendors seldom sold fish promised to a customer, and customers were responsible for all sales they had verbally agreed on.

Most market participants were invested in engaging in productive transactions; productivity was affected by the flow and content of communication between participants during the course of a sale. Vendors were generally silent and negotiated only when potential customers—peixeiras or not—appeared committed to the sale, or if the peixeira frequently purchased fish from them. Some vendors, generally small-scale distributors, tried to sell their fish as potential customers passed by. These were never loud solicitations; they generally occurred only within the ear reach of the targeted party. Exclamations such as "Beautiful grouper, let's make a deal!" or "Sardines, just perfect for grilling!" or "Let's negotiate!" were common to these scenarios. If a potential customer stopped to inspect the fish or to request prices, vendors generally used two strategies to prolong the potential negotiation: they would either focus on something unfamiliar to them in the customer, or they would focus on something that they shared with the potential client. Either strategy was meant to develop a context for empathetic dialogue based on each customer's uniqueness. If a vendor and a peixeira negotiated with one another regularly, the unstated rule was that no one owed anyone anything—business was understood as the first priority. In these instances, vendor and customer, regardless of background, greeted each other by asking about the other's health and family: "Are you well?" or "How is your family?" In such cases parties would generally not ask questions about the other's difference, as such information was assumed known. Yet vendors commonly emphasized a familiar peixeira's difference, using this information as a bargaining tool. In these moments, difference could emerge in the form of jokes: "I'm not making you a good offer unless you speak to me in Portuguese," or "Why are you negotiating with me in Kriolu?" When peixeiras felt comfortable with the vendor, and when their peers were around, they would sometimes ask for prices in Kriolu—"Kantu e kel pexe?" rather than the Portuguese "Quanto é este peixe?" The Kriolu version was often addressed as a bastardized form of Portuguese. Importantly, speaking to a vendor in Kriolu, despite proficiency in Portuguese, presumed that a bargaining request would be understood; it could also be interpreted as allowing vendors to engage in more familiar and intimate exchanges with peixeiras.

Other scenarios expressed familiarity after a negotiation had been finalized. In the following, typical example, which occurred at around 4:45 a.m., the vendor, Mário, was popping in and out of a tiny makeshift office positioned opposite the entryway of his enclosed stall. Some of the peixeiras approached him to request lower prices, but it was clear that he would not budge: one after the other the women slowly walked away, discouraged. For the next twenty minutes a discussion buzzed in Kriolu. The peixeiras all agreed that the vendor was in no position to bargain. Mário had about forty crates of exposed, thawing fish, and there was absolutely no way that he would sell them all before the beginning of cleanup at around 6:15 a.m.; so they decided to sit him out. As the minutes passed, Mário grew anxious about his thawing fish. He remarked, "So, are you going to buy my fish or what?" Everyone in the room started to pass subtle smiles back and forth;

Mário noted this. On realizing what was happening, he walked over to a large table next to the entryway and sat on it. With a smirk on his boyish face, he crossed his arms tightly while dangling his legs under the table, and exclaimed, "So we'll all wait. I guess we all have all day, right?!" Minutes later, Patrícia, a veteran peixeira, approached him. Standing to his left, in the same direction in which he was facing, she extended her right arm to his right shoulder and held it tightly. Embarrassed, Mário squirmed in an attempt to escape, but to no avail. Patrícia then said, "You know we should go out!" after which she leaned to her right to kiss him on the top of his head. Pleasantly stunned, he jumped up and yelled "OK! You win!" Patrícia—much taller and bigger than Mário—joyously spun him around in two dance rotations. Within seconds negotiations resumed; it was about 5:30 a.m., and at least ten other women now entered the space to renegotiate. By 6:15 a.m. Mário had sold all but two air-exposed crates of frozen fish. During the forty-five-minute sales period, conversations ranged from the financial negotiations leading to a sale to the vendor's familiarity with the peixeiras' country of origin. While Patrícia made her purchase, Mário initiated the following conversation.

MÁRIO: Cabo Verde! São de Santiago, não?
[Cape Verde! You're from Santiago, right?]

PATRÍCIA: Sim, você já esteve em Santiago?
[Yes, you know Santiago?]

MÁRIO: Não, mas dizem que é um sítio muito bom, boa gente. A senhora vai fazer katchupa com peixe, né?
[No, but I hear it's a nice place with nice people. Are you going to make *katchupa* with the fish?][1]

PATRÍCIA: Sabe alguma coisa de katchupa?
[What do you know about katchupa?]

MÁRIO: Conheço alguns Cabo-verdianos e de vez em quando como katchupa.
[I know some Cape Verdeans, and I've had katchupa a bunch of times before.]

PATRÍCIA: Bem, olha, nós fazemos katchupa, mas com outro tipo de peixe. Tem que ser um peixe com muita carne, tipo bife. Ás vezes fazemos com atum, ou mesmo carne de porco ou bife, sabe? Se continuar a portar-se bem, posso ver se consigo trazer uma katchupinha para o senhor.

[Well yes, we make katchupa, but not with this kind of fish. It should be meaty, so sometimes we make it with tuna, if not with pork or sometimes beef, you see? If you continue to behave well, I'll bring you some katchupa!]

MÁRIO: Combinado!! E sei que sabe dançar, a senhora tem de me ensinar, a mexer o rabo e tudo!

[It's a deal! And I know you know how to dance, so you have to teach me—you know, the hip stuff!]

PATRÍCIA: O senhor fez muito bem hoje; é uma pessoa boa, mesmo boa. Eu gosto de pessoas que gostam de ajudar os outros. Não vale a pena não nos ajudarmos uns aos outros, não acha? Todos têm o direito a trabalhar e cada um tem de alimentar os seus filhos. E assim, não é?

[It's a good thing what you did today—you're a good person, a very good person. I like people who like to help other people. There's no point in us not helping each other, don't you think? Everyone here has a right to work, and everyone here has mouths to feed. Those are the facts, right?]

MÁRIO: Sempra às ordens! Sempre às ordens!

[Always at your service! Always at your service!]

PATRÍCIA: Algum e sertu!

(directed and whispered to me, the ethnographer, in Kriolu) [Some (referring to whites) are good!]

Some elements here are obviously important, such as Patrícia's emphasis on a shared economic sensibility: the need for kindness and assistance, as everyone has to make a living and feed their families. Here we get a sense of how peixeiras understood themselves in relation to vendors in particular moments in this setting. That both parties were in need could put them on par with each other in the interactive moment. Further, Patrícia's use of her age, and especially the fact that Mário positively acquiesced to her seniority, put on display a moment of respect for one's elders across racial lines, thus further establishing the context for a mutually beneficial exchange. But I also want to emphasize Mário's use of ethnic and racialized signs, such as katchupa and hip dancing, in this scenario.

Here, the establishment of equal grounding enabled the "safe" relay of information associated with the explicit recognition of difference. Because such references had become increasingly taboo by the late 1990s—in restaurants, malls, and in homes—I want to call attention to the social possibilities enabled if and when a sense of common grounding existed. While the performance of mutual recognition was never a given in this facility, even when a successful transaction was underway, the reality of economic precariousness was never hidden in this setting. It was a fact of life openly discussed among the vendors themselves and with peixeiras.

In interactions between parties who did not know each other or who did not interact with each other regularly—after a company had hired new personnel, or if the peixeira herself was new to the scene—the vendor might talk about other fish available for purchase or begin to discuss the best ways to prepare that particular fish. These initial probes could lead to the identification of something in common with or different from the customer. In cases where both customer and vendor mutually identified each other as Portuguese, differences between regional cooking techniques often emerged. In cases where the customer was Cape Verdean, questions sometimes arose regarding the archipelago's cuisine. A vendor might ask: "How would you cook this?" or "How do you do it in your country?" or "You would eat this with hot spicing, right?" And, if the vendor had lived in Africa or was born there, he might insert this information into the negotiation: "This fish is good, but nothing like the fish *we* can get back home in Angola." Here peixeiras might nod in agreement, saying little to confirm the information—mainly because they are not Angolan (though many Cape Verdeans lived in Angola during the late colonial period)—as they continued inspecting the fish, deciding whether to bargain.

Even given the hegemonic terms under which a race-racism distinction was publicly regulated in this space, the accomplishment of appropriate race usage among Docapesca actors was a momentary, nonreplicable circumstance that could never be rehearsed or crafted in advance of the actual situation or transaction (Fikes 2005a). In that the subject does not exist independent of the discourse in which it is embedded and named (see Butler 1993) it would be the desire or need to buy or sell in a given moment, on the one hand, and the use of publicly authorized information, on the other, that produced the potential for ethical interaction in this space. And yet, on some days vendors were ambivalent about negotiating with peixeiras, especially if they had already met their daily sales quotas. Such financial forecasting could impact a vendor's conduct and his observance of the ethical principles in question. Though there were moments when peixeiras bargaining in Kriolu was tolerated, there were also times when vendors would add, in all seriousness, "We can negotiate if you speak to me in Portuguese" or "Don't you know how to speak Portuguese?" These statements often came when a peixeira made a grammatical mistake in Portuguese, or if she mixed Kriolu with Portuguese with no perceptible strategic intent. Such statements almost always jeopardized the negotiation. In some instances, the vendor simply chose to stop acknowledging the peixeira; in other instances, the peixeira might end the interaction by walking away. The latter often occurred when peixeiras found a vendor's statement to verge on meanness, cynicism, or racism. They would commonly walk away on their own accord, often at the very moment at which the vendor uttered the sales price, in a move that likewise undercut the vendor's presence. Thus while circumstances such as the time of the day could influence a vendor's willingness to negotiate, the vendor-peixeira relationship went beyond a supply-demand logic. If a peixeira sensed disrespect, she might think twice about doing business. Furthermore, if a peixeira's peers knew of the tense situation, they might boycott the vendor for some time, generally twenty to thirty minutes. Such displays made the vendors in the vicinity anxious, largely because they feared being publicly identified as racists themselves. Their anxiety, importantly, did not simply concern the loss of potential peixeira business, however temporary. It concerned the personal experience of embarrassment that came from having one's social face damaged and one's personal ethics thrown into question. These were the moments that illustrate how life beyond this specific setting was intermittently integrated into everyday activity at Docapesca: emergent discourses of political correctness variably managed tropicalist authority. More telling, as illustrated below, is how value was increasingly produced through claims of racism, whether by regaining the offer of fish just denied, or by the power of publicly shaming the responsible vendor. In either scenario, discourses external to the immediate setting were shaping predictable outcomes.

One morning, for instance, in August 1998, I accompanied Bia as she purchased her fish for the day. Shortly after entering the facility she got into an argument with a vendor from whom she often bought fish. She shouted at the top of her lungs, "Vocês patrícios se defendem!" (You countrymen, you protect each other!). The vendor, stunned by her intensity, shouted back, "You're crazy!" Minutes earlier Bia had made a verbal agreement with this vendor for a box of fish. As a rule, verbal agreements counted as legitimate sales contracts, and fish was seldom taken immediately after a sale. Once the transaction had been completed the vendor was expected to mark the box as sold on a small square of paper. Bia went to another vendor directly across from the one with whom she had made the verbal arrangement. After unsuccessfully haggling with the second vendor, she quickly moved to the next stall, but not without noticing the scenario unfolding at the original stall at which she had accepted an offer: two men and a woman, all of them Portuguese, asked the vendor if they could purchase the box that Bia had just requested; it was one of the last of that variety of fish. I am not sure whether the box had already been tagged as sold when the Portuguese customers made their request, but I did observe the vendor look over at Bia to confirm that she was not aware of the goings-on. He then told the three customers that they could have the crate, though I did not hear at what price. He urged them to take the box immediately, as it had already been tentatively promised to a peixeira, and he looked in Bia's direction. The three buyers also looked over their shoulders for the peixeira in question and then quickly turned back to the vendor. As the woman in the group reinspected the fish, before positioning the box to be lifted by the two men, Bia screamed at the vendor from a distance. The exchange took place at about 2:30 a.m.

BIA: Este peixe que está a vender é meu!
[That's my fish that you're selling!]

VENDOR: Pois, mais estão aqui agora, às vezes é assim.
[Well, they're here now, and that's how it goes sometimes.]

BIA: Não é justo, a forma como negoceia com os seus patrícios, a forma como se juntam. Temos um negocio!
[That's not fair, the way you negotiate with your countrymen, the way you stick together. We had an agreement!]

The vendor, in an apparent effort to redeem himself in front of the growing crowd, started to roll his eyes and shrug, as did the new owners of the fish— "I guess she was really attached to this box," said one. "Let's just get out of here and move on," another commented. The peixeiras in the vicinity closely monitored the incident. One mumbled in a strategically forced and elite nasal Portuguese accent, "You KNOW what you did was wrong." As the seconds passed, and justice, from Bia's perspective, would not be served, she became irate. The vendor addressed Bia in the familiar *tu* form, a mode of address sometimes used among friends or among those who engage in conversations that go beyond haggling.

> BIA: Não, nem pensar, não!! Não faça isso. Vocês associaram-se nas minhas costas e isso não se faz!
> [No, don't even think about it, no!! This is not how one acts. You have collaborated behind my back, and that is wrong!]

> FIRST MAN: Deixe estar! Quantos lugares temos cá? Qual é o teu problema?
> [Let it go! How many stalls do we have here? What's your problem?]

> BIA: Non!!!
> (In Kriolu) [No!!!]

> WOMAN: Porra! Devolva o peixe pá! Caralho!
> [Fine! Just give her the fish! Gosh!]

> VENDOR: Mulher, pare de gritar. Já disseram que pode levar o peixe. Que drama, está tudo resolvido!
> [Woman, stop screaming. They just said you could have the fish. You're so dramatic, and everything is resolved!]

> BIA: Eu não quero este peixe sujo! Nem que fosse de graça!
> [I don't want your dirty fish! Not even if it were free!]

> VENDOR: Qual é o teu problema?
> [So what's your problem?]

> BIA: O meu problema é a tua falta de honestidade, de carácter, nunca mais compro peixe aqui.
> [My problem is your lack of honesty, your character, I will never buy fish from you again!]

VENDOR: É contigo . . .

(Head down, blushing, and embarrassed by the growing crowds)
[Suit yourself . . .]

Bia turned her back and walked off. Another peixeira approached her to ask if she was alright. Bia responded loudly, mocking an elite or Lisboeta accent by overpronouncing her Portuguese with forced nasality, her back to the vendor, "I just lost some fish because of a RACIST vendor and his RACIST countrymen." The vendor overheard this; he seemed both embarrassed and disgusted. He looked over at another vendor who was now looking at him, as if to question his move and wondering whether the incident was indeed racist. The first vendor thus decided to defend himself: "Racista! QUÊ!? És mesmo maluca!! Sou Moçambicano! Como sou racista? Por que é que sou racista? Qual é o teu problema? Estás a dizer coisas sem sentido, merda!!" (Racist! WHAT!? You really are crazy! I'm Mozambican! How am I racist? Why am I a racist? What's your problem? You're talking nonsense—bullshit!!) The other vendors immediately took a different approach—the air grew tense. Bia then swaggered off, grinning, as she mumbled in a low voice, "I guess the problem is yours now." The other peixeiras broke the tension by beginning to chuckle audibly. They slowly strolled past the angry vendor, boycotting him for a good thirty minutes.

Mocking Portuguese through the performative use of an overly nasal accent is a common practice among Lusophone Africans, both in Portugal and in Lusophone Africa. It generally performs Portuguese authority in a way that temporarily endows the speaker with that very authority often denied in the Portuguese-African encounter. In theory, everyone is supposed to receive equal treatment at Docapesca. But by enacting a Portuguese voice of authority, Bia made reference to the very real nature of hierarchy—both material and political—thus indexing the tenuousness of performances of respect and recognition in this space. In this sense, the negotiating ritual creates the idea of mutual recognition. The mocking of Portuguese oddly engages a hierarchy that is not supposed to exist.

Also interesting is the value that being Mozambican is supposed to yield. Here we have an attempt to recall the colonial past for redemptive purposes. But it does not work in this scenario because the vendor has already been temporarily identified as a racist. The use of the colonial past here helps us think through how to go about historicizing it in postcolonial settings. The use of the past as something that can help interpret events in the present is a construction that depends on consensually identifiable rules. Thus what matters is not that the peixeiras called the vendor a racist, but that racism has been collectively identified as inappropriate and intolerable. It is the rule of equal recognition—a product of the successful sales encounter—that enables the past to cohere with the present.

But what seems most important here is that peixeiras and vendors enacted a rule that ethically mediated a distinction between race as a neutral descriptor and racism as the misappropriation of such recognition (see Seshadri-Crooks 2000) within the course of sales. The neutral performance of race recognition was thus a process whereby race assumed exchangeable value: it could be used to add or subtract value to or from a sale. At a time when the two concepts became conflated in other contexts, and were thus either emphasized to injure or avoided to prevent harm, peixeiras and vendors cultivated a social universe in which the performance of a concrete distinction permeated the meaning of an ethical transaction. But engagement with ethical conduct still remained complicated: a peixeira's claim of racism did not effectively damage a vendor's social face if no Portuguese participants corroborated her claim; only they could ultimately confirm the injustice and establish, through participation in a collective act of shaming, that an offense had been committed. The importance of Portuguese corroborators was indicative of the impact of political correctness —as modeled by municipal government—on Docapesca.

In the following scenario from the late summer of 1997, I observed an aggressive encounter between peixeiras and a frozen fish vendor. The Docapesca closing whistle had just sounded, and it was nearly 7 a.m. Searching for additional fish, we found ourselves near a large walk-in refrigerator on the outer perimeter of the facility, a space we seldom ventured into. There, four peixeiras began negotiating for frozen fish from a vendor preparing to close. Time was running out, and the encounter began badly. First, the vendor would not allow the peixeiras to inspect the fish. He told one peixeira—addressing her in the familiar and nonrespectful *tu* form, as he did not know her—that if she were really serious about buying the fish she would make her purchase and be on her way. Djina stressed her responsibility to her clients, saying that she was not going to lose money or business over fish she could not sell. The scenario unraveled as follows:

VENDOR: Cale a boca! Peixeira . . . você não sabe como atender clientes!
Eu vivi em Angola, SOU ANGOLANO! Não podem brincar comigo!
[Shut your mouth! Peixeira . . . you don't know anything about
clientele! I used to live in Angola, I AM ANGOLAN! So you can't
fool me!]

DJINA: Eh, ki boca k'el tem! N'ka ta odja ninhum pex ki n'podi bendi!
(In Kriolu, directed at the other peixeiras) [What a mouth on this
one! I don't even see anything that I can sell.]

VENDOR: Anda! Mexam-se!!
[Hurry! Move it!]

PATRÍCIA: Olha! Podemos TODOS ganhar dinheiro, vamos com calma
para acabar depressa.
[Look! EVERYBODY here can make money, let's calm down so we
can move quickly.]

VENDOR: Foda-se! Saiam daqui! Esqueça! Deixe o peixe!
(The vendor grabs Djina by the arm and thrusts her toward the door.
She falls.) [Fuck it! Just GET out! Forget it! You (to Djina), put that
fish down!]

DJINA: Que bom! Que grande negócio! Um grande negociador!
[That's good! Great business! A real business person!]

VENDOR: Vocês, fora!! Estou farto dessas pretas, putas!! Não me en-
ganam, CONHECO-LHES! Voltem para merda da vossa terra, Angola!!!
Ou da merda do sítio donde vocês vêm . . . !!
[All of you, out!! I'm so tired of these niggers, whores!! You won't
fool me, I KNOW you! Just go to the shit hole of your country,
Angola!!! Or whatever shit place you're from . . . !!]

The four of us walked away, remaining silent for a very long few minutes.
    The Angola reference, not unlike the use of Santiago or Mozambique in
the previous scenarios, was invoked to express a sense of intimate knowing.
But this knowledge served the purpose of racially situating the vendor's
authority to halt a sales transaction: the rules had been broken. Throughout the ensuing silence, Patrícia and another peixeira looked straight on as
they tightly gripped their bucket handles. Djina shook her head, sought eye

contact with each of us, and then continued to walk what seemed to be a fraction of an inch behind us. We meditated on an appropriate response to the ethical rupture—perhaps there was nothing more to be said. The vendor had asserted his authority using a logic that did not cohere to the rules of fair market practice at Docapesca; he had played on his peers' absence. Accordingly, the possibilities for resolution here had no social or political life; politically correct discourse is supposed to prevent the need for resolution, not perform it. Therefore the aftermath of such confrontations depends on the individuals involved and how they—from their various social locations—manage to mediate or diffuse the situation or not.

The reference to Angola did something else. Angola, and the vendor's attachment to it, was called forth to authorize his use of racism, even though the peixeiras were not Angolan. Conflating race with time and geography—the vendor essentialized the women in accordance with his own experiences in another time and place—the vendor took advantage of the isolated setting that rendered the rules of confrontation unclear. This instance speaks to the fragility of antiracist rhetoric and especially to the conditions of possibility needed to be in place for such rhetoric to accomplish its assigned political and ethical work, that is, the copresence of white and black audiences. The peixeiras' silence meant that at that moment they operated from the assumption that nothing could be done, said, or proven. They had been interpellated into imaginary roles—"unscrupulous Angolan subjects"—that obscured their professional status as peixeiras. I pay attention to the copresence of white citizens and black migrants to observe the interactive requirement of antiracist practice. Here, black agency is dependent on publicity and grounded in the ability to claim racism, while white agency is spatially independent and comes to life through the practice of delegitimizing such claims (see Fikes 2005a).

This example is meant to negate any tropicalist romanticization of the tensions at Docapesca. Sexual harassment also ran rampant in this setting, although I do not associate it with Lusotropicalism per se, but to the general invisibility all women in Portugal experience (see Ferreira 1994, 1995, 1998). The concept of feminism or of a woman's autonomy in relation to her body are often trivialized in Portugal, as evidenced by media portrayals of women's domestic responsibilities and especially the power of anti-abortion politics. What I found interesting about Docapesca was the asymmetrical relationship between racism and sexism: racism could damage one's social fact, but sexism did not. Here was a predominantly white male setting where an unrecognized form of social aggression—sexism— could be used to harass black women in a context self-defined as antiracist. Explicit sexual attention to peixeiras draws no crowds: flirtation voids racism and sexism does not exist (at least not in this space) as a working concept. If anything, tropicalism is an alibi for sexism.

It was around 1 a.m. one spring morning in 1998. Both black and white audiences observed the scene. In this instance, however, the interaction was not meant to prevent a sale. Instead, a vendor used the context of the sale and the empathetic rhetorical strategies built into it to capture a peixeira's attention: he was romantically interested in her and had made similar advances before. This scenario is important because it speaks to the limits of the moral purchase of race in this setting. People thus played with the moral parameters in which difference could be invoked to accomplish other, *depoliticized* goals.

VENDOR: Psssssst. . . . . . .Pssssssssssssstttt.

DJINA (looks over at the vendor, annoyed)

VENDOR: Anda cá, minha flor. Ou já és boa demais para comprar o meu peixe?
[Come here, my flower. Or are you too good to buy my fish today?]

DJINA (without a word nods at me, and we walk over to the vendor)

VENDOR: Olhe para este polvo! Não o queres?
[Look at this octopus! You don't want it?]

DJINA: Quanto?
[How much?]

VENDOR: Para ti, quase nada!
[For you, almost nothing!]

DJINA: Quase nada!?! Quanto!?!
(eyebrows raised) [Almost nothing!?! How much!?!]

VENDOR: Tanta educação numa flor tão simpática. Porque é que não tomamos um café? Podes levar a tua amiga. Quem é ela, é tua irmã?

[Such control from such a lovely flower. Why don't we have a coffee? You can bring your friend (referring to me). Who is she—your sister?]

DJINA: Ehhhh. . . .

VENDOR: Então vamos tomar café. Que mulata bonita, mesmo bonita, sabes isso, né?
   [So let's go and get coffee. You are a beautiful *mulata*, really beautiful, you must know this, right?]

DJINA: Hoje não tomo café. Quanto é o peixe?
   [No coffee today. How much for the fish?]

VENDOR: Tu partes o meu coração! Por que é que nunca aceitas tomar café comigo? Sou um homem simpático! Não sejas fria comigo!
   (jokingly) [You're breaking my heart! Why don't you ever want to have coffee with me? I'm a nice man! No need to be so cold.]

DJINA: Não preciso de comprar o seu peixe. Kesh, nu bai!
   (stern, but with a smile) [(in Portuguese) I don't need to buy your fish. (in Kriolu) Kesh, let's go!]

Here, the vendor manipulated the commodity field of the market setting. Seeing him embed his attraction for her in the discourse of business, Djina questioned the price of the octopus, presumably to determine the fate of the interaction that she already anticipated. Was this octopus—which peixeiras seldom purchased because it was costly and spoiled quickly—really affordable? Or was this simply about a coffee date? And was the expression of the vendor's authority, in this way, a violation of the rules?

In this situation, heterosexed politics—treated in this space as if operating outside of racialized practice—could override the market rules for social conduct. Sex was not politicized or ethically coded at Docapesca and therefore could slip in and out of raced encounters without publicly disrupting the race-racism rules. Attention to this phenomenon helps us consider how expressions of tropicalist intimacies—iconicized by the mulata figure—actually ride on the uneven political relationship between race and sex as projects, or rather on the hyperpoliticized status of race when compared to that of sex.

Vendors could choose to mask their romantic or sexual intentions with the ritual code according to which the recognition of difference was legitimate, for example, in sales interactions. This suggests that the underpoliticized locations of sex and gender placed real limitations on peixeiras' bargaining power, thus undermining the operative potential of the race-racism distinction all together. That sex and gender were not recognized as potential sites of contestation—in conjunction with or independent of race—speaks volumes to the importance of collectivized or consensual understanding (in a Gramscian sense) in the production of practices associated with ethical conduct. Tellingly, as Djina and I left the scene of the encounter, she rolled her eyes, looked slyly at me, and grinned. Slowly, we strolled away, in search of the next bargain.

KILLING INTIMACY

At midnight, on October 31, 2003, the Ministry of Agriculture and Fisheries permanently closed Docapesca. A group of wholesale fishmongers and their labor representatives protested along the fringes of the gated facility. Those who wanted to maintain their businesses, the ministry offered, should relocate to the new, advanced facility built in 2000 in distant Loures, a Lisbon suburb partially stretched along the shallow end of the Tagus River. But fishmongers and angry unionists cried that some five thousand individuals would be affected, many of them vendors who lacked the resources to commute to what they called the "fish pavilion" or who had small-scale business clients who would have to carry additional costs to make purchases in Loures. As I later learned, those tied to Docapesca were not the only ones forced to make the trek to Loures. The ministry had also built other pavilions, designated for produce and meat, in a huge suburban market complex called MARL (Mercado Abastecedor da Região de Lisboa, Market Provider for the Region of Lisbon). Each of these pavilions had been equipped with the newest technology guaranteeing utmost product freshness.

The ministry's decision to close Docapesca after nearly fifty years surprised many, especially because of the facility's accessibility. The decision to construct the Loures facility (for fish) was made in 1993, costing the state about 1.6 million Euros, a sum cofinanced by the EU.[2] At the time, it was the only facility to meet all the EC's sanitation codes: the inside of the facility boasts appropriate climatization for fish conservation; a machine produces saltwater for cleaning fish; and an ice factory produces tons of salted ice at an unprecedented speed. The facility opened to the public in 2000, and shortly thereafter the city of Lisbon applied to host the America's Cup in 2007. If selected, Lisbon would designate Docapesca the official venue of the event. After the Cup, the site would be handed over to the highest-bidding developers and their urbanization designs geared toward integrating the Pedrouços waterfront with the nearby city of Algés (and its highway network). When the bid for the sailing competition went to Spain in 2003, Lisbon classified the land around Docapesca a "public dominion" with the intent of requalifying the area for urbanization purposes or *espaços verdes* (green spaces) for eco-friendly leisure (Supremo Tribunal Administrativo, Lisbon, no. 1726/03, January 27, 2004).

But the ministry did not just publicly announce its decision to close the facility. It made a large financial investment in the new pavilion and assigned a veterinary research team to the old facility to check the cleanliness of the product on sale (by testing fish and mollusks for harmful bacteria). The results of the first report appeared in 2001: images on television and in newspapers seemed to revel in fish stalls next to unsanitary bathrooms. Most alarmingly, the study concluded that some 220,000 kilos of spoiled fish had been consumed in 2000 and that another 33,000 kilos had been identified and rejected by the veterinarians before being circulated in the market.[3] The team of biologists recommended the facility's immediate closure to prevent any further health risks. The ministry then followed suit, claiming that it needed above all to safeguard the public's well-being.

Accordingly, the protest in October 2003 concerned many things. Wholesale vendors were outraged by the city's unwillingness to remedy what labor supporters argued could be easily fixed. They were angry about the misrepresentation of their professional integrity in the media and about the city's disregard for the lives to be financially disrupted by the closure. The ministry, however, holding firmly to the arguments culled from the scientific assessment, continued to espouse the argument that its decision was made in the best interests of the general public.

Everyone at Docapesca knew of the city's alternative plans for the space, plans tied to the city's luxury urbanization vision. The state secretary of fisheries even leaked to the newspaper *O público* that there were "other interests behind the closing of the facility" (June 4, 2001). And the city had already told the press earlier that it wanted to use the Docapesca site after the America's Cup competition, if Portugal's bid was successful. When

Spain was chosen over Portugal, most believed that Docapesca would remain a wholesale facility, if simply for practical reasons.

But the city had already invested in the fish pavilion at the MARL facility and, along with private developers, had already envisioned what was to become of Pedrouços (though to date no urbanization project has become of it). Thus on October 31, 2003, what clashed were the rights of the honest and hardworking fishmonger and what had become a messy and ambiguous relationship between the city of Lisbon and its responsibilities to its people. Furthermore, private developers could now call for the previously unthinkable: the increasing marginalization of the small-scale merchant.

Unlicensed peixeiras deeply felt the sting of change because many did not have driver's licenses, let alone own cars. They ranged among the most precariously situated workers because they generally did not have the resources to arrange sales licenses, and the law thus already criminalized their activities. The driving network discussed earlier that linked unlicensed Cape Verdean women to Cape Verdean and Guinean men could barely sustain the larger distances to Loures. Many of the men participating in this network borrowed cars from friends and employers. They earned money making multiple trips to and from nearby shanty residences and the Docapesca facility in Pedrouços. The long trek to Loures, and the two highway tolls required en route, made it unfeasible to make more than one trip. While some Cape Verdean women quickly got driver's licenses and arranged for or purchased cars to commute themselves, the move to Loures would prove a major factor in the dismantlement of the economy they participated in.

Travel to Loures thus involved numerous obstacles. Drivers had to pay tolls once they reached the outer limits of Loures. They also had to arrive at the facility earlier to return downtown early enough to beat the suburban morning rush-hour traffic and the arrival of the police. While some unlicensed Cape Verdean women continued their peixeira work, their numbers fell by 75 percent overnight. Some said they could have continued but chose not to because "this time the city really means it. Sales are coming to an end very soon. I might as well get out now and start looking for work when I can at least continue relying on some fish sales for income. I'm tired and getting too old for this, running from police, everything."

In terms of timing, the move to Loures could not have come at a more difficult moment. For one, the city had begun bulldozing some of the last shanty communities, housing that tended to have a predominant African national group, such as Cape Verdean or Angolan. The state did not pay attention to the deep national-ethnic networks operating in these communities: in many cases, children born in Portugal or having arrived at an early age were connected to their parents' language and cultural practices through single-nationality bairros. The new state housing projects, sprinkled across the outer limits of the city, generally pulled in people from diverse shanty communities, thus mixing these neighborhoods with working-poor individuals from multiple backgrounds, including some Portuguese and some Portuguese Roma (who would be relegated to the vulnerable status of outsider because of their state-defined welfare needs). Certainly these new settings created new networks, enabling the potential of class- or raced-based solidarities. Yet the move also ultimately put migrants and society at large on the same page in terms of the emergent concepts of identification described in the previous chapter: African nationals, youths in particular, increasingly identified as "black migrants," rather than as Angolan or Cape Verdean, for instance, thereby matching their self-categorization with that imposed by public discourse. The changing work environment for peixeiras indicated a similar shift: networks exclusive to Cape Verdeans, including some Guinean men, would dissolve as new labor (and housing) options effectively homogenized African differences into a single ethnic-cultural category.

As I revisited hours of video I shot at Docapesca—collected originally to simply document where and how peixeiras purchased fish—I started to see that "African" modes of sociality were not the only things that changed in connection with the structural transformations mentioned above. For instance, Cape Verdean women had working relationships—some deep, others insignificant—with the Portuguese men who sold them fish. Some of the women I knew had been in the business since the early 1970s, prior to democracy and decolonization and before vending laws were aggressively enforced in the late 1980s. So they had seen these vendors almost every day over a very long period of time.

Bia, for instance, maintained an intimate friendship with a small-scale vendor named João and his wife Marília. Bia never purchased fish from him because he specialized in shellfish, something peixeiras hardly ever sold due to high cost and perishability. But Bia would stop at his stand almost every time she passed it, about three to four times per morning. In those brief, five-minute encounters, they had the most intense conversations. On one occasion João told Bia, without any introductions, about the distress his teen daughter's pregnancy caused him. As he went on about how irresponsible she was, and about how he did not believe she had the aptitude for motherhood, Bia consoled him. She told him that that was the way of life for working folk who did not have the means to constantly monitor their children. She also told him that she knew he had done all he could as a father, but that his only option now as a good man was to support her. When he said that he might close shop early because of his grief, Bia told him that leaving early would solve nothing, that he needed to deal with the situation and move on. And so he stayed.

On another occasion João offered Bia emotional assistance. One of Bia's family members, a young man in his twenties who had just arrived from Cape Verde, had died after falling multiple stories from a construction site. As he was undocumented, the firm he worked for kept the accident secret. Bia, understandably, was concerned about his family. João consoled Bia by stressing the inherent gamble of construction work and suggested that the family now make sure they receive compensation. At this point Bia schooled João on the precariousness of nondocumented living and ex-plained that the extent of the firm's intervention would be the shipment of the young man's body back to Cape Verde. João, disgusted, wanted to know how such an injustice could happen. He cried, "That's unfair, the way some people get treated. . . . It's racist."

I began thinking about how the facility's closure would diminish the possibility of these and other types of interactions between working-poor Portuguese men and Cape Verdean women under conditions not tied to a labor contract. The Loures facility favored a particular type of vendor—the mid- to large-scale one whose clients could manage and afford the com-mute. As the demise of these networks transformed the communicative possibilities with Portuguese and Guinean men—given peixeiras' new, lon-ger work schedules as domestics—I wondered about the kinds of social engineering that the city's intervention enabled. City sponsored political correctness had already effected how people variably brokered difference for profit. That communication would be further tamed by the occupa-tional separation of these communities is a direct consequence of city intervention. The city's efforts closed down a space where practices easily associated with tropicalism thrived, while creating the infrastructure for encounters that abided by political correctness, like the waged household setting.

The ministry's actions—having established a preference for companies, and thus for certain kinds of moneyed national subjects—designated who should play the intermediary role of wholesale vendor between the fisherman and the public. The fate, too, of arrastas—the retired, poor Portuguese men who made their living transporting and circulating the wooden crates that hold sold fish—confirmed the biopolitical effect of the ministry's actions. At MARL these men suffered a 70 percent decrease in their earnings, their work now yielding, they claimed, too little income for them to buy food. They were also angry about having to pay two hundred Euros a year to enter the facility—why should they have to pay an entry fee if they worked there, that is, "belonged" to the facility? Further, in Loures, they no longer had access to a changing room with showers, as they had had at Docapesca. In response to the criticisms, MARL's director claimed that some time ago an arrasta had attacked one of the facility managers and so the entry fee helped maintain security by "limiting the number of aggressive people that might enter" the facility. Further, MARL management had never anticipated the arrastas to make the move to Loures, as the new setup gave companies the space to store their own boxes, rendering the arrastas obsolete.

The closure of Docapesca also had the effect of regulating how the fishmonger interacted with and handled fish before the public consumed it, as the use of new ice and saltwater machines and of climate-control technology altered fishmongers' relationship to their products. The state, in effect, became intimately involved in the means and conditions by which fish would be distributed to the public. In the process, fisheries practices became "modernized" as informal, unregulated, and "unsavory" acts and individuals were increasingly weeded out.

Again, I could not help but wonder about a connection, however indirect, between the city's support of particular types of citizens and particular kinds of work and especially about the types of social arrangements that resulted from this new form of management. The political and economic circumstances that had enabled the unique demographic "cocktail" at Docapesca—one composed largely of Portuguese men and African women—had now disappeared, constituting conditions that no longer fit Lisbon's profile. The city did not, of course, consciously work to prevent such encounters. Yet a variety of actions taken by the state (alongside developers) had mutually enforcing effects, such as the eventual routing of Cape Verdean peixeiras into waged women's work, one of the few alternatives open to them.

The Cape Verdean peixeiras' transition from street entrepreneur to citizen-managed waged-labor is a consequence of local government's response to the accession process. The original Docapesca was closed by the government as part of its efforts to transform economic activity in Lisbon into practices expressive of EC standards and capable of generating commercial profit. The team of scientists inspecting the fish, the new MARL facility distant from both the public and residential housing, and the middle-income companies that MARL targeted, were each modernizing measures with large social implications. Cape Verdean and Guinean male social networks tied to peixeiras dwindled; the arrasta was weeded out; and the peixeira economy likewise declined. Accession put into motion a reconfiguration of the workforce through moves as simple as regulating the types of subjects authorized to thrive at MARL. Controlling who could handle fish mediated how fish would be exchanged in transactions between the clean, upgraded fishmonger and *his* new median-income clientele. Entrepreneurial labor tied to daily subsistence—to making ends meet— was no longer sustainable; nor were the small-scale businesses of the working-poor who relied on wholesale prices at the old, centrally-located facility.

The weeding-out of the working-poor entrepreneur was, importantly, a broad trend; for instance, it affected small-scale agricultural cooperatives in the countryside that could not beat the discounted prices of mass produced items from Spain. In this sense, Cape Verdean peixeiras were by no means exceptional. They were caught up in the whirlwind of change where regulations would transform the successful male fishmonger into a new professional while altering patterns of product distribution and public consumption. The work that went into structural changes, such as infra-2structural upgrades, yielded new subjects and thus new conditions for psubject visibility.

The whirlwind spun numerous actors—white citizens and black migrants alike—out of the old arrangement. In the next chapter I attend to the mechanics of this process: How do citizens and migrants on the fringes of society collectively make sense of the modernizing project from which they have been ejected? What bits of information become the communicable or consensual sites in which belonging and exclusion become knowable and transparent? Finally, how and why did this information necessarily inform individuals about ways of inhabiting EU modernity through Portuguese citizenship?

three

BLACK MAGIK WOMEN Policing Appearances

Before it was permanently closed, Docapesca in Lisbon closed at 7 a.m. every morning. After gutting fish and bagging pre-ordered product, separated by variety with ice, Cape Verdean peixeiras positioned themselves on the streets to sell throughout Greater Metropolitan Lisbon. In general, the women sold fish outside major public transportation facilities that generated pedestrian traffic. The most common locations were outside of the Cascais train stop (serving middle- and upper middle–class Portuguese women), the Algés train stop (within walking distance from Docapesca and servicing a diverse mix of working-poor and middle-class Portuguese and African clients), the Carcavelos train stop (servicing a primarily Guinean shanty community, with some middle- and upper middle–class Portuguese women), and the busiest and most diverse train stop, Cais do Sodré, where I did my fieldwork (servicing primarily working-class and working-poor African and Portuguese communities).

The Cais do Sodré station is the only station connecting people from throughout the greater metropolitan area. A ferry connects a working-class suburb on the other side of the river to Lisbon, which docks at Cais do Sodré. The location also boasts one of the most frequented bus terminals; its buses transport people all over the city. And the train station itself is linked to a coastal region in the west, with final stops in Estoril and Cascais, cities with elite Portuguese, and British and German expatriate communities. As I did my fieldwork a subway station was in the process of being built at Cais do Sodré, which would link the Cascais train line to the metro system of Greater Metropolitan

Lisbon. It created the potential for more fluid connection and a sense of uniformity among these locations.

On a late spring morning in 1998, we stood near the east corner of Cais do Sodré. I observed a Portuguese woman—perhaps in her sixties and dressed casually—approach six peixeiras. It was about 9:30 a.m., and police had already arrived on the scene. They stood around the north corner of the station and thus pushed sales activities into less visible places. I did not recognize the woman, but I suspect that she had purchased fish from Cape Verdean peixeiras in the past. As she approached them, she kept looking over her shoulder to determine whether she was being watched. Once the vendors invited her to inspect their supply, a cold and unbalanced dialogue ensued. The potential customer asked questions while the peixeiras responded with one-line affirmative and negative responses, variably adding in nonconfrontational sales pitches. The woman would not touch the fish; she just pointed at it as the peixeiras manipulated it for her viewing. There was little eye contact between the parties, and they kept their bodies at awkward distances from one another. Neither party wanted to enter the other's space, so each person leaned into the outer limits of her own imaginary physical space—from the torso up—as information about the fish was exchanged.

Manuela was the one that the potential customer seemed to trust. Manuela showed off a medium-sized fish by pushing against the eyes to show buoyancy, opening the gills to reveal their deep red color, and pressing against the flesh on both sides, revealing its firmness and freshness. "Fresquinha a minha senhora, faço um bom preço para si" (Very fresh, my lady; I'll make a good price for you). As Manuela continued telling the potential customer that she would gut and scale the fish at no extra charge, three young male police officers approached—all three of them Portuguese, two white and one black. Immediately the woman took a few steps back and then straightened her posture, head cocked, as if she were preparing to salute. She gripped her shopping bag with produce and her medium-sized black leather purse with both hands, one on top of the other, right up under her diaphragm. Her lips were pursed. She looked the officers dead in the eyes, as if to dare them to say anything to her. Meanwhile, the peixeiras began to scurry as they picked up their buckets of fish and ice and then made for the opposite direction. The black officer and one of his white colleagues slowly chased after them, more to scare them off than to catch them; they maintained a strategic distance behind the peixeiras. The other white policeman stayed behind, looked about the place, and then nodded and tipped his cap to the would-be customer. She nodded back at him and then went on her way.

In this chapter I discuss the political importance of scenarios such as this one that defined the nature of interactions in a heavily policed setting. I find intriguing how the potential customer played on her whiteness and her age to neutralize her presence in this scenario. Yet age and whiteness alone did not do the trick. What did was the reading of her body *in comparison* with those of the peixeiras she had been dealing with. Specifically, the customer's social location in relation to the peixeiras positioned her actions within the limits of the law, while the peixeiras' location in relation to the customer located their actions outside the permissible. In the process, the customer and peixeiras played out a mutually enforced encounter that aestheticized not only the categories of belonging and exclusion, but also the very practices and habits that render such demarcations. In other words, both parties knew their relationship was constituted in that moment through the performance of the good and bad. Furthermore, police authority seems to have no color; the presence of the officers established the visibility of the law through the customer-peixeira encounter (see Rancière 1999: 29–31).

The previous chapter provided an example of the ways in which the state used infrastructure development and public health standards to alter the profile of the nation's primary wholesale fish market and of the fishmonger. This one illustrates how the explicit presence of the state motivated the assumption of diverse public stances that pivoted on an agentive potential, one made available through the abject status of the black peixeira.[1] I also illustrate, more importantly, the relationship between these stances and how diverse actors were simultaneously informed by both the agentive process of emulating EU modernity, and the agentive process of practicing a diasporic version of migrant status. As opposed as these two processes were, the practice of one had the effect of reinforcing the other. Individuals in the vicinity of Cais do Sodré were forced, by the presence of the police, to experiment with their agentive potential, and so their actions said something important about the role that policing played in establishing new parameters of distinction. The police presence did this by clarifying what righteous and modern behavior is supposed to look like and by elucidating the practices that enable actors to carry out their respective objectives.

POLICING: ENFORCING THE PUBLIC'S DIVERSITY

In 1989 the city of Lisbon established an urban interventionist committee called the Sétima Coluna, the Seventh Hill Project. It aimed to revive and upgrade a section of Lisbon that stretched from Cais do Sodré through the Largo do Rato, near the city center (Dacosta-Holton 1998: 187). As Dacosta-Holton writes, the committee formed part of an elite and politically fractioned group of Lisboetas who were committed to the city's outward appearance due to Lisbon's debut as the City of European Culture in 1994. Preparations for this event occurred between 1989 and 1994, a period that coincided with the beginnings of violent police intervention at Cais do Sodré. In addition, dozens of developers hoped to cash in during these years on the city's planned development along the riverfront.

Other players were also invested in the transformation of the Seventh Hill Project, for reasons represented as separate from urban development. The Ministry of Agriculture and Fisheries, even before closing down Docapesca, wanted to stop small-scale local fishmongers from selling in this area to supposedly improve the city's public health standards. Until the late 1980s, local fishermen had sold fish to peixeiras and the general public along the ribeirinha and behind Cais do Sodré for at least a century. My fieldsite, I soon learned, did not jive with the city's objectives for a modern Lisbon, in which food distribution would be relegated to stores and licensed markets and in which urban spaces would be sites of leisure rather than of subsistence. The drive toward licensed markets had begun in Lisbon as early as the mid-1960s, but the city had turned a blind eye to the activities of its poorest, who could rarely participate in more regulated food distribution. By the time I entered the scene, city and state police had been assigned to safeguard the new spaces of upgraded urban leisure most days of the week.

The presence of police, and hence the specter of criminality, had a curious effect on multiple audiences—ranging from different types of customers, to the supposedly uninvolved and colorless pedestrians who moved along the fringes of these scenarios, to a small community of neglected elderly Portuguese women outraged by the policing of black peixeiras.

These groups' diverse responses proved important because the legal parameters of the setting ultimately marked each of these players politically as either for or against the law. People's decision to present themselves in these ways said something about their relationship to changing, regulated market practices, and to the greater context of modernization and European integration. Paul Passavant (2005) has commented on the interdependent roles that market intervention and crime play in the neoliberal state. He notes that nonstate actors are often involved in the regulation of crime, in ways that instantiate the state's anti-interventionist stance on a successful market. In the case in question, the actors are not "subcontracted," as the ones Passavant refers to, but rather include individuals, such as ordinary pedestrians, who *choose* to assume certain roles, often in passing. Below I explore why some individuals would choose to participate in these scenarios and what it says about the new relationship between citizens and their government.

Police

The two officers I had the opportunity to informally interview stated that Portugal had to clean up its streets because of integration. Neither provided specifics, however; they referred to Europe in the third person. They also mentioned the importance of the city's appearance, particularly for tourism. They stressed that vending was an option for all within the stipulations of the law and that there was a legal process through which one could acquire licenses and sales spaces. They emphasized that selling fish on the street meant that the product was not properly or sanitarily stored and that their jobs were also about enforcing public health standards. One of them mentioned the lingering odor of fish remains, which he said could prevent pedestrian gatherings or pose serious threats to the city's health.

The character of police intervention varied daily, thus making street sales a daily gamble for peixeiras. Rare were the days completely without police presence; and on Thursdays through Saturdays, when peixeiras sold larger amounts and more varieties of fish, generally more officers, often from the *paisana* (state police), patrolled the area, in combat gear. On days with less police, one to four municipal officers might stroll slowly in the direction of sales exchanges. Such strolls would serve as a type of warning: peixeiras would immediately pick up their buckets and supplies and move to an out-of-sight location. Some officers would thus limit their interventions to simply moving the Cape Verdean women out of sight.

Peixeiras often had nonaggressive conversations with such officers. Police would tell them, "fora daqui" (get out of here). If such exchanges occurred during the holidays, they might part with "Happy holidays to you and your family" or "May everything prosperous happen for you." Such conversations could begin with peixeira pleas, such as "I know you're not here to take fish from us today—tomorrow is Easter," and the officer would reply with, "I'm just doing my job and making sure there's no trouble." Most of these encounters involved multiple peixeiras who often played off of each other. One might be sarcastic and reply with, "Of course, feeding one's family is a crime!" while another, often a veteran like Bia or Patrícia, would attempt to mediate the situation. This very character of mediation would enable the insertion of a moral voice: "She certainly knows that you're just doing your job, just as she is doing hers." The general police response, particularly to women such as Bia or Patrícia, might be, "OK, but make sure you clean up—I don't want a scale in sight." And police would then leave as a couple of the women might see them off, sincerely, with, "Good/That's right," "Thanks," "May God accompany you," or "Much appreciated."

Yet the more common type of interaction turned verbally aggressive, though peixeiras only rarely received fines or were taken into custody. For instance, in one interaction a paisana officer aggressively marched up to Manuela and Djina, who remained immobile because of their heavy fish supply. Manuela responded to their approach with, "Oh, come on! I've been here all but thirty minutes!" That particular day she had more fish than usual because she had made arrangements with a client to purchase a large supply for a Guinean social event. The possibility that such a large order might be confiscated or destroyed clearly flustered her. The police officer yelled back, "You know very well that you are working outside the law." Manuela thus did her best to gather as much fish as possible and then quickly leave the scene. As she lifted one bucket and put it on her head, grabbing two others in each hand, she looked worried because she could not take her other two sacks of fish: they were unusually heavy because they had lots of ice, as the client had requested. Djina, who realized what was happening and sympathized with the situation, decided to give up two of her own buckets of fish (she had a total of three) to carry Manuela's two sacks. The officer then shouted, "Forgot something?!" to which Djina replied, "I have two arms. TWO

ARMS!!" He then said, sarcastically, "So use them." Minutes later the officer left the scene without taking Djina's fish. Djina ran to retrieve it and then moved to a different, out-of-sight location. Police actually did more harassing than confiscating, illustrating the theatrical importance of their presence; and I never observed an officer actually give a fine. Bia, however, had received two in her several years of fish selling.

When peixeiras came under physical attack, at least once or twice a week during the late 1990s, they fought back. Physical confrontations could last between five and seven minutes. Sometimes police caught peixeiras while running, and both parties might fall when officers lunged at the women to grab their clothing or a body part, thereby losing their own balance. Once on the ground, there was nothing for officers to take. Peixeiras would push them away, but the officers might grab them by the front of their shirts— "missionary style," as peixeiras remained defenseless on the ground—and warn them about future sales. In these heated moments, *Africa* or other raced inferences popped up without fail from white officers. I regularly heard comments like "Sua preta!" (Your niggerness!), where 'preta' was used in its most extreme and derogatory capacity, and "Sua feia!" (Your ugly niggerness!). Also common were statements like "Why can't you Africans obey the law?!" or an infamous comment that peixeiras found amusing, "Go back to Angola!" And one officer regularly stumbled through the words "niggers" and "bitches" as he vocalized with rage and frustration that he had killed folks like peixeiras during the colonial wars.

In a country that at the time was just beginning to question the existence of racism in Portugal, these comments went unscrutinized by most pedestrians. Not unlike the references to Angola that emerged at Doca-pesca, the ones here pointed to the officers' past, not to the immediate present. Cape Verdeans made up by far the largest African immigrant community at the time, not to mention the group most commonly referred to in the media, and Angola thus had nothing to do with them, though everything with what certain officers remembered: Angola had the largest white colonial settlement. Importantly, these comments occurred in earshot of countless citizen and migrant commuters passing by on their way to work. This meant that one did not have to intimately participate in either the vendor or customer role to think about the racialization of righteousness in these encounters, whether one agreed with the association or not. Regardless, the association had been rendered legitimate because of the noncontested agents who codified it, the police. While some officers chose to make the association for personal reasons, things everyone passing by heard, the effect did not necessarily encourage pedestrians to reflect on the colonial past. Instead, these routine references constitutively identified white subjects as exempt from police scrutiny. In practice, the effect was the public construction of opposing alliances—those for order and cleanliness, and those against racial discrimination and state-induced poverty.

Public support for order and cleanliness, expressed by the vocal pedestrian passing by, created an air of intolerance for peixeiras. This nonoffical form of surveillance, one enabling white civilians to publicly partake in migrant policing, had important consequences: policing enforced white inculpability. There were two male communities who experimented with this potential as they consciously attempted to align themselves with the police—addicts and garbage sweepers. Addicts assumed the roles of informants, and sweepers also served as collaborators of sorts. Attending to the character of these groups' participation illuminates the particular role that whiteness came to play in the articulation of Portuguese modernity: addicts and street sweepers, each white in this setting, were otherwise seen as occupying the lower rungs of society. People generally regarded addicts as unscrupulous criminals—defying the law through narcotics consumption and for profits to cover their habits—while sweepers were considered dirty and untouchable because of their connections to urban refuse. The criminalization of the peixeira through a language of exclusion, a language that, by default, suggested the inclusion of otherwise marginal subjects, would prove oddly productive for the latter. As addicts aligned with police to divert attention away from themselves, while street sweepers relied on an imagined solidarity among other whites, their actions played some role, however marginal, in diminishing what a peixeira could potentially earn each day at Cais do Sodré. In this sense, racist speech acts had inclusive powers: as locutionary acts they involved not only attempting to injure the excluded target but also simultaneously naming and identifying "the mechanisms by which a certain citizenship was enabled to occur" (Rancière 1999: 31) through white, nonmigrant status.

Addicts

Since peixeiras generally arrived in the area some thirty to sixty minutes before the police, they spent that time hiding heavy sacks of fish in chopped ice behind construction sites and in bushes behind and around Cais do Sodré. By the time I left the field, a few women had gotten driver's licenses and purchased minivans to secure their fish and ice. But those who could not afford this luxury still put much time into identifying shaded and out-of-sight locations for storage. Peixeiras had to put effort into these choices because they could never rely on the same place: they generally hid their fish in the same spaces in which addicts slept, dealt, or consumed substances and to which sweepers were assigned for cleanup. I never interviewed addicts or sweepers; at the time I never imagined their participation as meaningful because I focused so much on police and peixeiras' interactions with their clients. I did, however, have daily contact with them and regularly observed how they disrupted peixeira business. Addicts appeared to be young Portuguese males, perhaps between the ages of twenty and thirty, and they operated in clusters of two to four.

Addicts often alerted police to hidden fish locations. Interestingly, they did not seem paid or commissioned by the police. Yet their own underground lifestyles allowed them to closely observe the operations of the peixeira economy, and quite a few of the addicts in the vicinity would run up to police—high, often with leaves and debris in their hair—when they saw peixeiras; they gave the police information, which was generally followed. They did this individually rather than as a group, presumably to present themselves as harmless. When they were too high, they might skip facing the police and simply steal or destroy the sacks they found by dumping the fish onto the street or by putting them in sweepers' garbage receptors. On the rare occurrence that the police did not act on addicts' informing, they simply shooed the addict away, often without giving him eye contact. Hence, their inclusivity relied on the default status that peixeiras momentarily provided them.

There were a number of sites throughout Lisbon in the 1990s where addicts consumed and purchased drugs, mainly cocaine and heroine, but also hashish (Chaves 1999; Vasconcelos 2003). I do not know whether or how Cais do Sodré was understood by addicts (or by police) to be included in the network of consumption sites. I never saw more than four addicts congregate there, and they were all men. But their early-morning sleeping patterns in this location suggested homelessness. They had dirty hands and faces, and their hair was often matted with debris, on the verge of dreading. They wore old, torn clothes and shoes. Roughly three miles from this area, there was a predominantly white shanty community called Casal Ventoso. In the 1990s heroine and other substances were readily available there (see Chaves 1999; Vasconcelos 2003). When homeless addicts had nowhere to stay, they often slept there temporarily. Thus they may have purchased their products in Casal Ventoso and then consumed or resold them behind the station at Cais do Sodré. According to the interviews done by Miguel Chaves and Luís Almeida Vasconcelos with addicts who lived in or frequented Casal Ventoso, these individuals came from diverse class and educational backgrounds. Most consumers had gone through multiple cycles of relapse, recovery, and family reunification. Those involved in dealing had sometimes spent time in prison.

I highlight these details to suggest the broader social universe in which addicts were already embedded as citizens, aware of ongoing changes and their representational importance to the nation. They moved in and out of worlds in which they did and did not count as social agents. But what was the precise point of contention that addicts had with peixeiras? What was meaningful about their actions being effective, if only momentarily?

Peixeiras exposed addicts' consumption practices to the general public (potential buyers of fish) and the police. When police chased peixeiras behind the station in the middle of a sale, the client or potential customer would follow the peixeira if the officers simply wanted the women out of sight. On the other hand, if the police followed the peixeiras, they might spot someone shooting up, thus potentially discovering a criminal activity. Further, when peixeiras ran to their hidden locations, they sometimes ran up on and startled the addicts. Thus peixeiras and addicts competed over the hidden spots behind the station. Addicts would respond with racial slurs or by destroying the peixeiras' fish. Such moves drew on the indexical capacity of racialized visibility to establish who did and did not belong. The addicts thus inserted themselves into a realm of inclusive visibility that they otherwise no longer belonged to, at least not in this setting. Though police did not interact intimately with addicts, the unsolicited willingness of these "abject" individuals to provide the officers with information on illegal peixeira activities created a communicative network that oddly tied these individuals, however temporarily, to state authority.

What matters here is the emergence of a realm of authority tied to a broad concept of citizenship and national membership. Police alone staged the disciplinary limits of the city. Addicts' participation in the act of policing established a racialized link between criminality and non-national membership. In this sense, the terms of audience participation solidified and named what was being policed in bodily terms. It also proves meaningful that the addicts' actions did in fact contribute to the state's goals, however minimally. While they did not necessarily tie their efforts to "state" interests, their assistance lent to state authorities required that they recognize someone consensually interpreted as lesser. This relationally constituted production created material consequences for the Other, the peixeira, in terms of profit loss. In many ways this observation speaks to the argument that John and Jean Comaroff (2004) make concerning the complicated relationship between politics-as-theater and biopolitics. They argue against separation of "symbolic from instrumental coercion, melodrama from a politics of rationalization" (822–23). Dividing these two political processes obscures how one would qualify the political status of addicts, making it difficult to count their temporary and staged embodiments of whiteness as meaningful contributions to the broader demographic transformation occurring in the labor market.

Sweepers—who seemed to have little contact with addicts—likewise partook in the presentation of order; yet they differed in that they attempted to assert an ideal of authority through their relationships to white civilians, in addition to police. Whereas addicts asserted their citizenship through their momentary alliances with police (in which whiteness temporarily rendered their drug habits irrelevant), sweepers attempted to appeal to a common sensibility concerning appropriate conduct in this space through their roles as street *cleaners*. Sweepers not only played with the limits of their own inclusion in the nation as members of a stigmatized profession, but their actual calling out to civilians involved a collective, preexistent sense of who was and was not included in the nation. The ability to call out to a pedestrian, in the hopes that that person would dutifully respond as a concerned citizen—thus reconfiguring (whether in reality or only in the imagination) the social status of the sweeper at that moment— speaks to another possibility: a sense of Portuguese community knowable in relation to righteous practice, to, in other words, following the rules.

Garbage Sweepers

Garbage sweepers, whose task was to manually sweep the street and pick up garbage that the street machines had missed, felt frustration at having to clean up fish remains five days a week. Because police forced peixeiras to constantly rotate their sales locations, they left debris in many areas. The debris consisted of scales, fins, and fish guts that sweepers had to manually scrape to remove; on hot days, the remains often melted into the pavement or fell between the cracks of Lisbon's famous cobblestone sidewalks. If the sweepers happened to cross paths with police while cleaning they might mention to the latter where a transaction was occurring or where they had identified a fish stash. The responsibilities of their job thus positioned them in opposition to peixeiras.

The city of Lisbon hires dozens of sweepers. They generally work alone in the morning hours, sweeping the streets with straw brooms and large green plastic bins. Most of the men were between forty and sixty. The nature of their publicly visible work often made people think of them as lowly or untouchable.[2] I regularly observed three men assigned to an area within a quarter-mile radius of Cais do Sodré; they often mumbled to themselves that fish debris violated their rightful list of chores.

When sweepers came across a group of women selling fish, they yelled the same racial slurs heard from addicts and police. Yet their behavior differed because they attempted to engage pedestrians. If police were not in sight, sweepers might authoritatively demand that a pedestrian seek police assistance. This attempt at interpellating pedestrians into the policing activity by requesting that they seek out help occurred under the assumption that pedestrians in fact shared the sweepers' dislike of peixeira activity. Interestingly, civilians hardly ever listened to street cleaners; they would just look at them strangely, sometimes pointing to themselves to determine if they were the target of the request. At other times they would simply look away, perhaps smirking, and keep walking, thus suggesting that they did not want to be pulled in the conscious frame of these encounters, and especially not with the likes of sweepers. The few times that I observed civilians respond, the pedestrians were middle-aged Portuguese men apparently from modest backgrounds. These men might enter into a brief conversation about how despicable Lisbon had become, but that was as far as the sweepers' requests succeeded. The police would heed sweepers' requests, but after disbanding the peixeira activity in question, police rarely continued to interact with the men. While sweepers might greet members of the police, the officers would generally limit themselves to a nod, without much eye contact, and keep patrolling.

Pedestrians

Beyond street sweepers and addicts, pedestrians, passersby who did not buy fish and thus the audience to these policed scenarios, would also contribute to the latter. Most pedestrians, comprising a socially diverse group, appeared unmoved by the scenes in front of them. While a minority might also yell racial slurs at peixeiras, most simply strolled by, seemingly involved in their own thoughts as they made their way to work, school, or other appointments. In this sense, they were passive participants ratifying this performative context. With the exception of the curious tourist who seemed bewildered by the theatrics of this scenario, these events for most became a habitual part of their morning scenery.

At least five times a month, however, I observed the paisana swoop down on peixeiras from an unmarked van. The sliding door would fly open, giving a clear signal of violent aggression about to occur. Peixeiras would scream to alert their colleagues in the distance who were not in hiding. In general, the state troopers would attack the peixeiras by pushing them to the ground after chasing them and then confiscate their fish. Only in these moments did passersby react with alarm or shock, transforming this normalized ritual into a momentary spectacle for which no one seemed prepared, as suggested by the wide-eyed fear and apprehension that witnesses exhibited. Yet still, with the exception of poor elderly Portuguese women, some of whom relied on peixeiras for food and who openly critiqued police as unethical and racist, no one openly criticized troopers' full-speed chases, and so they continued on without question. These events did not generate public reflection; there were only marginal notes in newspaper and magazine stories that off-handedly made reference to them. For example, features on immigrant lives, and on the experience of racism in Portugal, might open with a photo of a peixeira balancing her fish on her head or sitting on a couch in her humble home. The accompanying caption might read, "the women who run from police," signaling, almost cynically, that *everyone* had in fact been watching the aggression, but they had assumed stances after the fact that depoliticized an interpretation of the encounters, forgetting the visceral responses they might have had upon passing one morning through Cais do Sodré.

Peixeiras were thus operating in a complicated environment. On the one hand, the banality of daily municipal intervention, as established by a largely black pedestrian response, disrupted peixeiras' income potential. On the other, when individuals chose to engage in sales they were inserting themselves into a theater that potentially put them on the wrong side of the law and of the pedestrian audience. Peixeiras, too, of course, had to manage themselves in this divided world of good and bad, a world in which they themselves stood in for the bad, in which black clients risked harassment, and in which white clients had to choose whether to risk their evolving privileges. Peixeiras moralized the act of buying fish as a working-class necessity and thus as a righteous *political* stance. They thereby embedded themselves in the national working-poor narrative about the right of the poor to maintain themselves, using whatever resources were available to them.

PEIXEIRAS AND THEIR CLIENTS

Between 1989 and 2001 peixeiras had to be savvy about how to keep their customer base and stay afloat. When working, the women wore traditional Cape Verdean market gear: brightly colored head scarves, broad pieces of cloth, or *panos*,[3] wrapped about the waist, and large, multipocket aprons that held utensils, money, miniature plastic balancing scales (as fish was sold per kilo), and various sizes of plastic bags. Certainly this attire gave the peixeiras away to police immediately; however, they were also working to attract customers, especially when they were stationed in less visible locations.

Peixeiras had diverse relationships with different clientele. The tensions between blackness and whiteness had to be played out carefully to maximize profit potential. With their black clients, for instance, the women relied on the moral-political dimensions of black solidarity. By contrast, with their white clients, who included pedestrians and other unlicensed vendors, they relied on the signifying properties of whiteness and the decriminalized status of white women's bodies. Thus everyone involved in the activity of peixeira fish sales, immediate or distant, brokered the dialectic capacity of race as established by policing.

Working-Poor White Portuguese Women

Peixeiras relied heavily on the friendships they developed with elderly and middle-aged working-poor Portuguese women, some of whom also sold products without licenses such as flowers and candy. Peixeiras let these women pay for their fish in installments. In exchange for this trust, their Portuguese friends would sometimes stash a bundle or two of unsold fish behind their own unlicensed setups. These setups, different from those of peixeiras, were generally stationary. Poor Portuguese women used one or more rectangular, open-topped crates that they converted into tables for displaying their wares. The openings of the crates faced the vendors and so these were ideal places for storing supplies, as well as for hiding fish. In general, the police did not regularly confiscate their supplies and instead issued harsh warnings. Peixeiras relied on the fact that candy and flower vendors ran less frequently from the police. They knew the ritual between poor Portuguese women and officers: the women would stage their preparations for departure, that is, they gathered their products to give the impression of the intention to pack up and go. Once the police had left the vicinity, the women would put their products back on display, all the while keeping the fish supplies hidden.

In addition to hiding fish, poor Portuguese women and peixeiras also alerted each other to oncoming police. When police officers harassed the Portuguese women, peixeiras further played with the privilege in whiteness by ridiculing the officers: "How could you, how could you bother this poor woman? Imagine!" Peixeiras were able to do this because commotions concerning poor elderly women could draw angry attention from pedestrians, or the few licensed vendors selling newspapers or flowers in the vicinity. At times, poor elderly women were "sacred" life, to borrow from Agamben (1998), when they were positioned in scenarios framing them as defenseless. Civilians might not have disrupted police activity, but they would certainly authorize themselves to step in to confirm that they had all the facts.

These relationships partially enabled peixeiras to remain on the street for the time that they did. Peixeiras drew on the opportunities inherent in whiteness on a daily basis to avoid fish confiscation: they managed to strategically separate themselves from their fish by temporarily handing their supplies over to older, poor white women, the bodies of which disassociated the product in their possession from contraband. Importantly, elderly white women stumped police officers' ability to use a regime of racial visibility to target Peixeiras. Officers might suspect that a Portuguese woman had fish, but they generally just paced in front of her in frustration, as if she were an object that was protected behind a shield. Without fish, police could take no action against peixeiras, because it was the possession of fish that ultimately criminalized peixeiras in this public setting. The process of tying fish to white elderly bodies momentarily decriminalized the peixeira. Not surprisingly, elderly women were also deemed sacred by peixeiras.

Peixeiras' conversations with elderly Portuguese women tended to center on their mutual struggles as women who made ends meet by "hustling." Bia, Patrícia, Manuela, and Djina each had a special relationship with one woman in her late seventies, Dona Ângela. On most days, Dona Ângela methodically strolled by the women with her cane, a plastic bag of old bread pieces dangling from her opposite wrist. On days during which she remained absent, people would always inquire about her. Bia and Djina even visited her once—as she lived close by—when a candy vendor told them that she was ill. At least twice a week one of the peixeiras would give her free fish; they were each disgusted by the fact that her adult children did not take better care of her. When Dona Ângela passed by, she would go on poetically with one or more of the peixeiras about her humble life. The conversation would evolve as one of the peixeiras repeated her words in a show of respectful agreement. I jotted down the following conversation one day:

DONA ÂNGELA: No one cares about us.

BIA: No one cares about us.

DONA ÂNGELA: Such a difficult life, so difficult.

BIA: I mean difficult, so difficult.

DONA ÂNGELA: We try to make our little (what little we can).

BIA: We try to make that little.

DONA ÂNGELA: Oh, life is so hard.

BIA: It's just so hard, so hard. Ooh so hard, . . . but God is like a father.

DONA ÂNGELA: THAT'S TRUE, GOD IS LIKE A FATHER.

With "Deus é pai" (God is like a father), suggesting that all will be taken care of, the conversation would move on. Bia and Dona Ângela would greet each other in this way in a shared ritual that prefaced their reflections on high rents and food prices in Lisbon. When police were present Dona Ângela would add racism to the discussion, noting that preventing peixeiras from subsisting was plain racist. In fact, Portuguese women who supported peixeiras often explicitly identified racism as the motivation behind police action. They further implied that keeping people from subsistence earnings was highly immoral.

I have illustrated how peixeiras channeled whiteness through their solidarity with poor Portuguese women in ways that helped them protect their fish supplies. This observation is significant because it reflects how information on the new properties in whiteness, in regard to income accumulation, mutually intercepted the imaginaries of citizens and migrants alike. The situations in which Portuguese women acquired new knowledge of their political locations, under transitioning urbanization practices, was not independent of the process in which peixeiras were informed of their abject identification. Notably, poor senior white women, from time to time, continue to sell candy and flowers without licenses at Cais do Sodré today, while Cape Verdean peixeiras had disappeared completely by early 2005. The biopolitical ramifications of the police presence says something about the evolving status of citizenship in the early 2000s: it seemed that the subjects occupying various jobs, as opposed to the persistence of supposedly antiquated forms of work, were what mattered most to the city.

Working Middle– and Middle-Class Portuguese Women

Sales exchanges between peixeiras and working-middle to middle-class women were quite different; here, the properties in whiteness were not momentarily shared as they were exclusively possessed by their "original" bearers. In this sense, the negotiation between peixeiras and their more economically stable women customers was restricted to the racial locations scripted by their original positions. While working middle– to middle-class Portuguese women also feared being caught by police, their very proximity also decriminalized the fish. But here the concern was different than the

Selling fish, 1995.
VIDEO STILL BY
THE AUTHOR

examples above. While poor Portuguese women were worried about being caught themselves, working middle– and middle-class women most feared their association with peixeiras. When police approached and peixeiras ran, they simply stood still, sometimes indignantly, before walking away slowly. They performed their inculpability on their own terms, for themselves. When peixeiras chose to negotiate with them, the peixeira followed the Portuguese woman's lead by staying at a distance and thus enabling these potential customers to control any kind of proximity.

Sales pitches to working middle– and middle-class Portuguese customers included polite and socially respectable utterances that focused on the quality of the fish and its price. Peixeiras might begin a negotiation with "Minha senhora" (My lady) or "Dona" (Miss), before saying "Olha, linda Garopa. . . . Faço duzentos" (Look, beautiful grouper . . . I'll give it to you for 200 escudos). They employed these strategies after sizing up their customers' attire. The middle-class Portuguese women who approached them tended to dress conservatively. They often wore two-piece women's suits of wool or polyester fabric, leather shoes with a low heel, and blouses made of cotton, silk, or the like. After scrutinizing them, peixeiras commonly followed their pitches with several nonverbal cues. These included silences, performances of deference such as noncommittal gazes, and the intermittent use of honorific lexicon. These utterances occurred as the peixeira held the fish, pressed its eyes, and opened its gills, so that it could be inspected from afar. A successful sale generally had peixeiras saying,

"Thank you very much! Remember to ask for me the next time you're looking for fish." Or, "Know that I can always prearrange a supply for you." But if a sale failed, and especially if the peixeiras considered the potential customer rude or disrespectful, a peixeira might tell the person to "go to hell" or give a sarcastic "Yeah, thank you *very* much!" in a move that generally caught the prospective customer off guard. Such interactions almost always ended badly, though they might last for short or long amounts of time.

Bargaining with middle-class Portuguese women generally took longer than with other customers, often because peixeiras ranked each other in terms of who the potential customer first approached; the first peixeira that the customer oriented herself toward had priority. They believed it honored the client's space. By contrast, in their interactions with black clients, peixeiras' verbal finesse trumped the ranked order of vendor-customer interactions. Peixeiras also often gave middle-class Portuguese women higher quotes, which meant that negotiating down took more time. The process by which the lead peixeira kept lowering her prices often occurred in response to one-lined, negative statements from the potential customer: "No, that's too big"; "No that's too much"; "I don't like that kind of fish." The emphasis on what the customer did not like or want generated a dialogue in which the peixeira worked to meet the customer's personal needs, rather than explicitly negotiating a price in ways that recognized both parties as equals, however temporarily.

Peixeiras sometimes used other approaches for negotiating with working middle– to middle-class Portuguese women that refused to haggle. One strategy involved two to three peixeiras bargaining while the others turned their backs and appeared uninvolved in the sale. This move, where large supplies of other varieties of fish were then restricted from the customer's view, was used to pique her interest. Another was to acknowledge the customer's behavior via signifying eye contact with other peixeiras, directly in front of the customer. This approach could make the customer self-conscious, fearing that she might become the subject of judgment. Sometimes peixeiras simply chose to stop acknowledging and/or communicating with the potential customer, until the individual would eventually walk away.

All this came down to a kind of game. Before police arrived on the scene, sales scenarios had evolved very differently because there had been far more customers available for bargaining. Drawing on racial and/or class-based rank had of course always defined sales encounters, but the element of aggressive policing fitted the setting with new social opportunities, new limitations, and new messages. Racial profiling, accompanied by police use of racial slurs, sealed a different kind of relationship between race and citizenship—working middle– and middle-class Portuguese women were asserting a political choice, as odd as that might sound. In actuality, these women were not engaging in any new or unfamiliar activities. For those raised in Lisbon or in or around fishing towns, going to the docks to purchase cheap fresh fish was an everyday occurrence. What had changed was how this practice was now viewed and what it was thought to reflect. When middle-class customers chose to buy fish from peixeiras in the 1990s, they were walking a fine line between reproducing the familiar and behaving in ways supposedly inappropriate to upgraded urban standards. This in-betweenness is perhaps what was most meaningful about this setting and it helps clarify the role that police played within it. Without the police, and the need to constantly look over one's shoulder, the roles that these negotiations hardened would not have been the same. This is not to say that the interactions would have been more respectful; rather, the police presence enabled, in their enactment of superiority, the potential to signal something different. The performances of inculpability did more than keep these customers safe: they underscored the conditions under which officers policed—"Portugal was now part of Europe." While information on good and bad forms of urban behavior became legible, in part, through racial profiling, the deeper connection made between European modernity and the meaning of Portuguese citizenship also became legible.

Black African Women and Men

There was something special about exchanges between African immigrants and peixeiras. Until the mid-1990s most African communities lived in nation-based shanty communities, making work sites the spaces where Africans of diverse national backgrounds came together. Since many African women worked as domestics in isolation, it meant that most of them were not connected to or even aware of the various African communities that lived in and around Lisbon. In the mid-1990s the city began to sponsor African cultural and musical festivals at which Africans of different national backgrounds came together in public, as discussed in chapter 1. Before that, however, peixeira sales offered one of the few instances, spontaneous ones at that, that allowed Africans, including African women, to come into contact with each other.

The only other popular site for such coming together during the day was the Rossio commercial square in downtown Lisbon, in an area called the Baixa, not far from Cais do Sodré. There, from the Praça da Figueira to the pathways leading to the Rossio and along the steps of the national theater house, well over one thousand Africans, primarily men, would gather to socialize, discussing everything from business to politics. The Rossio was targeted for recommericalization in the late 1990s, notwithstanding a modern two-story McDonald's and remodeled old coffee houses like the Suiça that had been there for over a century. The city did not directly dismantle this particular setting; instead, the new construction projects that blocked off the spaces in which Africans congregated simply made it impossible to "hang out." By the early 2000s only about a hundred or so men, many of them Guinean, would remain. Rumor has it that they will not be removed because they are members of a Muslim ethnic group that fought with and for Portugal during the colonial wars in Guinea-Bissau, from the late 1960s through 1973. Many of these men are awaiting pension checks—which they may or may not receive—and hence are tolerated, for now, by city officials and elites.

Thus fish sales under police surveillance at Cais do Sodré not only became one of the few spaces where Africans of diverse backgrounds came together but likewise constituted an important site of politicization. The exchanges between peixeiras and their African clients—even in the midst of transactions—directly and indirectly made reference to state-inflicted racism, questioning the narrative of equality. This meant that while addicts and sweepers improvised the meaning of national authority *in opposition to peixeiras*, African immigrants asserted a belief in their economic rights through their willingness to patronize peixeiras on the streets. As some officers did not make a distinction between peixeiras and their customers, these African immigrants also often had to run from police. Thus their actions, when read in comparison to those of addicts and sweepers, revealed that peixeiras had indeed emerged as a site around which a type of polarization had taken shape.

Peixeiras knew that they could not remain in business without their African customers and long-term clients. Clients likewise understood how much money they were saving by patronizing peixeiras. The peixeiras created payment installment plans for their African clients, as they did with poor Portuguese women. They gave them two-week to one-month supplies of fish that they could freeze and consume throughout the month, for instance. On Saturday afternoons or on Sundays, when some peixeiras did not work, they might visit their clients' homes to exchange money, deliver fish, or wish an ill customer well. Thus fish vending built a sense of social community among Africans from multiple national and sometimes class backgrounds—Cape Verdean peixeiras residing at the center—where politics and culture gradually became intertwined.

Yet the intertwining of politics and culture was never a given. Fish sales constituted carefully negotiated encounters during which one's dedication to this type of racialized community was a moral commitment. Given the social and political climate in the country, peixeiras in effect relied on their clients to make political decisions about the types of political subjects they wanted to be in Portugal. At the same moment that policing equated whiteness with political rights, it also established the grounds for a heterogeneous expression of African community, with its own moral-political guidelines. So while policing pushed middle-class Portuguese women to assume a revised stance as citizens, it likewise guided African nationals and first generation black citizens into a politicized migrant category, one signifying more than simply migration. Peixeiras' activities would be among the sites that could propel this mutually agentive process for citizens and migrants alike.

This sense of community proved paramount to peixeira survival on the streets in the late 1990s and early 2000s. Understandably, African customers and longtime clients felt pressed to run when police intervened. To ease their anxieties peixeiras engaged in carefully orchestrated transactions where the exchange of fish and money might occur at different locations or different times. Such operations required a commitment and the investment of time from both the customer and the peixeira. The time that it takes to weigh, scale, and gut the fish could easily have proved too much for immigrants to risk under strict police surveillance, destroying peixeiras profits. Yet the Cape Verdean women continued to thrive, underlining the sense of diasporic community that had been building through sales. Since police could intervene prior to the exchange of money and/or fish, trust in and by the peixeiras needed to be in place to maintain the customer-vendor relationship. Here I do not aim to represent diasporic community building as simply functional; rather, I wish to illustrate the types of circumstances under which nationals from different countries and with different languages come to recognize a shared predicament, as I show in more detail later (see also Fikes 2008).

Importantly, prearranged transactions not only involved identifying safe exchange locations but also acknowledging how police understood race as a criminal marker. Tellingly, peixeiras offered the same special treatment even to new African customers, under the presumption that the client would understand and comply with the rules. This willingness to gamble with income is suggestive of the degree to which they commonsensically relied on an ideal of racial morality, or what I refer to as *diasporic governmentality*. Here, the police and the policing actions of civilians, in their assertions of Portuguese privilege and citizenship, would not alone inform the sense of exclusion that blacks experienced as customers in this setting: the politicization of exclusion as something with agentive potential happened simultaneously (see Povinelli 2002; Brown 2006). So the counteremergence of a diasporic consciousness also played a role in the moment at which minority status became the visible grounds for effectively determining communities of exclusion and belonging. In this sense, the commodification of a shared racial consciousness—one unique to the changing context of Portugal—prolonged peixeiras' survival on the streets through the creation of real communities, hence contributing to the basis on which Euopean modernity and Portuguese citizenship could converge.

The process by which peixeiras accessed a multiethnic and multinational diasporic sensibility occurred through the venting of their frustrations as they capitalized on what they called a "racial predicament" that extended beyond policed street transactions. The point here is not to suggest that there was no predicament, but instead to focus on the productivity of this recognition among potential customers. For instance, peixeiras would say things that might not specifically speak to policing but that indirectly referred to the conditions of a shared blackness in Portugal. Clients would confirm the women's observations, generally by nodding as they looked fearfully over their shoulders, and give sales-related rebuttals that linked their "clandestine" activity to social issues. Prior to addressing a person in Portuguese or in Kriolu, peixeiras used aesthetic markers to assess a person's country of origin, and thus the language most appropriate for initiating a sale. They focused on clothing, jewelry, and hairstyles in

The sales pitch,
Cais do Sodré, 1995.
VIDEO STILL BY
THE AUTHOR

Bagging fish after
negotiations, Cais
do Sodré, 1996.
VIDEO STILL BY
THE AUTHOR

attempts to guess the potential customer's national and class identity. When a peixeira assumed that a prospective customer did not come from Cape Verde, they often initiated the sale in Portuguese with "Não és Cabo-verdiano, pois não?" (You aren't Cape Verdean, are you?). In cases where they could not assess a background, they asked general questions about the types of fish their clients might like, which almost always made for a dead giveaway. Even listening to customers' pronunciation as they responded helped situate them. After a negotiation began, peixeiras used Kriolu words and phrases such as *kunhadu* (in-law), *patrisiu* (compatriot) or "Bo e di Guinea?" (Are you from Guinea?) to integrate an ideal of moral responsibility that could help influence the fate of the transaction. During a sales pitch these terms and turns of phrase were meant to invoke a sense of familiarity and trust, particularly if a client lost interest or when police drew closer. Here is a typical scenario:

BIA: Ouí querida!
[(in Portuguese) Hey dear!]

PATRÍCIA: Ouí bem leba pexe. Anda bem leba pexe!
[(in Kriolu) Hey, come get (some) fish. Come here come get (some) fish!]

BIA: Ei! N' tene Carovina nha patriciu!
(Points to targeted client) [(in Kriolu) Hey, there is Carovina, my countryman!]

PATRÍCIA: Ei!
[(in Kriolu) Hey!]

BIA: Ei! N'tene Carovina pssssss anda! Anda! N'tene Carovina nha kunhadu. Anda! Bo é di Guiné!?!
[(in Kriolu) Hey, I have Carovina psssss come here! Come here! I have Carovina, my in-law. Come here! You are from Guinea!?!]

Certain terms are used exclusively with Guineans, the peixeiras' primary clientele. Cape Verde fought for liberation from Portugal in a unified struggle with Guinea-Bissau. The goal was to symbolically unify the Cape Verdean archipelago with the African continent, via Guinea-Bissau, under the slogan "Uma Pátria, Dois Países" (One Nation, Two Countries). *Kunhadu* and *patrisiu*—the latter also used among Lusophiles more broadly—were used by Amilcar Cabral during the colonial wars to nationalize kinship: he aimed to build a family of citizens who resisted Portuguese colonialism. These political goals have been out of vogue since the late 1980s, when the one party system uniting these two countries—the Partido Africano da Independência da Guiné e Cabo Verde (PAIGC)—fell apart. But that these terms would still surface in exchanges between people during sales interactions suggests an ethnicized understanding of moral fraternity. Peixeiras variably commodified such meanings to enhance their sales opportunities. The phrase "Bo e di Guinea" confirmed and established the context in which *kunhado* and *patrisiu* could be used affirmatively.

Similarly, in interactions with other African clients—from Angola, São

Tomé and Príncipe, and Mozambique—the women also deployed terms that referenced their common colonial past. In addition, language choice constituted an essential marker of difference and belonging. Clients from Guinea-Bissau, São Tomé and Príncipe, and Cape Verde were addressed in the mutually intelligible Cape Verdean Kriolu. By contrast, Angolans and Mozambicans, who are not Kriolu speakers, were addressed in Portuguese.

Once a sales pitch evolved to the negotiation stage, bargaining strategies intertwined the transaction with "African" sayings that have become unique to contemporary Portugal. For instance, if a client seemed unwilling to negotiate a proposed price, one woman might say, "Nossa gente" (My people). Semantically, this phrase equals "Come On!" The peixeiras used it in Portuguese with prospective African clients who may or may not have been Kriolu speakers. "Nossa gente" operated differently from its literal Cape Verdean Kriolu translation, "Nha genti." In Cape Verdean Kriolu, it is an exclamation that one might use to respond to tragic news. Hence, the use of this reference with blacks in Portugal (exchanged in Portuguese) layered the original with additional meaning—the simultaneous use of familiarity to mildly call a person out while brokering fraternity to keep the sale going. Thus the use of "Nossa gente" moralized solidarity; it could be used to save potential sales that were under surveillance or going sour.

So establishing common *racial* ground proved essential to the successful sale. The inability to establish cultural familiarity within the context of a sales pitch could limit a peixeira's bargaining strength and jeopardize a transaction with police in the vicinity. Moreover, customers expected this skill of integration, and peixeiras were supposed to deliver. By the same token, potential customers who failed to collaborate in the appropriate construction of solidarity ran the risk of embarrassment. Such embarrassment occurred when the client recognized that he or she had failed to display a sense of community in the exchange with the peixeira.

As the loss of social face was real, there were also strategies mediating national and/or racial hierarchies (i.e., black- and mestiço-identified differences) among customers. Specifically, Angola in many respects constituted the privileged territory in the African empire, being the richest in raw materials and the place with the largest Portuguese settlement in the mid-twentieth century. Sometimes Angolan customers would reference this sense of colonial entitlement in their bargaining strategies, or at least the peixeiras believed or claimed that Angolans were doing so. These attempts, apparently marked by tone of voice rather than actual historical references, were not tolerated. Customers who acted as if contemporary Portuguese society made a distinction between themselves and peixeiras were reminded of their social "place." If they did not respond appropriately, some peixeiras would stop the transaction; they would go about their business or attend to other customers, which generally made the target self-conscious. Customers often saved face by reinitiating their interest in the sale.

BIA: Quer levar peixe, querida?
[(in Portuguese) Want some fish, dear?]

CLIENT: (makes offensive face)

(a pause in the interaction—a few seconds go by)

BIA: Não é preciso fazer beiço assim porque NÓS SOMOS Africanos!
[(in Portuguese) It's not necessary to flip up your lip/sneer like that, because we are ALL Africans!]

(another brief pause)

PATRÍCIA: Leve peixe.
(to potential client) [(in Portuguese) Take some fish]

(another brief pause)

KESHA (nervous laughter)

CLIENT: Kel e di bo?
(referring to Bia's fish) [(in Kriolu) That's yours?]

BIA: E bo e Badiu?
(to the potential client) [(in Kriolu) Are you Badiu?]

CLIENT: Eeee vocês são Badjuda?
(directed at each of the peixeiras) [(in Portuguese) Oh, you are (all) Badjuda?]

At first, the familiar term of endearment *dear* is used to attract the potential customer, who reacts with an offensive "flipped lip." Bia responds with surprise as she raises her eyebrows and then nearly turns her back on the potential customer to establish eye contact with her colleagues. She then reaches out her arms and dramatically flips her head back, stating, "It's not necessary to flip up your lip like that, because we are all Africans," calling out the potential customer. Silence ensues. The customer's embarrassment becomes evident by the way she then chooses to approach the peixeiras. When Patrícia commands that the customer, who is perhaps ten or fifteen years her junior, "take some fish," the customer attempts to display her alignment with the peixeiras by uttering in Kriolu, "That's yours?" referring to Bia's fish. Bia then responds with "Are you Badiu?" But it is immediately clear that the woman is not Badiu once she asks if the peixeiras are Badjuda, which refers to non-Santiaguense communities who are ethno-racially and culturally positioned in opposition to Santiaguense, or Badius. Hence it appears that the potential customer, soon to be identified as a Portuguese-speaking Angolan, is attempting to save face after being ridiculed. The response "Kel e di bo," in this sense, works as an indirect messenger (see Morgan 1996; Yankah 1995); it establishes the potential connection between each actor present. Though the customer does not personally know the peixeiras, the humiliation of being called out encourages her to repair the interaction prior to negotiating. When less than five minutes later she gets out of line again, Bia enacts an elite nasal Portuguese accent to return her to her place. The play works immediately.

What I have tried to show with these scenarios are the terms under which a sense of African community emerges through interactions under surveilled conditions. These interactions partially relied on moral-political ideals of solidarity that were variably referenced through the colonial past and contemporary expressions of knowing one's place *within the community*. The collective aim was to counter the consequences of policing—the shaping of a revised citizen-agent—and so policing, in this context, orchestrated a divisive citizen-migrant sociality. Because policing demanded that civilians take a stance, at a difficult economic moment, the presence of officers positioned a worthy citizen (and those hoping to appear as such) and the criminal migrant (whether peixeira or customer) in opposition to each other. While tensions certainly existed between these communities before police intervention, policing transformed an economic practice that previously attracted multiple communities into a statement about one's commitment to Portugal's modernity. The *paired* stances of worthy citizen and criminal migrant that polarized these communities in relation to labor practice reified the justification regularly voiced by the police: "Get off the streets—Portugal is now a part of Europe."

DISSOLVING A NEED-BASED ECONOMY

By the early 2000s policing had slowed down. Police were still present and addicts continued to attempt to out the few peixeiras who continued to make a living in this space. But police had stopped caring and no longer bothered to chase after the women; suddenly they had ceased to pose a threat. In 2001 only eight of the twenty-plus women remained. By 2003 only three or four of them chose to continue selling at Cais do Sodré. Some worked five days a week, while the others sold fish on Fridays and especially Saturdays when the Docapesca facility in Lisbon received the largest quantity and variety of fish. Many people had just stopped buying fish from the peixeiras: before 2003, some drove to Docapesca themselves to deal directly with wholesale fishmongers, while others simply relied on the grocery store. Reasons may have ranged from negative media coverage on unsanitary fish supplies in Lisbon to policing, but attitudes about where and from whom to buy fish had shifted drastically. Whatever the culmination of reasons, the theatricality of police intervention—where few women were ever fined or taken into custody—proved useful. Over time, poor citizens and migrants alike participated in retail consumption.

In the previous chapter I focused on how changes in industry, a result of Portugal's EU integration and modernization objectives, transformed the social face of the market, in part through new government-enforced food conservation and distribution practices. These practices were mediated through the types of subjects allowed to partake in the new trends and through a weeding process that further underprivileged the low-income Portuguese fishmonger. I thus argued that the closing of the Docapesca facility and the move to the pavilion in Loures stood as an example of how the state regulated the market through subject-specific measures. In this chapter I have highlighted another means through which such measures are applied to market practices in the production of the urban leisure setting. That the enforcement of social practice occurred through non-related individuals, like pedestrians, suggests the ways different spatio-temporal modalities of biopolitical regulation are constantly at work (Povi-nelli 2002: 204). Here, small-scale production among familiars and urban subsistence among strangers—independent of the different social worlds pertaining to each—both disappear in the momentum generated by their joint destruction. Together they exemplify the necessity of new versions of difference in Portugal's modernizing scheme.

Each of the scenarios above is tied to practices, direct and indirect, of racial profiling partially enabled by the vending laws that criminalized the Cape Verdean peixeira. They each also speak to an ambivalence surrounding the meaning of Portugueseness, as both officers and civilians were either stumped by and/or began to play with the new link between Portuguese whiteness and European citizenship. Here, the state plays a more explicit role (through police authority) in equating whiteness to a brand of citizenship, but the state's increased presence is also at the same time mediated and enabled by the actions and decisions of those new citizens. Hence new practices of racial profiling help disclose a *concealed gap* between each group and the state. In each instance described, the parties apparently experimented with the limits of this gap for different reasons. Middle-class white women tried to play both sides as they worked through how to maintain respectable appearances while continuing with familiar practices. In a different vein, though with similar consequences, addicts and street sweepers attempted to acquire some recognition or respectability by partaking in the upkeep of the law. In both cases people played with the undefined limits of a connection between citizenship and race, a connection policing came to refine.

Whites used race to play with or maintain their appearance as citizens, while blacks likewise used it to consolidate a sense of community. These determinations, importantly, parallel the citizen-migrant distinctions justified through emergent discourses of tolerance and respectability. Thus while it may appear that the strategies police used were in opposition to politically correct trends, the consequences of their actions productively enabled the definite distinction that the city of Lisbon supported through its multicultural activities—involving rational, civic-minded citizens and a controllable, homogeneous community of black migrants.

four

BEING IN PLACE Domesticating the Citizen-Migrant Distinction

Peixeiras left Cais do Sodré and headed home between 10:30 a.m. and 11:45 a.m. Most boarded public transportation, buses and trains, with all their gear: buckets, unsold fish, their miniature scales, and plastic bag supplies. They tucked away their knives and scrappers in their aprons. When they boarded, everyone knew who they were; few fellow passengers would sit next to them. Once peixeiras sat down, many people in the close vicinity would give up their seats; they preferred standing to sitting next to the women. During the ride some passengers closely scrutinized them. They stared at the random scales that glistened on the sides of their buckets, in addition to the bloodstains inside and around the rims. They stared at the women's arms, huge and muscular, a product of years of lifting sometimes over one hundred pounds of fish and ice each day, often while running. Scales were also randomly attached to their hands, and sometimes distributed about each arm, maybe even on their clothes. Some passengers stared at the women's bodies with disgust, finally lifting their eyes to the peixeiras' faces, as if to confirm or question the women's humanity. Looking on with raw and unmonitored repugnance, these passengers might twist their faces with abhorrence when they heard the peixeiras communicate in Kriolu.

Other passengers, of course, felt disgust at the intolerance of their fellow riders. I once observed a middle-aged white Portuguese woman indirectly criticize a white passenger who was staring at a peixeira and the blood and scales on her hands. As she looked into the peixeira's eyes, she said firmly, "There's nothing wrong with working hands, BECAUSE THEY'RE *WORKING* HANDS!"

When peixeiras noticed the scrutiny directed at them, they often looked elsewhere, avoiding the passengers' stares; yet sometimes they might return the confrontational gazes, making the other passenger self-conscious. Routinely, the embarrassed passenger would look away, indignantly, waiting for the right moment to start staring again. Unless peixeiras could catch rides home from their sales locations, they endured this treatment as a normal part of their lives during this portion of the day, five days a week.

As most peixeiras before the mid-1990s lived in the more affordable outskirts of Lisbon, generally in a shanty settlement, it generally took them between forty-five and ninety minutes to get home. Rides on city buses were often followed by travel on the less frequent suburban buses that went to their neighborhoods; most cabs refused to enter these areas for fear of being robbed, and most taxi drivers did not want fish products or utensils in their vehicles. When the peixeiras got home, those who worked part-time as waged workers would begin preparations for their next job.

Before departing a second time, they might visit friends and family for some five to ten minutes each day. They might also drop off fish to neighbors who had requested it the day before. Other neighbors, realizing that the peixeiras were home, might peep through their windows and ask if any fish was available for purchase. In their neighborhood communities, regardless of the other types of work they did, the women were known as *the peixeiras*.

To people they did not know, from the afternoon onward, peixeiras who worked part-time were different types of subjects. They dressed in ways that did not distinguish them as peixeiras: they wore modestly patterned cotton or polyester button-up blouses, polyester pants or skirts that generally covered or came to their knees, and modest sandals or low-heeled women's work shoes. They removed the head scarves they wore while selling fish that sometimes concealed rollers. Most slicked their pressed hair back into a tight bun or combed their curls down behind their ears before adorning themselves with jewelry—medium-sized gold earrings, a bracelet, and a necklace or two with crucifixes and evil-eye protectors. In short, they looked nonthreatening and respectable. As they boarded the same buses and trains that they had just left an hour or two ago, no one, not even police officers, noticed or stared at them. Suddenly their bodies melded into the background of the city; they were there, but they remained invisible at the same time.

What happened once they arrived at their waged jobs could not have differed more from the types of interactions described in the previous two chapters. As wage earners they were employed primarily as maids (or household workers), nannies, janitors for small businesses and large cleaning corporations, kitchen help in large restaurants, and as cooks in small ones. The discourse in these settings was instruction driven. In restaurants and with large janitorial companies, the women received instructions from both Portuguese men and women. But the individuals they reported to in most of these jobs were white, lower middle- and middle-class Portuguese women. The women I worked with generally characterized them as polite and sensible employers and supervisors. Though peixeiras encountered women from similar backgrounds in their roles as pedestrians and customers at Cais do Sodré, their descriptions of these women in waged encounters were light years away from those they recounted during sales interactions.

These two income-earning jobs—fish sales and waged work—gave Cape Verdean women a sense of security: the state recognized their waged work, allowing them to collect social security that was transferable to Cape Verde. Wage earnings also meant they had proof of legal employment in Portugal, which they needed for their residency visas and for reentry into Portugal after travel abroad. At the same time, if one employer did not work out or if they were asked to change their hours to times at which they could not work, they could also leave that employer and search for another because of the financial cushion that fish sales provided. Many women worked at least two waged jobs. If they lost or had to give up one of them, they still retained proof of employment with the other. In effect, living on the margins of waged labor and nonregulated vending financially worked to their advantage. As rough and tiring as it was to work twelve to eighteen hours per day, they did it with the knowledge that it rendered them financially flexible and hence gave them material options.

In the mornings the women thus worked *djunta mon* (in solidarity through community practice), in the company of their family and peers at Docapesca and later on the streets. They had known many of their acquaintances since childhood in Santiago and thus fish vending reproduced social networks dear to them. In the morning hours at Docapesca, for instance, they would share news as they passed each other. In the afternoons and evenings they worked waged appointments that paid them roughly 30,000 escudos per month, some $200 to $275, which covered monthly household expenses for up to seven individuals or perhaps rent. Their fish-sales income, totaling between $400 and over $1000 per month —earnings that technically placed them in the middle-income bracket at the time—went into savings accounts or was used for monthly remittances to family, children's expenses, emergency household costs, long-distance phone bills, and lots and lots of land (for future home building) in the interior of Santiago and in the outskirts of Cape Verde's capital city, Praia. Life was incredibly hectic and exhausting, but the women had in many ways come to experience it on their own terms.

This small community of women willing to sell fish—*sem vergonha* (without shame), as they would say—had identified a niche in the Portuguese market. What the fascist and later democratic state had previously identified as petty work not worth strict regulation, peixeiras shrewdly approached as income opportunities. In fact, some Cape Verdean women, generally those recently arrived, would dabble in fish vending until they found a steady waged job. But fish sales and domestic labor describes a more general situation, beyond the opportunities of a small community of Cape Verdean women. These options reflected the conditions of the Portuguese labor market at one time, when migrant labor laws had yet to bind residency to pre-established, state recognized labor contracts, a new legal process taking effect in 2001. Their lives, in this sense, tell us something about the height of economic transition in Portugal, where numerous kinds of urban income schemes co-existed through the early 2000s. Their lives reflect how these opportunities were amplified at one time by the conditions of migrant labor laws, which positioned migrants as active participants in the reproduction of creative earning strategies. As such, the decline of the peixeira market and the insertion of peixeiras into low-wage "women's" work is a story about the standardization of market practice. It suggests how the homogenizing effects of this process would culminate in the professionalization of dichotomized citizen and migrant profiles that reified these standards, clarifying any blurriness.

My objective in the previous two chapters was two-fold. First, I emphasized the productivity of this blurriness where citizens and migrants participated in similar labor and consumer practices. I illustrated how encounters between citizens and migrants were mediated by a market increasingly regulated by new standards and by the engagement of local officials with the meaning of EU influence in Portugal. Second, I considered how individuals' use and reception of raced information went beyond shaping encounters between citizens and migrants. The exchange of raced information in an emergent antiracist environment elucidated how selves were variably interpellated into the state's restructuring schema. This information was exchanged with the very subjects assigned to take up hierarchized labor profiles, and so we must now consider the different nature of discourse in scenarios characterized by the waged encounter. Thinking about self-other relations under declining welfare conditions, the meeting point between neo-liberal market practice and the autonomous individual gives way to more than compassionate recognition of the "lesser" other. Specifically, it appears that compassion and respect, as media for governing, are tied to the *mutual* experience of placement and settlement for citizen and migrant alike.

This means that respect and its forms of expression are not practices exclusively determined by the privileged subject. Diasporic migrant subjectivity and the liberalism inherent to the contemporary enactment of citizenship are mutually mediating forces. Their connection is negotiated not just through their joint rationality—where "diversity" and recognition meet in the cosmos—but especially through the daily repetition of immediate, ordinary encounters between those positioned in these asymmetrical roles. In this sense, compassion is at one end of an uncomfortable social terrain. The other side, at its extreme point, is *compliance*, or dare I say, obedience and submission. By placing the Other's compliance at the other end of the spectrum, as opposed to the cruelty of the compassionate person, compassion can be read in alternate ways that shore up a bigger picture of the social dynamic at play. These ethnographic chapters describe how the meaning and practice of Portuguese citizenship, under EU conditions, would increasingly involve the taking up of "sensible" state-recognized activities that were mediated by or consumptive of migrant compliance.

In this chapter, where instruction-driven interactions characterize the encounters I observed, sensitive and politically appropriate language emerged. Neither facing disbandment nor policing, waged domestic work has emerged as a constant for African immigrant women and represents a realm of social life not in conflict with the state. The latter, in fact, supports it through the labor contract, leading to questions about the relationship between state-sanctioned labor and the social arrangements it entails, on the one hand, and the interactive performance of tolerance or antiracism, on the other. Below I highlight what the particular bodily arrangements under discussion enable.

THE DOMESTICA INDUSTRY

As I followed Patrícia, Djina, and Bia to work during the week, I had the opportunity to observe three different work options.[1] Patrícia did what I call latchkey domestic work. She had limited contact with her employer, a single Portuguese woman, Rosa, with a twelve-year-old daughter. Rosa would leave notes with daily instructions. Patrícia cleaned her home twice a week. Most of their communication took place via lists and telephone calls. Rosa had found Patrícia through her neighbor's household employee, a Cape Verdean woman in her sixties. Patrícia would be Rosa's first African employee. All the others, four in total, were working-poor Portuguese women near retirement whose waged incomes probably resembled Patrícia's, as these women also worked multiple households.

Djina and Bia did different types of janitorial work. Djina worked in a large grocery chain alongside some forty-plus other Portuguese and African women who worked on the store floor. When I left the field she began working full-time, six days a week. The team leaders of this facility were all working-class Portuguese women who supervised work activities. Interestingly, only certain activities were officially monitored: arrival, departure, breaks, and talking to people while working. Thus workers became invisible to supervisors when they followed certain rules. They also remained invisible to customers. They all wore the same uniform, and workers' uniforms differed from those of their supervisors. Generously sprinkled throughout the store, at the end or in between the isles, women janitors blended with the background of the setting—in malls, supermarkets, or office buildings—as they moved about slowly with their brooms and mops.

Bia, by contrast, was the only janitor at her work site. She worked in a very small branch of one of the nation's leading banks situated on a major, centrally located street in Lisbon. The bank consisted of three small sections: the front with two ATM machines, a section with three teller stations, and a third office section separated by a wall (and accessible only to employees). There was also one small bathroom with a utility shelf. Bia cleaned the bank between the hours of 3 p.m. and 6 p.m., Monday through Friday. As banks in Portugal close at three o'clock, her only interlocutors were bank staff. She received instructions from one of the seven Portuguese bank employees there, who happened to be the only woman employed. These three examples represent the diverse ways in which black women have been inserted into the Portuguese waged labor market.

Latchkey Domestics

Patrícia generally expressed satisfaction with her employment situation with Rosa, who was younger than her. As I followed her and helped her clean, she said that while Rosa was somewhat rigid, she liked that trait about her. She said that rigid people were meticulous and that meticulous employers kept their homes clean. For Patrícia this meant that the bulk of her labor involved laundry, ironing in particular. And it meant that she could generally complete her assigned tasks in three or three and a half hours. Rosa originated from the Alentejo in the southern central region of Portugal. She had come to Lisbon to study economics with state funding; she was the first person in her family to go to college. On finishing her degree in 1987 she got pregnant with Sara and decided to stay in Lisbon. During my fieldwork she lived in a middle-class condomunium complex on the outer limits of Lisbon, her mortgage covered by her income as a civil servant in a state ministry. Because the Portuguese state allows single mothers to arrive to work an hour after regular commencement hours, her daily work schedule involved leaving her home by 9:20 a.m. to arrive at work by 10 a.m. She drove herself to the subway stop in a new five-door Peugeot and then took the train to work. Monday through Friday she worked until around 4 p.m. Her daughter, whose school was located near their home, walked home after four o'clock.

Patrícia generally arrived at their home at 2 p.m., and she worked there until around 5 p.m. Tuesdays and Fridays. She would thus likely run into either Sara or Rosa during her final fifteen to thirty minutes of housework. Rosa's home had four bedrooms; one of them served as an office. Patrícia thus made sure that the kitchen was the last task, while the bedrooms and the living and dining rooms were done first. She started off in the kitchen by organizing the clothes, sheets, and tablecloths that needed ironing and then would start a laundry load. In general, Rosa would wash clothes the night before. Since she did not have a dryer, she would put the damp clothes on the clothesline before leaving home. If the weather was warm, and if there was no rain, the clothes would be dry by the time of our arrival.

So on arriving we gathered the clothes, sorted them, and then put in another load. If the load was finished before 5 p.m. we would put it out to dry, and sometimes Sara helped us. If not, Rosa would take the damp clothes out, retrieve them the next morning, and leave them for Patrícia to iron on Friday or Tuesday afternoon.

The tasks that Rosa gave Patrícia varied each week. Certain things she had to do twice a week, but other things she was assigned only once a week. Twice weekly tasks included ironing, dusting, vacuuming, putting things in their place, and cleaning the entire kitchen, the toilet room, and the shower room. Once-a-week tasks involved changing sheets, cleaning the windows, mopping, beating rugs, and cleaning the veranda (which involved scrubbing mud from its tiled floor and removing dirt from the outdoor furniture).

Once clothes were sorted and prepped for ironing, Patrícia removed her shoes and vacuumed the entire house. Then, if it was time to clean the shower room (the one task she sometimes did once a week though she was assigned the task twice a week), she would sprinkle water with cleaner into the tub, on the shower curtain, and on the shower walls and then let the cleaner go to work. Then she moved onto the toilet room and then back to the shower room. She could do both in less than thirty-five minutes, moving briskly, always mindful of the time. Next she moved into the bedrooms, which were rarely out of order. Thus her basic tasks involved changing sheets, making the beds, and dusting. After the bedrooms and the office, she cleaned or wiped down the windows. Then she dusted the remainder of the house, which included two ebony statues of nude women, artworks Rosa had recently inherited from an older cousin born and raised in Angola. These types of encounters with colonial artifacts, as Patrícia dusted off a wooden black female body that could have been her own, were among the few moments that subliminally referenced the colonial. While the dusting perhaps appeared more ironic to me than to her—given my role as observer—the abounding silence of such moments indicated something. The growing irrelevancy of the colonial past, as knowledge used to inform or to justify actions and intentions in the immediate present, was partially constituted through mundane and repetitive exercises, like the seconds it took to dust an object. What seems important here is that the figure had little relevance for both its cleaner and its owner.

Next she moved to the veranda, which took a good twenty minutes, and then she addressed the kitchen. She removed the dishes from the washer, cleaned the oven, the refrigerator, the counters, the microwave, and the stovetop. This took about twenty-five minutes. The remainder of the time, anywhere from forty to sixty minutes, was spent ironing. The speed with which Patrícia accomplished her tasks, constantly checking the clock while making sure that every hair stayed in place, made an impression on me. She changed the rhythm and pace she assumed while purchasing or selling fish—here she was operating on *someone else's* time, not her own.

By the time Rosa or Sara arrived, Patrícia had done every room and about half of her kitchen work. Rosa and Sara would *lanchar*, have a midafternoon snack before dinner. So between 4:15 p.m. and 5 p.m. the three would run into each other as Sara made herself a ham-and-cheese *tosta* and Rosa made her own snack, generally some cheese on fresh multigrain bread and some black tea. To stay out of the way and to iron without disruption, Patrícia positioned herself in the back of the kitchen, away from the refrigerator and the sink. Everyone went about their business autonomously. Rosa would offer us tea or bread and cheese as she prepared it for herself. Sometimes she did not even verbally offer it: she would just prepare a large plate from which the three of us ate at our leisure. Patrícia took what she wanted, often taking the last bite and eating the largest portions. She never seemed to think anything of it. Rosa would continue to conscientiously fill the plate until it seemed that we had all had enough: "Patrícia, you know there's plenty; you know to make yourself at home, right? And take some cheese home with you, if you'd like." Sometimes Patrícia would.

As Patrícia ironed and Rosa moved in and out of the kitchen, their interactions strictly touched on surface issues, like the weather or the latest telenovela. But the conversations did not build familiarity or intimacy; responses were polite but short on both sides. Rosa might observe, "Looks like beach weather this weekend," to which Patrícia would respond with, "Sure does." Rosa would continue with, "Any plans this weekend?" And Patrícia, looking distant, perhaps ironing, would reply with, "Oh, nothing special." And that would be it. Rosa would pop out, get on the phone, or scold Sara for watching TV and not doing her homework. Sometimes when she left the room she would leave her purse on the sink, wide open. Patrícia told me that this bothered her because she generally had to move it to finish her work and that she feared that if anything was ever missing, it could easily be blamed on her. The burden of possible accusation eluci-dated the very tension so carefully concealed by the civility of the women's encounter.

At 5 p.m. Patrícia would assess her accomplishments. If the remainder of the work would take her fifteen minutes she generally chose to finish. If she was nowhere near finished she might stop as early as 4:50 p.m. She would then call Rosa as she walked through the house. Patrícia would report on her tasks by tapping each lefthand finger with her right forefinger, address-ing her employer in the formal third person: "Miss Rosa, I've changed the sheets, cleaned the veranda, the windows, cleaned the bathrooms, and the rugs are done. I put in a load of sheets for you." And if something went wrong or seemed abnormal, Patrícia would report, "But there's a yellowish color that I can't scrub out of the tub. Maybe Miss Rosa could buy a stronger product?" Rosa would reply, "Very good, Patrícia. Don't worry about the tub, it's not going to get whiter, it's just old. And did you get the chairs on the veranda?" "Yes, Miss Rosa," would be Patrícia's reply. Rosa would continue, "Very well, so I'll see you on Tuesday/Friday? Oh, and could you get the cobwebs in the ceiling corners in the living room then?" Patrícia would respond with, "Of course, it will be the first thing that I do on Tuesday/Friday." And indeed it would be.

Conversations about Africa tended to emerge under circumstances rele-vant to the immediate moment. For instance, Patrícia wore a pair of ear-rings with three charms: a fist—representing Cape Verdean resistance and unity; fish—representing the peixeira economy; and a cross—representing Catholicism. One day Rosa complemented Patrícia on her earrings. The conversation, begun by Rosa, went something like this: "I can tell that those earrings are made of good-quality gold. They're beautiful; are they heavy?" Patrícia: "A little." Rosa then asked what the charms meant. Patrícia—who later told me that she had never thought of what these charms represented, or rather, had never discussed their meaning aloud—stated, "Well, this one means *djunta mon*, Cape Verdeans working together; this one is my faith; and this one is . . . my survival." When Rosa asked which one represented survival, Patrícia answered, "The fish." Rosa admitted her lack of under-standing, until Patrícia explained that she was a peixeira. Rosa expressed surprise, asking, "And you run from police and everything?" Patrícia, smirk-ing and still ironing, responded, "That's what we do!" in a light singsong of sarcasm. When Rosa asked her daughter what she thought of this revelation, Sara, politely and sincerely said, "Cool!" Two weeks later Rosa apparently discussed Patrícia's fish vending with the woman who had connected her with Patrícia, in fact also a peixeira. Things did not seem to change after Patrícia was outed; conversations remained the same—polite but impersonal.

Still, Rosa did actually know quite a bit about Patrícia. Rosa had filled out all Patrícia's family residency documents, census information, and even Patrícia's pregnant teen daughter's welfare forms (for her daughter was a Portuguese citizen). Patrícia would coordinate this kind of assistance with her a few workdays in advance. She would bring her residency, employment, and housing papers to Rosa's house, where the two women would sit down together to piece through the information, filling in the blanks on the appropriate forms. In such instances Africa would surface in conversations regarding the amount of savings transmitted as remittances, whether Patrícia needed to go to the Cape Verdean embassy for additional documentation, or the number of times Patrícia had traveled to Africa since establishing legal residency and employment. This information, importantly, was immediate—relative to the present. And this immediacy established the terms of the women's difference, as it partly informed Rosa of the specifics of her citizenship through markers not tied to her life experience such as the need for proof of employment, proof of residency, or proof of registered housing to operate in the confines of the law. In 2001 these details would take on an intensified tone as employers became surrogates for the state in managing migrant matters. Prior to 2001 the route to legal residency involved filling out the appropriate paper work and including a letter from an employer, serving as proof of employment, that documented the applicant's wages. In this way, proof of employment was not tied to job conditions. In theory, if the migrant was fired or chose to leave their job, they simply had to make sure they had another means of verifiable employment when they renewed their visa. A new law, D.L. 4/2001, aimed specifically at men in the construction industry from both Africa *and* Eastern Europe, was passed in 2001 to enforce controllable labor quotas that responded directly to industry needs. While the campaign around the legislation leading to the law was framed around the curtailment of illegal immigration and the protection of the migrant worker, the new process of applying for a labor visa suggested other motives, as noted by SOS Racismo (2002: 177–85). Under the new law employers were required to state that they would guarantee one full year of work. This meant that the labor visa not only had to be updated yearly, but that the employer controlled the migrant's residency. According to the law non-national adults without employment, who previously held work visas, had to leave the country. Not surprisingly the consequences for domestic labor was devastating, particularly for women who worked in the confines of households or during after-business hours in corporate offices where janitorial work was beyond public viewing. If the employers was unscrupulous they could control the migrant's life, creating the conditions for bondage.

In this light, such access to Patrícia's personal information, including her family's cumulative income and her children's eligibility for state assistance, was the building block marking divisions between her and Rosa, in concrete ways. Nothing about either party's material reality would remain open to the imagination. This uneven exchange of personal information— where Patrícia knew Rosa because she worked in the intimate space of her home, and where Rosa knew Patrícia because she established her salary and was privy to the details of her residency and migrant status—expressed the terms of their difference each time they were together. Furthermore, there were evolving legal structures in play that intercepted each role in ways that consolidated their relationship through their diverse experiences of connection to the Portuguese state.

The interesting thing about Rosa and Patrícia's relationship was that they needed each other differently and that the terms of their engagement —from the exchange of money for work to providing free assistance with state bureaucracy—constantly reified the terms of their connection through an experience of difference. Regardless of how they chose to manage themselves or of their individual politics, there existed concrete, typed actions that hierarchically recognized them as separate kinds of mutually dependent subjects. The repetition of these actions in their Tuesday and Friday encounters produced conditions replicated next door and in other similar household situations. The simple fact that Rosa's role in the encounter was by choice—the choice to hire a domestic—while Patrícia's role would be progressively bound to need paired them in a cycle that reproduced their relative difference, one mediated by the tension between leisure and subsistence.

Custodial Work

Janitorial work, by contrast, differed because most employees worked in teams or within nonisolated settings. Most companies and offices that hired cleaning services contracted janitorial companies who assigned temporary and permanent cleaning teams to them. Other janitorial services were made available through commercial malls that hired workers to maintain the common areas of the facility during opening hours.

Bia

Bia had a very specific situation. She was the only janitorial employee at a tiny bank branch in an upscale shopping district in the heart of Lisbon. She worked alongside seven other bank employees. One of them—the only woman—was a thirty-nine-year-old divorcee named Cândida; she served as Bia's unofficial supervisor.

Bia sold fish with the other women, from 7 a.m. to around 11 a.m. Whatever she did not sell, she brought home with her on ice. She had an arrangement with a Guinean friend, a man who regularly bought fish from her. He picked her up between 10:30 a.m. and 11:30 a.m. and dropped her at another sales spot, some forty-five minutes away and near her home. Bia lived in one of the few remaining shanty communities situated next to a working-poor suburban neighborhood, quite distant from the center of Lisbon. Many of her neighbors, Portuguese individuals of working-poor and working-class backgrounds, purchased her remaining fish. In general, the fish would be gone within the hour, as people valued fresh fish for lunch. Then Bia would walk home, which took about fifteen to twenty minutes. At home she would give away her unsold fish to her African and Portuguese neighbors and then disinfect and put away her sales supplies and utensils. Next she would nap for some twenty minutes before preparing to take the bus and then the subway to the bank.

Bia did not have her own key, and the bank closed at 3 p.m., so she had to use the buzzer and wait. Sometimes she waited for up to seven minutes before someone attended. Bia was greeted by Cândida, who worked at a large information desk near the teller machines in the front room; there she did some kind of accounting. Their daily greetings would start with Bia asking, "Miss Cândida, how is your body today" (O corpo está bom?), a Cape Verdean greeting. "I'm very well, Bia, and you?" Bia would respond:

"Thanks to God [sometimes to the Virgin Mother] I can't complain today; today is good." And Cândida would tell her she was glad to hear it, as Bia moved through the room with the teller stations, on her way to the bathroom that stored the cleaning supplies. As she walked by, she greeted everyone she passed, and they each greeted her: "Hey Bia! How's it goin' today?"; or, "Hey Dona Bia! Good to see you!"; or "Hey Bia, another day!" Two of the employees appeared to be considerably younger than Bia, and they prefaced her name with Dona. Bia greeted each of them by name, using *você*, or as her colleagues: "Colleagues! How are your bodies today?" And everyone would reply with, "Great Bia, thank you!" Or, "Thanks Bia, and you?"

Bia's tasks included cleaning all the windows, including the outside of the front window, cleaning the bathrooms, vacuuming, sweeping, dusting, and polishing all countertop surfaces. She also emptied all the trash cans and ashtrays, and removed disposable cups, and candy and food wrappers atop desks. She started by picking up the trash at each station, then emptying each trash can into a giant garbage bag. The interesting thing about this space was that each worker rushed and moved about quickly, resulting in a lot of comfortable but obligatory surface conversation as people whisked by and bumped into each other, moving from one task to the next. I constantly heard "excuse me" or "pardon me." After collecting all the garbage in this central room, which took about fifteen minutes, Bia retreated to the bathroom to clean for another fifteen minutes. She then added the bathroom garbage to the larger garbage bag and moved on.

Next, she cleaned the windows. She then dusted and polished all the countertops in about an hour. As she cleaned she engaged in small talk with whoever stood beside her, if they were available to speak. Conversations generally focused on the weather, family, or planned weekend activities. Bia's communicative style, both poetic and empathetic, charmed her workmates.

Once it was clear that no one was doing work that required concentration, something Bia would inquire about, she would begin vacuuming the tiled and carpeted areas. After that she mopped and finished whatever was left to do. This generally took under twenty-five minutes, and Bia would be out of the door by 6 p.m., if not a little earlier.

Bia found the bank to be the perfect job because it not only gave her access to benefits but let her work in an environment in which each worker focused on his or her respective job. She said that even if a colleague seemed testy or irritated, she knew that the sentiment was not about her or her work because everyone was running on their own clock. And she especially appreciated that Cândida hardly gave her instructions; she trusted that Bia knew what to do, and she let her do it. Thus the only time they interacted in a different manner than how Bia interacted with the other employees was when Cândida gave Bia her paycheck or when Bia had to request refills for cleaning products. Yet even so, Bia and Cândida did have a few awkward moments that were interestingly tied to expectations around Bia's status as a janitor.

One instance I observed happened when Cândida asked Bia if she was going home to Cape Verde for the holidays. Bia told her that she would visit Cape Verde in the next six months and that during the current holiday season she planned to fly to Paris and then take a scenic route to Marseille, to where her daughter's fiancée had just relocated to work in construction. Cândida, who did not know that Bia sold fish and thus had the means for such a trip, asked Bia how she might afford her two weeks away. She said something like, "Two weeks in France will be quite an expensive excursion. Is that feasible?" Bia politely told Cândida not to worry and that she had been saving for the trip for quite some time. Cândida then added that she did not know Marseille but hoped to visit it someday. They then continued with their respective duties, seemingly without a second thought.

As we left the bank Bia turned to me and said, "African people aren't supposed to do anything nice or have anything nice!" She said that if Cândida had any idea that she sold fish, or worse, if she knew she could make *at least* the equivalent of $300 per week selling it, that Cândida would "flip." She said this had become clear the year before, when Bia's daughter's fiancée pulled up in front of the bank in an older but well-kept BMW to pick up Bia. Bia had asked Cândida to call her if she was in the back when her ride came. Apparently Zé, her daughter's fiancée, sat in his car waiting for nearly ten minutes, blocking heavy rush-hour traffic on a major boulevard. When Bia happened to walk by the entryway she saw Zé in the car, irritated. So she grabbed her stuff and moved toward the door, asking Cândida why she had not called her. Cândida appeared flustered and embarrassed when she realized that the BMW was for her.

After the incident, Bia observed that, Cândida would periodically ask her questions to figure out just who she was. Cândida knew that she lived in a shanty community, and Bia noticed that she was consistently puzzled by the things Bia had or knew. Yet still Bia said she would not trade her job for the world; she felt independent in her work, and it afforded her another source of income. Most interesting was Bia's decision to keep her income potential to herself, and thus away from Cândida's curious radar. She said that she did not fear losing her job, but that she was concerned about how this information would affect her relationship with Cândida, and thus the quality of the independence that she felt as a worker at the bank. In this sense, she situated her independence in two seemingly paradoxical realities: first, in the fact that she had other income, being one of the most financially successful peixeiras in the Cape Verdean peixeira community; and second, in the façade of her subordination to Cândida, which made her feel protected and not intruded upon. In that Bia could easily amass between $1,500 and $2,000 a month in total income, she probably made the rough equivalent of what Cândida earned as a bank teller in the late 1990s. Yet she managed herself as the sole waged worker in a salaried setting to obtain a sense of peace, suggesting that the performance of migrancy, like that of citizenship, had its own effective script for enabling the appearance of normalcy.

I knew little about Cândida's story, except that she was a recent divorcee who had just reentered the job market. She also had two adolescent sons and a Cape Verdean maid from Santo Antão. She often spoke of this maid to Bia, generally describing her appreciation for her. In addition to doing housework, the maid would prepare food that Cândida could easily toss together on returning home from work. Thus when Cândida arrived home after 6 p.m., all she had to do was mix the ingredients together, something that facilitated her life.

Cândida's periodic questions further prove interesting because they emerged in moments of misrecognition, moments in which Bia's position as a waged janitor did not coincide with her supposed consumption practices. Hence I want to emphasize that Cândida requested personal information from Bia when she believed that she did *not know* Bia. Bia suggested that Cândida did not ask for personal details so long as her image of her as a janitor was not challenged. Instances in which information was requested thus suggest moments of rupture; the practices imagined to solidify the citizen-migrant distinction often did not match up, particularly in the late 1990s. The two previous scenarios equally pointed to confusing contexts in which people tried to figure out who they were independently and in relation to others. The policed scenario in particular emphasizes this point because it concerned the regulation of urban space and designated the contexts in which legalized commerce could take place and with whom. There is thus a connection between the effort to put things in order, on Cândida's part, and the policing efforts aimed at disbanding peixeira activity at Cais do Sodré. The two activities pertain to a common regulatory force, or potential, whose outcome would locate the black migrant woman as a waged, domestic worker.

Djina

Djina worked as a janitor in a grocery store in a large mall completed in the mid-1990s. This mall at the time was hailed as one of the EU's largest in terms of square footage. Djina worked for a janitorial company that had a contract with this particular store. Right before finishing my fieldwork she started working there six days a week, from noon to 6 p.m. At 9:45 a.m. her companion, who owned a small-scale construction company (that catered to projects in city-recognized shanty communities), would pick her up where she sold fish and take her home. He then went to work. She arrived home before 10:15 a.m. and would be on a bus by 10:50 a.m. to get to the subway station close to her job.

When Djina arrived she had to punch in and report to a supervisor. Her supervisor, Joana, a working-class Portuguese woman from Lisbon, managed fifteen other women, ten of them Santiaguense Cape Verdean. The others were two white Portuguese women and three other black women, an Angolan and two Guinean. As a team they were responsible for sweeping and mopping the premises. At any given moment at least twelve women were cleaning on the store floor. They were primarily stationed near food and household items. The store aimed to have them well spread out so that any spills or other accidents could be taken care of immediately. The women's two-piece uniforms—pastel button-up blouses with matching darker skirts—were a snug fit. The sleeves ended right above the elbow and the skirt hovered right above the knees. There were no jewelry restrictions, and they all wore high-grade gold. The women, including the supervisor, wore earrings, rings, bracelets, and necklaces, though the charms on their jewelry differed. The Angolan and the Portuguese women had crucifixes, in addition to evil-eye protectors, butterflies, puppies, and other kitsch items.

The Cape Verdean and the Guinean women also had crucifixes and evil-eye protectors, in addition to anchors, fish, and fists.

Each woman had to monitor her assigned spot with a mop or a broom and a long-handled dustbin in hand. On receiving their daily location instructions, they generally stayed close to that side of the store for most of the shift, unless called to another section. The Cape Verdean and the Guinean women spoke to each other in Kriolu as they worked. When the Angolan or Portuguese women were present, the Kriolu speakers generally only switched to Portuguese when directly addressing the others. One Portuguese woman lived in a predominantly Cape Verdean community and so spoke a mixture of Kriolu and Portuguese with the Cape Verdeans and Guineans. The non-Kriolu speakers were rarely collectively addressed in Portuguese, but instead in Kriolu, the lingua franca among the workers. I asked them if they understood Kriolu, and they each said that they could understand it or were learning to do so; in group settings they would respond to Kriolu in Portuguese, illustrating linguistically how practices tied to carrying out this work had been codified as thoroughly African. At times two or three of the Kriolu speakers would congregate if they passed each other, but Joana would ask them to disband. With a hint of fun in her voice she would stroll by without stopping and say, "OK, girls, let's go," or, "Chat on your own time, back to work." Sometimes she would show off the bit of Kriolu she had learned and tell them "Dja kaba!" (It's over!). The women would then disperse, reluctantly.

As did the other workers, Djina had an interesting relationship with Joana. The women called her Joana, with no Dona prefacing her name. They also used the familiar *tu* form with her. Importantly, Joana did not set the terms of work, nor was she involved in the hiring; she simply supervised and made sure that the job requirements were fulfilled. Thus her position explicitly involved managing women whose economic circumstances did not differ very much from her own. But her relationship to the terms she was hired to enforce and manage was telling. In addition to deciding where the women should be stationed, or when they could take their breaks and lunch periods, she was also tied to a system of punishment that could lead to job termination or suspension if workers failed to show up to work or to arrive back on time from breaks or lunch periods. Since the employees she managed were for the most part financially struggling mothers, Joana's job required that she make daily decisions that pitted the welfare of the working-poor mother against new work principles that favored responsibility and personal accountability. In essence, Joana did much more than supervise tasks; the consequences of her actions enforced work habits that could potentially lead to terminations in a country previously unaccustomed to them.

Joana was under pressure from her supervisors to enforce the rules strictly, so she had to weigh the gravity of reporting problems to them. Her superiors could monitor worker productivity on their own by simply browsing through the hours a particular worker punched in. Thus Joana's own job security relied on her ability to supervise and manage efficiently. Workers knew that Joana was empathetic to struggling mothers' experiences, as she was one herself: she had four kids, rent to pay, and the father of her youngest child had left her the year before. Thus the women she supervised knew they could appeal to this side of her, which was real and heartfelt. It created a struggle for Joana, however: she felt morally obliged to honor the workers' experience, but she resented that they did not recognize her own vulnerable position.

Djina was one of the women who gave Joana a hard time. The two of them regularly exchanged short-lived but very tense words about Djina's tardiness, in displays that both compromised Joana's authority and piqued the curiosity of customers passing by. The two women repeatedly argued about Djina's arrival time: if Djina missed her 10:50 a.m. bus, which happened about once a week, she would arrive to work twenty minutes late. Djina would explain that this was her second job and that she was doing everything she could to arrive to work on time. And Joana rebutted with her own, similar work situation, pointing out that she managed to avoid being tardy. Under previous legal conditions it was very difficult to get fired: terminating someone's work contract was considered extreme until recently. But Joana had been involved in a woman's dismissal. And Djina's tardiness forced her to contemplate the benefits and disadvantages of old and new ways of management. Had Djina not stood out as a great worker once she got out on the store floor, she probably would have been fired. To her credit, she took her work very seriously and moved quickly. She was also known for compassionately consoling customers who were embarrassed about spills they made, although it was not part of her job description. Had she not made Joana look good by extending herself to customers—in displays of customer service highly valued under new management practices—she would have likely lost her job.

The interesting thing here is that Joana was not supposed to rely on her intimate knowledge, those things essential in the scenarios of previous chapters in settings on there way out. Her job would have run a lot more smoothly had she not connected with the economic hardships of her workers. In fact, her job demanded a distance between herself and the other women, an emotional detachment considered rational, safe, and objective. It is helpful here to compare Cândida's distant conduct vis-à-vis Bia with Joana's particular role as a supervisor. The tension Joana experienced was largely tied to the fact that her own hardships were transparent —she shared them with her workers as opposed to concealing them. She felt that this decision, which she shared with Djina, compromised her role as supervisor. In thinking about how race, class, gender, and national status variably meld into the role of janitor or domestic in ways that enforce citizen-migrant distinctions, it is useful to reflect on the parallels between this scenario and that of Cândida and Bia. In both scenarios employee and employer were bringing home roughly the same amount of income, taking into account Bia's and Djina's fish sales. This relative income equality, however, highlights that a particular practice of social distinction was present in the first scenario and absent in the one between Joana and Djina.

Joana's crisis emerged from not seeing herself in the "new" light or in the very realm of authority that the male addicts and street sweepers described in the previous chapter had embodied, for instance, by participating in the policing of peixeiras. If anything, this situation teaches us about the tenuousness of citizenship as a possession: addicts and sweepers needed to participate in racial profiling, while individuals like Joana were forced to question and abandon certain moral values if they wanted to be included in the workforce.

THE LAST STANDING SCENARIO: NEW ROUTINIZATIONS

What the scenes described in this chapter reveal is a curious slippage. I observed a moment at which one's political subjectivity did not quite correspond to one's labor worth because of the unevenly regulated character of the market, as evidenced by the profit in public fish sales. The interventions that followed, from the closing of Docapesca to intensified policing, would fix this incongruity so that domestic labor and the other forms of low-waged women's work associated with it were codified in the image of the African migrant woman. The examples just illustrated are standing scenarios today in the late 2000s. The women I worked with now fill these waged positions fulltime, including Manuela.

The income of former peixeiras in the mid-2000s averaged from $500 to $800 per month, in an economy in which the cost of living has more than doubled since the mid-1990s. Most of the women now send remittances twice or thrice a year, rather than once a month. They speak less often to family in Cape Verde because many cannot afford the phone calls, and some feel shame at not being able to send money as before. Some dependent family members in Cape Verde see them as ingrates: persons who no longer support their family back home, where the cost of living has also more than doubled. In Cape Verde, homes remain half built or have been abandoned; people can no longer afford the guards who watched their property to protect the sand and bricks from theft at night. In effect, the material distinctions between former peixeiras and the women who hire and supervise them have never been more real.

My objective is not to leave the impression that the lives of African immigrant women are worsened and Portuguese women are better because of this. Many African women are now Portuguese citizens and many white, working Portuguese women are not better off than African immigrant women. The point is to emphasize *the depth of information that is produced through the waged encounter between black and white women*. Attention to former peixeiras enables this introspection: it is one thing for a group of immigrant women to find that the jobs they encountered are also their niche; it is another to be positioned, and repositioned over time, in the market. The time period I have documented, from the mid-1990s through the early 2000s, when Portugal's economy was integrated into the EU, is an odd moment characterized by "transparency." Activities involving policing, scientific experts, and especially civilians, ranging from addicts to working-poor supervisors, suggest that the space between domestic work and popular ideals about black womanhood had yet to be filled. This study aims to understand how individuals responded to and took up this information in ways that codified the association while solidifying (in part) the citizen-migrant boundary.

If, by the early 2000s, material divisions did not neatly map onto the citizen-migrant divide, what enabled subjects to sense this division? What practices normalized this perception of the social landscape? Most migration studies detect power through the impact of unforgiving laws on migrants; they render migrant subjectification a code word for repression under the law. The migrants' "docility" emerges through the ways they *alone* are forced to comply with the law or make amends with it. In these studies, the citizen emerges in expressions of intolerance where the conversation is limited to affect. I have tried, rather, to consider the means through which citizens' roles as social managers bridge the separation between affective stance and institutional authority, consequently performing the law with institutionally mediating effects. I have identified the sites where citizens are called to such action by assessing how state-regulated market changes impel civilians to assert a version of citizenship whose effects do not simply mimic the law, but rather enforce it. The field of domestic labor, I have argued, is one of these sites. The resilience of the moralizing core in racial knowledge—information that neutrally orients both racist and antiracist practice—constitutes the space in which civilians make connections that amplify the idea and the appearance of citizenship.

The amplification of a revised version of Portuguese citizenship occurred at the same moment when a sense of diasporic consciousness was emerging. When peixeiras went to Docapesca, for instance, they connected on average with over three hundred Cape Verdean peers on any given work day. These encounters kept them abreast of social events and family affairs in Cape Verde. This kind of encounter is no longer a social possibility, at least not in this specific form. While waged jobs mean that Cape Verdean women are increasingly tied to a network of Portuguese citizens, corporations, and the state, it also means that former peixeiras are increasingly tied to other African national communities through labor practices generically codified as African. Thus labor restructuring and new state housing projects that absorbed African immigrants from various nation-based shanty settlements have led to a diminishing distinction between these national groups. This likewise enforces practices of diasporic recognition at the same time that the apparent ties between citizens and the state are consolidated through the 2001 nonnational labor law. Diasporic recognition and its ties to migrant identity, while also powerful and recuperative, is a governing site that necessarily engages with the practice of citizenship.

The transformation of the former peixeiras runs deeper. Today they do not look like the same people they were in the early 2000s. Many have lost the incredible upper-body strength required of them to carry, balance, and run with fish and ice. Their once muscular frames have shrunken considerably, and for a few lost muscle tone has transformed into medically monitored obesity. Many suffer from chronic neck, back, and hip pain that they themselves attribute to the policed conditions of their sales activities and that requires frequent visits to the doctor and pain relief medication. These physiological or carnal traces, something that Elizabeth Povinelli (2006) draws our attention to, further solidify the citizen-migrant distinction. Here, we can see not simply the policing of bodies, but the turning of the body's own defenses against itself.

five

REGULATING THE CITIZEN, DISCIPLINING THE MIGRANT

Rummaging through the national archives in Cape Verde's capital city, Praia, I came across an interesting series of correspondence among ITPAS administrators (the colonial labor placement office that oversaw the migration branch for Portugal), CATU, Cape Verdeans in Portugal or ones hoping to travel there, and Portuguese employers. I found a letter of complaint (of which there were many) dated September 29, 1971, written by a coed group of twelve young Cape Verdeans employed at Lisbon's old Hotel Ofir. The letter explains that not only had each of them been asked to work long hours, day and night, without clear instructions on their job duties but also that one of them had been asked to clean a huge *sala* (dining room) by herself, right after it had just been cleaned. A section of the letter responds to this harassment as follows,

> E está por sua vez dirigiou-se a menina, obrigando-lhe que fosse lavar sozinha aquela tão grande sala. E a menina por falta de mentalidade disse que sozinha não ía passar a sala.
>
> [And then she turned to the girl, forcing her to clean that huge room by herself. And the girl for lack of knowing (her place), told her that she wouldn't do it alone.]

> A dona Mercêdes insistiu com ela, e empurrou-lhe dando-lhe palmadas nas costas. E está ficou tão . . . que não foi levar a sala. A patroa foi chamar o Director e este veio nas meninas com aspecto zangado. . . . Mais antes a D. Mercêdes dísse as meninas que elas são negras, palermas, e mandigas. As meninas foram ao Sr. Director e disse-lhe que já não que íam trabalhar, e o Sr. disse-lhes que deixassem o trabalho dia 18 e que entregassem as

farads. Chegado este dia deixaram o servico, e entregaram as farads, e nesse día não as pagaram o vencimento e ainda fecharam-lhe as portas do quarte e nos e que tivemos de ir alugar uma casa para elas se dormirem.

[Dona Mercedes pressed on, and pushed her giving her a slap on her back. And it was so hard that she couldn't clean the room. The boss then called the director, who then went to the girls angrily. . . . But before that D. Mercedes called the girls blackies, idiots, and *mandigas*.[1] The girls went to the director and told him they would work, and he told them to leave on the 18th and to return their uniforms. When the day arrived, they left their jobs, returned their uniforms, and on that day they didn't get paid and they were locked out, and we had to rent a place for them to sleep.]

When this letter was written ITPAS was trying to figure out whether they could use Cape Verdean women as domestics; this occurred some two years before many would enter Portugal through the new family unification decision mentioned in the introduction. The Hotel Ofir was one of the few businesses at the time that recruited both men and women for hotel work and thus its employment of this coed community was in many ways experimental. Because ITPAS's activities spanned Cape Verde and Portugal, paying attention to its confusions about the social location of poor Cape Verdean womanhood in colonial Cape Verde helps elucidate the tensions arising in Portugal. In Cape Verde, for instance, ITPAS was trying to identify work opportunities for women; emigration to São Tomé and Príncipe —to where thousands of women had been recruited—had just about ended, leaving women with fewer income opportunities. In 1968 elite Cape Verdean housewives had complained to ITPAS about their "insolent" maids who spoke back to them or who would not do as they were told. Correspondence between ITPAS in Praia and a local office in Santo Antão reveals that the agency did not know how to proceed because they did not know what types of subjects they were dealing with. Though legally the maids were Portuguese nationals, they worked in the same positions as "indigenous continental subjects" in São Tomé and Príncipe; some managers referred to them in their labor reports as *cabo-indígenas* in some moments, while expressing shock at some northern islander Cape Verdeans' high literacy rates in others. The officer responding to the complaint rationalized disciplinary action against one maid by referring to indigenous labor codes that did not apply to Cape Verdeans and had been outlawed in continental Africa in 1959. The Portuguese colonial administration outlawed indigenous legal status in continental Africa in 1961, a move that rendered all subjects of the empire Portuguese nationals. Accordingly, the inherent contradictions in colonial Cape Verdean identity—a product of tensions between literacy, mobility, indentured servitude, and the possession of Portuguese nationality for those beyond Portuguese colonial space—would rise to the surface in moments when the coed group described above were reduced to the indigenous status of mandingas.

I raise this discussion for two reasons. First, I want to stress that Cape Verdean women's association with low-waged women's work was contested by Cape Verdean women themselves, even while being taken as a viable possibility by the ITPAS office and Portuguese employers. The connection between African womanhood and domesticity had yet to be crafted or constituted as norm because it was an ideal that had yet to be realized in practice. Second, I want to emphasize the irony that their current labor positions (since 2001) as contracted workers do not differ much from those evident in the colonial period. The vulnerability they experienced as recruited nationals, through 1975; resembles the vulnerabilities imposed by the 2001 law here the absence of employer support puts the migrants' political and economic status in jeopardy. Thus we need to examine at least two factors to comprehend the process by which African women's labor would become codified as low-wage domestic help: the regulation of the inhabitance of Portuguese citizenship under EU conditions; and the changing nature of state intervention in the management of social life more broadly.

CAPE VERDEAN WOMEN'S RELATIONAL STATUS

Over the course of a thirty-year period spanning colonialism, decolonization, democracy, and European unification, Cape Verdean women have lived through a series of different relationships with different versions of Portuguese citizenship. Their presence disabled any stable concept of Portuguese identity prior to European accession, while partially constituting the potential of the nation's modernity and hence European citizenship following integration. Thus the relational potential in the idea of poor African womanhood, as an appendage determining the destruction or constitution of something imagined as whole, has had significant regulatory effects. Cape Verdean women's ever changing roles have contributed to the production of feelings of continuity in a country undergoing drastic transformations. The shaping of the Cape Verdean woman's relational potential, over time, provides us an opportunity to consider the roles that particular kinds of relationships have come to play in the appearance of normalcy, or in the production of those signs equating the appearance of social action with the law. In this sense, the quality of their relationships to Portuguese citizens tells us something about the character of power at that moment, the means through which democracy was exercised, and the forms of cultural practice that constituted the signs of citizenship or belonging in that period. The story I tell thus treats the diverse temporalities through which the appearance of normalcy comes to the fore, as well as the means through which social relationships are necessarily re-engineered in the process.

I want to suggest how we might read these shifts, particularly in the context of Lusophone studies. The tricky thing is that tropicalist myths of racial-cultural intimacy existed as an ideal; and to state that racial-cultural intimacy is disrupted means to argue in some way that it actually existed at one time. Important here is that the idea of intimacy *did* exist. It circulated in the form of popular knowledge that Portuguese nationals utilized to explain relations of affectivity constituted through difference. Thus the question is not whether racial-cultural intimacy ceased to exist, but rather how and why a respectable distance between the white citizen and the black migrant constitutes a form of conduct that makes one's possession of citizenship legible. We have to move beyond the all-or-nothing argument that needs to establish definitively whether racial-cultural intimacy was "real" in the Portuguese-speaking context. What matters is that many believed it to be real. In this ethnography I have tried to show the circumstances under which people were directed, either forcibly or out of personal interest, to change their relationship to this idea of intimacy. Each labor setting discussed in this book represents the ways in which some individuals were rerouted to networks tied to new ideologies of the appropriate proximity with Otherness.

Chapter 2, on the regulation of product distribution and food-conservation technology, provides one example of how and with whom business dealings were reconfigured. State interventions selected and disposed of targeted subjects. This action not only led to a new labor demography in Lisbon's fishing sector but to the end of a form of relationality (between vendors and unlicensed entrepreneurs) that was not tied to a state-mediated labor contract. It was not that there was "less" power at Doca-pesca, as evidenced by the role that the simultaneous presence of black and white actors played in the formulation of racist grievances and the ensuing disclosure of the limits of any genuine equality. Rather, the move to Loures configured a different kind of power, one in which the state was more intimately engaged and one in which Cape Verdean peixeiras lost their access to a non-waged market.

In this sense, efforts privileging a middle-income subject had the effect of clearing "scavengers" from the vending space. But the impact of this lost labor flexibility only comes to light in connection with the following two scenarios (in chapters 3 and 4) that demonstrate how this was actually tied into strategies that generated the same outcome—the routing of peixeiras into waged women's work and their employment or management by Portuguese citizens, women in particular.

The city's regulation of public space, through the enforcement of new conservation and food-consumption principles, had other consequences, however, effects that pointed to the criteria of belonging through the policing of urban locations. Though policing began before the push for multicultural practice and Alcino Monteiro's death, such that politically correct discourse had yet to assume the moral importance it bears today, the phase that I documented raises questions about what police were actually performing, as well as about the relationship between their actions and the new wave of antiracist consciousness beginning at the time.

Policing contributed to a new polarization of political communities by facilitating competing forms of political consciousness: it harnessed a black diasporic consciousness grounded in the collective observation and experience of racism; and it harnessed a Portuguese consciousness grounded in the preservation of the nation's modernity. Neither of these forms were absolute: peixeiras and their black and white clients needed to sell and buy fish, while the white individuals that harassed the peixeiras sought to lessen their stigmatized status as abject nationals, however temporary. Racialized policing in many ways positioned these intertwined threads as less complicated, making it simply a black-white issue. Policing, ultimately, gave everyone a concrete language with which to understand and assume roles reflecting the meaning of the regulation of public space.

But racialized policing was not about enabling the polarized scenario that ensued. It was about enforcing the new principles that had enabled the polarized distinctions in the first place. As such, the scenarios in chapter 3 share something with those in chapter 4: each had cumulative consequences that ethnographically revealed a gap between the proposed intentions of regulation, as mediated by the law, and the effects of regulation, such as the way in which society responds as a collective. The "state," the entity represented by police, is precisely the elusive space between law and action (see Rancière 1999). Citizenship is a practice in which civilians enact ways that appear to bridge this space. Police serve to regulate this relationship through the enactment and/or threat of force (see Comaroff and Comaroff 2004). If we follow Jacques Rancière's (1999) logic, citizenship is the vehicle through which state and society appear as opposites—in the liberal "checks and balances" kind of way—hence manifesting the appearance of modernity, democracy, and the like. White civilians who participated in the policing, and the diverse pool of individuals who ignored it, enabled a particular message: they allowed police to perform orderly compatibility between state and society, regardless of the techniques policing deployed. These are the sorts of details we need to remain mindful of when critiquing the antidemocratic core of European citizenship. An exclusive focus on the migrant, or on those who are excluded, neglects to address the important role that the practice of citizenship plays in the production of marginal conditions. This is what I find fruitful about Ann Laura Stoler's work on the European self and bourgeois civility: the interplay constitutes an important strategy of government in and of itself. The most productive assessment of citizenship is one that grasps the interplay between those who have it and those who do not.

The defining feature of chapter 4 is the absence of police or pressures to modify anything about the setting under discussion. Moreover, each of the arrangements I observed was legally binding; each party's lawful observance of their role in the labor agreement occurred on the grounds of their willed participation. While it is certainly easier to regulate events and behaviors in public spaces, or in spaces sanctioned by state ministries, rights—such as the right to not be questioned—were actually given to individuals participating in state-recognized employment practices. Thus the allowances taken away from peixeiras in the previous two scenarios (rights that never *really* belonged to them anyway [see Rancière 1999]), were "given" back to them in the domestic/janitorial scenario. That these rights were "revived" through peixeiras' dependence on citizens is meaningful.

So while the two scenarios previously described did not *aim* to transform the peixeira into a domestic, they did just that. There was a social consequence in this chain of events, one transforming an understanding of the nation's labor demography in ways that did not recall the failures of the economy's past but that paralleled the types of social arrangements ongoing further north in Europe, as reflected in the shift from an emigrant to an immigrant nation. These new citizen-migrant pairings did not recall the colonial past, as the centrality of new consumer practices renders these relationships novel.[2] The avoidance of race in the last setting in chapter 4 enables an engagement of difference disassociated from the past. Of course this is not *why* the actors in these spaces avoid race talk. But there is something about the terms of the encounter that does just that. Why do these women not see the past? For there is nothing automatic about the gendered pairings under discussion. The general absence of explicit references to race speaks to the nature of a form of disciplinary conduct, one far more insidious than that present in the previous two scenarios.

In essence, uneven changes in consumption and product-distribution patterns enable us to observe the temporality of integration, or the diversity of seemingly disparate practices—like engaging or avoiding collectively recognized racial discourse—that culminate in a common project. Technological shifts that favor middle-income companies and workers, policing efforts that discipline product-distribution practices and consumer habits, and signs equating the possession of citizenship with migrant dependency are all tied to each other. But the process by which new and distinctively identifiable social types emerge through their new relationships to each other and to the state in work settings did more than add to Portugal's industrial and infrastructural transformation, or represent the Portuguese state's interpretation of the meaning of European integration. These shifts disrupted a series of market practices in which working-poor migrants and citizens not only interacted with each on a similar economic level (sharing vulnerabilities in a changing market) but also had similar relationships to the state (in terms of how the state cared for and recognized them as poor).

The antidemocratic core of citizenship reveals itself in the favoring of the middle-income subject, which occurs through the state's increasingly differential relationship to the citizen and the migrant: there now exists a distance between the two, migrants rendered subordinate *through* their attachments to "autonomous" citizens.

GOVERNMENTALITY

Having asserted how middle-class respectability and antiracism were connected through a new understanding of citizenship, I have tried to analyze those encounters and practices that sew these connections together as seemingly rational and normative. Michel Foucault (1994: 3) spoke of "the conditions that enable people, according to the rules of true and false statements, to arrange that a subject recognize the essential part of himself in the modality of his sexual desire." He argues here that various locations of social life—from the hospital to the prison to the home—served as sites at which the regulation of sex converged, becoming the reference onto which individuals crafted themselves as law-abiding, moral, and accountable selves.

I want to make a similar argument in relation to race: subjects recognize an essential part of themselves, not just through race per se, but through their treatment of race—whether as truthful or dehumanizing information —and thus in their moral relationship to it. And I am specifically interested in the historical conditions that enable this orientation through an individual's perception of what is definitive of racism—inclusive of words, attitudes, and other incriminating practices. Yet discourses do not exist unto themselves; they are tied to broader networks of information and thus as something that appears to operate in isolation from other discourses and practices seemingly unconnected to race or racism (see also Hesse 2007). Here I am speaking about those realms of discourse unwittingly tied to how selves know themselves through their closeness to or distance from popular understandings of ethical practices like antiracism. I am thus interested in the productivity of the excessiveness of race (see Brown 2006) as something that can conceal engagement with raced information in one moment while heavily emphasizing it in the next. This book has, after all, explored the role that EU citizenship has played as an apparatus binding the antiracist stance to contemporary middle-class respectability.

Today, waged labor continues as an organizing feature of social life—

through the hierarchies that constitute it—but the ways in which African women's roles in waged work are codified as normative, while white waged labor symbolizes backwardness, point to the effects of state intervention in the shaping of the appearances of Portugal's modernization. People began to experience themselves differently because the terms of relationality between themselves and others had been intercepted by various forms of state-induced regulations, as the relationship between Joana and Djina indicates. Middle-classness thus became the site through which subjects came to assume a more ambiguous relationship to the state and experience greater autonomy in the market and in society. It is in the way that the consuming and socially accountable individual stands in as the model of citizenship in Portugal. The state's projection of this model of citizenship concerns better economic performance through consumption and hence one's relationship to practices of leisure rather than of subsistence. In this sense, citizenship encompasses far more than issues of political legality; citizenship—a juridical category—is also about social engagement, its performance created through an elusive relation with others (see Ong 2003).

Stoler's work (1995b, 2002) proves useful when reflecting on the essence of Europeanness as a practice today, particularly when citizenship is commonly considered in terms of its exclusionary potential. By drawing on the consequences of not performing in particular ways, as Stoler has done, we can analyze the essence of European citizenship in the postcolonial present. Colonial studies, in general, have centered for some time on the role of the colonizer in the workings of colonial power. By attending to the latter's messiness, in which projects of social management were experiments rather than perfected schemes, colonial studies have emphasized the importance of appearances in understanding how power actually worked on the ground. Postcolonial studies, by contrast, and in particular those dealing with diasporic and / or migratory communities, have tended to focus on those "below": the agents of political and cultural movements or those excluded from democratic citizenship experiences. As David Scott (1999) has pointed out, however, these subject-specific patterns in both camps prove problematic because they are driven by moral-political agendas that require select subjects to fulfill their objectives. Minding this observation, it would seem that postcolonial studies would greatly benefit not just from comparing racisms, as is being done, but also from considering how the new parameters of citizenship, as an agentive practice, have taken shape. By not focusing exclusively on the exclusionary essence of citizenship, we can actually "see" those exclusionary practices conventionally taken for granted or concealed by the voluntarism of the labor contract between the waged and the salaried individual.

I have focused on the emergence of a social distance between Portuguese and African-identified subjects. Here the dichotomy between the citizen and the migrant has widened to the point at which subjects who imagined knowing each other have become increasingly unfamiliar with each other, even given their recent colonial history. The tenuousness of citizenship in Portugal, at a time of changing parameters of inclusion and exclusion, provides much insight into how to read this dehistoricizing shift. The immigration laws addressed in chapter 1, for instance, wanted to eliminate any vagueness about national belonging. What followed, interestingly, would be the dissolution of imaginaries of mixed racial categories. Thus analytically embracing the inclusive potential of citizenship not only offers a route to observing both citizen and migrant roles and their mutual relationship, but also creates an awareness of how treating citizenship as a mode of practice enriches the ethnography of a state's transformative process.

So it is meaningful that the state established platforms for asserting supposedly good and bad forms of work and that these concepts were mediated through publics that witnessed not the criminalization of particular work forms, but rather forms of policing that criminalized particular *subjects*. The vending law so emphatically enforced in the 1990s actually went into effect in 1979, but the public barely knew, and people continued comfortably purchasing clothes, food, and household items from unlicensed vendors in urban settings. While the law and the market thus operate as discourses defining an ideal, the embodiment of these discourses through figures like the "criminal" black peixeira—which circulated at one point as a tangible and legible piece of information—would ultimately constitute the consensual tropes of appropriate and inappropriate labor practices for all audiences as they passed through Cais do Sodré on their way to and from home and work.

The peixeira figure had thus become one of multiple sites through which modern ideals of social order turned into concrete principles available for people to draw on, as they rallied on the side of or against changes occurring in Lisbon. Thus I started to question the translatability of the black peixeira as a mutually recognizable cultural form, particularly given that she was not criminalized before; much to the contrary, she was imagined by 1973 as a pacifying agent to potentially unruly Cape Verdean men. By attending to changes in the representational values of black immigrant women's labor worth, I wanted to account for the mechanics of this process.

The growing distance between the African migrant and the Portuguese citizen suggests the emergence of new governing practices, ones in which racism not only becomes a social possibility but in which its avoidance has evolved into a form of self-regulation. Displays of distance and restraint here not only mark the new conditions of contact between migrants and citizens, particularly in labor encounters, but also stand in as self-referential evidence of a nation undergoing a progressive socioeconomic transition. It is in this sense that I position consumption as a political field through which all forms of knowledge can derive some truth, legitimacy, and meaning since accession. Transformations in socioeconomic practice, through citizens' use of or engagement with new services, objects, and imaginaries signal free will and European rationality, independent of those interlocutors, like migrants, whose political positions constitutively enable these engagements, imaginatively or materially.

THE RACE-RACISM DIVIDE

If the regulatory potential of the citizen-migrant dichotomy dialogues with the moralizing potential of antiracism, then the new governing practices in question also teach us something about race and racism. If, by the late 1990s, the social goal was to not conflate race with racism (see Seshadri-Cooks 2000) in Portugal, what is the process by which certain types of race-centered performances emerge as normative and safe—or wrong and thus racist? By this I do not mean to question when a targeted party interprets something as offensive. Rather, I am referring to the process of consensus, or to when dominant society understands that it will be held accountable if it partakes in actions or word choices previously deemed apolitical. While it might appear that this information is a given, it falls into a domain of knowledge so intimately personal to us that we often neglect to reflect on its actual ties to the law—ties that, as Wendy Brown (2006) explains, do not actually exist: the observance of antiracism largely resides in the expressions of good will that are codified by word choice, a tolerant attitude, and so forth. These events, poignantly, cannot be policed unless they fall within the realm of things that qualify as proven or *tangible* acts of discrimination. This introspection demands that racism be treated, for the moment, outside its moral-historical baggage. If we can approach how it operates in practice at any given moment as something that people define themselves in relation to (as opposed to something absolute or definitive), then we can learn to read it as a barometer that can tell us a lot about a society's moral sense of itself, in a collective hegemonic sense—or about how people come to fashion themselves not just in relation to others but more specifically in relation to how *they themselves* will be read by peers as civilized, ethical selves.

In Portugal, the moral status of racism and the neutral status of race thus locate these ideas in separate domains of knowledge. However, the interpretation of the distinction, as suggested in chapter 2, proves quite messy, as it can be determined by how the historically or socially injured group interprets raced information—questioning it or letting it slide—in the moment of its conveyance. Here, audiences play an important role, as the information has to be confirmed (see Fikes 2005a). In other instances, a series of norms has been established concerning which descriptives are consensually appropriate, which also shapes whether an act or inference is neutral or not.

Making sense of the distinction between race and racism—for the sake of unearthing the neutral status of race—proves especially important when dealing with other subject variables such as ethnicity, gender, sex, sexuality, age, religion, color, and class. I attribute this importance to the idea that the differential politicized status of each of these variables determines how they combine with others, or whether they become hidden or politically visible in the presence of others. My point, thus, is not to determine whether one of the variables is more present than others; nor do I aim to discover the "truth" that all of them are omnipresent. Instead, and in the context of contemporary Portugal, I have focused on the normative category that people use to politically instantiate who they are as ethical or conscious persons, hence illustrating that people understand these categories not to be operating on par with each other, giving individuals communicative leeway in some matters, though not in others (Williams 2007).

I noticed these details when actors "inappropriately" propositioned other variables outside of race, using sex or class to "front" their actions, precisely because of the underpoliticized nature of the identity category under abuse (Fikes 2005). In such moments, since sex and class do not have the moralizing capacity of race, it proved difficult to problematize the offense because there was no established political ground from which one subject clearly emerged as the offended party. To incriminate gender bias, in this sense, would be to generate an ethnographic picture in which race was tied to what was happening on the ground, while gender was tied to what was happening in conversations in the academy. Combining the two, given their differential weight in communicative action, felt awkward.

But my point is not that people do not know when they have been offended beyond the confines of race, but rather that the avenues asserting a grievance are affected by the possibilities of politicized resources and their differential moralizing potential. The tenuousness of gender as a recognizable site of politicization in Portugal is evidenced by the abortion referendum in early 2007 that barely passed, or by the current political frailty of feminist, gay, and lesbian politics in the country. In an effort not to universalize how one should include gender, I am attentive to the productivity of its absences, such as the meaning of the disappearance of the mestiça figure. I am also attentive to the dissolution of this figure in relation to a politicized concept of race, where the polarization of blackness and whiteness obscures the role that gender continues to play in the normalization of new discourses. The goal here is not to dismiss gender or sex, but to think through how one could ethnographically interpret the microsociological processes by which politicization and popular consensus take shape, inform the individual psyche, and emerge as essential practices that mediate how we interpret our daily environment. So where do we go from here?

Cape Verdean women's diverse history of association with different types of subjects in Portugal, at least since the mid-1960s, suggests that the limits of their inclusion are not in fact traceable to their identities as black women per se, but rather to how their identities are constituted in relation to the interlocutors who popularly enabled their appearance in certain ways, over time. This is why attention to the agentive potential in citizenship (in relation to migrancy) proves essential. But this also suggests, concerning the question of the place of gender, that the intersection of race and gender is not at stake—though it appears that way on the surface. Rather, at stake is what the perceived predominance of one over the other enables socially and politically in the management of civilized social relations (see Williams 2007). So race and gender should perhaps not be integrated within the unified subject when trying to describe the normative workings of power on that subject. Here the point is not to disrupt the wholeness of the subject, where in fact such integration is essential to questions of intersubjectivity; yet when dealing with the biopolitical character of the construction of difference, the specificities of "race" and "gender" do not matter from the perspective of regulatory power, because those specificities are effects of that power. What counts is the interpellative power of discourse to highlight and even politicize some constructed differences, while necessarily minimizing the constructed essences of others. In that the intersection of identity categories requires, in that moment, that we take those categories at face value, the scenario also poses problems at the level of analysis. Attention to the potential of citizenship enables us to capture, at least for a moment, how these surfaces materialize in action through distinctive social relationships and the norms that bind them (see Butler 1993).

Thus returning to the charged concept of race, and thinking through the productive relationship between race and racism—a relationship that today benefits or is "worked" by whites and people of color, albeit certainly not equally—it is important to revisit how this distinction has been managed within recent discussions on Europe. In general, the literature does not make a distinction. With the exception of Paul Gilroy's (2005) suggestion to focus on racism and to do away with race, *racism* is commonly dealt with in terms of changing configurations of *race* over time. These changing configurations tend to focus on a shift from biological to cultural definitions. This approach proves problematic because biology and culture are treated as dichotomous discourses. While the intentions are to show a historic shift between eugenics-inspired politics and the strategies associated with contemporary multicultural discourse, neither of these is definitively biological or cultural. They are both tied into each other through the odd matrix that connects or refracts the distinctive discourses of race and racism (see Gal 2002), as new and informative studies on race and medical illness have indicated (see esp. Fullwiley 2007).

The shift, it seems, occurs not in the status of race, whose operative and moral capacity still requires the fluid or recursive relationship between the biological and the cultural, but rather in the resourcefulness of a relationship that distinguishes between race and racism and in how the expression of this distinction does not just mean to prevent injury but also to preserve the social face and liberal integrity of a potential offender. So I would argue that the most dramatic shift in racial discourse has not in fact been about race, but rather about the way in which political correctness has transitioned into the intimate or self-referential realm of social life in the performance of the self as antiracist. The changing manifestations of race cannot be reduced or explained away through changing forms of racial description, though these changes do constitute important symptoms. Again, what is meaningful here is not race per se, but changes in the signifying value of racism—its performative status and what it is enabled to reflect back. For ontological form cannot explain, for instance, Gilroy's (2000) reflections on the simultaneity of commercialization and terror that marked the status of blackness in Europe in the 1990s, nor the British state's refusal to authorize a brown prosthetic leg to a working-class black British mother, while freely offering compassion and counseling instead (2005).

So anxiety around identity politics positions racism not so much as an object of contestation or aversion than as a contentious rationality and sensibility, a way of making sense of things in a totalizing way. Here racism is drawn on to understand the quality of a popular sensibility because of the moral-political value that is embedded within it. It is a frame of reference used to interpret the moral worth of the person referencing it, and thus not limited to the object/subject racially interpellated. Yet politicization and political correctness are not the end objectives of this study; methodologically, they offer a means of assessing changes in the collective perception of the meaning that racial distinctions have for the relationships that individuals maintain with their moral selves.

I have tried in this ethnography to unravel the seemingly disassociated processes by which people come to assume new practices through transitioning social relationships. Lusotropicalism and its previous capacity to void racist incrimination—through its ties to the individual and not the social whole—constituted one form of governmentality, one legitimizing the continuation of colonial practice at a time when formal colonial practices were in decline. Likewise, Lusofonia and its ability to operate as a sign for the celebration of Lusophone commonalities have their own potentiality: the recognition of *cultural* or *ethnic* difference from a distance in a way that clearly racially distances the Portuguese subject from the African one. I have tried to establish the context in which urban practices of employment and consumption in EEC/EU Portugal come to rely on particular labor arrangements and thus social relationships—relationships framed, in theory, as humane, but that in fact are grounded in the uneven distribution of goods and services (Povinelli 2006). Resistance to or compliance with these arrangements can tell us a lot about how people grapple with new representations of sociality that value a respectable social distance from others as one of many instantiations of Portuguese modernity.

This book started off being about Portugal, attending to the particularities of a colonial history whose residue surfaced in two scenarios I observed. But it ends on a note that lacks this historical distinction: the final ethnographic scenario could have occurred anywhere in the EU. In many ways this is precisely the point of this book. My goal has been to historicize a moment in time—from roughly 1994 through 2003—when racism in Portugal transitions from something effaceable to something incriminating. I have concerned myself with how this move aligned Portugal—in the local imagination—with other western European countries.

It is no coincidence that this time frame coincides with Portugal's economic integration into the EU financial structure in 1996. The neoliberal underpinnings of this market shift are what make Portugal look increasingly indistinguishable from other locations. Key here is a popular liberalism in a citizen-migrant distinction that characterizes many legitimate, contractual work relations. That this shift occurs, in part, through revised relationships with others, especially in southern and eastern Europe, tells us something about the engineering capacity of quotidian sociality.

The ethnography that does not mutually attend to the interactive practices of those categorized as migrants and those categorized as citizens not only eliminate from analysis the relational conditions that enable the categories in the first place, but also generate a one-sided picture of how norms are institutionalized through repetitive social practice (see Butler 1993). In the case of Portugal, an investigation into the historical terms under which it altered its orientation, from Africa to Europe, is essential to qualifying Portugal's interpretation of EU modernity in the expression of Portuguese citizenship. Tracking changes in ideology concerning ways of being with the Other as a rational, liberal EU citizen speaks to how citizenship operates as a potential for *everybody*—for those at the center and on the margins alike. The inhabitance of citizenship as a *social* category occurs because of, not in spite of, Otherness such as migrant status.

We tend to think about liberal sentiment along a sliding scale running from compassion to self-centered greed. The Other, for whom this scale is calculated, is dismissed from the equation because liberalism is about the self, the individual. But if social life is the product of encounters then perhaps the scale should be evaluated through its intersection with another scale, the Other's scale, to assess how the two scales necessarily operate on the same plane. The mirror reflection of compassion, in the context of the asymmetrical relationship, is compliance. Accordingly, a radical analysis of the rational, documented citizen-migrant encounter is about the institutionalized meeting between compassion and compliance—juxtaposed expressions of agency with productively cyclic and trite effects. As Patrícia commented in the summer of 2006:

> Remember those times, when I used to carry all that weight of fish!?
> GOD HELP ME!!!!!!!!!! We fought those policemen every day!? And we
> stood up to people who put us down. What a lifetime ago. . . . That was
> REAL work, those were different days, Portugal is a different place
> today . . . but I get these excruciating pains every day, running here, the
> right side, from the top of my neck down to my fingers. I know it's from
> those days, you know, lifting all that weight and running. TIRING!!! But
> hey, that's the life of poverty, right! I think everyone has some kind of
> physical complaint from those days. . . . I guess we're stuck with it . . .
> poor, immigrant, it's just that kind of fight, you know? You keep going . . .
> what else does one do?

NOTES

1. *Peixeiras* are also called *varinas*. Varina is normed as the more appropriate or respectable term, with peixeira making for a more taboo label. Yet the Cape Verdean women I worked with self-identified as peixeiras; I never heard them mention the word *varina*, a term historically ascribed to Portuguese women who were also called peixeiras. Notably, Cape Verdean women's loyal customers also referred to them as peixeiras.

2. I have highlighted "glance" because I want to address the tension between analyzing "race" as a social construction and the process by which the analyst comes to identify subjects in racially meaningful ways through "looking." When subjects do not self-identify, the ethnographic process of racially labeling subjects reproduces race as determined and truthful. Thus I single out "glance" to remain mindful of the danger in this process. As the text unravels I maintain these categories, which appear first as ethnographic observations, because they were brokered by the individuals themselves in interaction.

3. In *Buddha is Hiding*, Aihwa Ong has worked out a compelling argument that likewise observes a productive relationship between the effects of the polarization of raced distinctions and the practice of citizenship as a set of officially sanctioned social values. My argument also considers the effects of such polarization, but for different reasons. Here, polarization refers to the process where miscegenation is eclipsed from the social imaginary, severing imaginaries of contact tied to blood.

4. I want to thank Andrea Muehlebach for helping me think through questions of citizenship in the ways suggested in this section.

5. Susan Gal (2002, 2005) has stressed the problem of analyzing the world as if the categories "public" and "private" constituted separate domains of fixed knowledge. Arguing that the public and the private represent a single practice or institution in itself, one made legible through the contrastive and referential potential embedded in each, Gal's point is that we need to be attentive to what

these realms are enabled to signify, *relatively*, when they are used. Reflections on the transition of racism, from something effaceable to something incriminating, suggest that race identification had been inverted from a private issue between individuals to a public one mediated through social or institutional scrutiny. If tolerance can be imagined through the changing content in one of these representational realms—whether the public or the private—then the question may not be, How do people choose or come to incorporate state-supported tolerance into their lifestyles? but rather (or also) How they are subjected or interpellated into it? In this sense, Gal's argument asks us to recognize how we play with these distinctions at the level of argumentation, as well as how we can use them at the level of analysis due to people's meaning-making relationships to them.

6. See the historian José Ramos Tinhorão's (1988) work on the fetishization of black imagery in 18th and 19th century theater in Portugal.

7. The following paragraphs also appear in "The Cape Verdean Woman Worker," published in 2005 in *Revista: Revista de estudos cabo-verdianos*. UNI-CV: Praia, Cabo Verde.

8. In 1973, in an effort to encourage better organization on the part of the NA, the Overseas Ministry pushed for more centralized management, in the process also changing the NA's name to CATU. Employees at CATU attempted to micro-manage the lives of Cape Verdean workers. The center categorized work opportunities by salary and skill capacity (see Carreira 1983) and attempted to manage every social and professional aspect of migrant workers' lives, including transportation to Portugal, transportation to work, housing, receipt of salaries, monthly savings and remittances, family reunification, work and after-work scheduling, holiday activities, contract termination, deportation, medical exams, and the like.

9. In fact, the public display and circulation of photographs of dead peixeiras—the women having died in fights with other "commoners" or peixeiras—were popular in the 1920s and 1930s. Photos printed in newspapers are available at the Municipal Photographic Archives in Lisbon.

ONE: MISCEGENATION INTERRUPTED

1. The argument I am building, on the ways acts of othering are newly interpreted as incriminating in conjunction with EU accession, could be read as a statement about the correlation of economic development and social recognition. This very process has been ethnographically documented and theorized within critiques of liberal democratic practice and ideology (Povinelli 2002, 2006; Brown 2006). However, bringing these two logics together in Portugal is difficult. Beginning in the eighteenth century, competing European empires, Brit-

ain in particular, lead a de facto campaign asserting that Portugal was economically backward. The Portuguese colonist/settler was criticized for mixing with its native populations and not managing its finances. Dating back to Adam Smith's *Wealth of Nations*, the argument goes that the Portuguese never understood the connection between wealth accumulation and national development. (I want to thank Jeremy Jones for suggesting the importance of this connection.) Thus the adoption of the liberal democratic argument, where neoliberal market gain accompanies respectful recognition, cannot be heard in the Portuguese speaking setting without the thought that the Portuguese are "finally getting it right." My approach is not to test or question this idea, but rather to recognize the anxiety it produced in this empire and thus to examine how the Portuguese state has continued to uncomfortably dialogue with this idea through the present.

Non-Portuguese representations of Portuguese relations with others have varied widely, ranging from their supposedly easy intermingling with natives to the diluted constitution of Portuguese blood. These representations of hybridity, importantly, have not only been tied to relations with natives in the colonies, but also to various populations in Iberia that include Moors and Sephardic Jewish communities (see Arenas 2003). Further, a number of travelogues written by British aristocrats who vacationed in southern Europe in the nineteenth century commented on Lisbon's decaying social face. Their prose often connected a failing empire to the "deviant" and "impoverished" Portuguese individuals with whom the writers crossed paths on their journeys. In a *Journal of a Three Months' Tour in Portugal, Spain, and Africa*, Frances Anne Vane (1843) the Marchioness of Londonberry writes,

> I had always heard of Lisbon as a detestable residence, but the reality far surpassed my expectation; the smell; the noises, the discomforts of all sorts, the impossibility of walking, driving, moving, and breathing without having every sense offended becomes very tiresome; and the noise day and night precluded all rest and sleep. (4)
>
> The shops that are dignified by the title jewelers, would be unworthy of the booths at a fair. . . . The filth and poverty of the people is very striking; they are a miserable decayed looking population; the soldiers here and there seen give an indifferent idea of what the troops must be at present. All the while ruins, heaps of rubbish and unfinished buildings shew the want of energy and the slothful nature of the people. . . . The carriages are the worst I ever saw. Wretched height cabriolets, drawn by two mules, though, the mules here are beautiful and appear very gentle. . . . (6)
>
> Nothing could be more amusing than the collection of different servants

that waited at dinner, including, among other extraordinary specimens, a Moor, a small boy dressed like an English tiger, in boots and leathers.... (9)

These critiques, denigrating the Portuguese as indolent and backward, circulated as popular knowledge by the late eighteenth century, a moment marking the rise of British imperialism and Britain's rising interest in the African and Asian territories under Portuguese rule. Other tales of Portuguese mixing that recall the absorption of Sephardic, Moorish, and various indigenous communities often blur into a single stereotypical narrative inattentive to the diverse historical moments that generated these representations. More confusing still is the post-1950s Portuguese national narrative that ambiguously associates this practice of absorption with its discovery missions in the late fifteenth century. This mishmash of ideas or discourses, coupled with Portuguese censorship under fascism, continues to obscure information on actual Portuguese colonial practices.

There is however one text that reformulates these British critiques as strategic advantages and human virtues; Brazilian sociologist Gilberto Freyre's *Casa Grande e Senzala (Masters and Slaves)* (1933). Ideas from this book informed how Portuguese nationals popularly understood race in Portugal, at least through the late 1990s. Thus one has to contend with the ways in which a fascist Portuguese state mediated the idea that it practiced racial democracy in the colonies through an antiracist imaginary that it drew from elsewhere, namely Brazil. It is also important to understand the relationship between this ideological legacy and the representational status of inter-racial intimacy in Portugal before the 1990s. This relationship is so important that no discussion of intimacy in the twentieth century could surface independent of a conversation about race or miscegenation. It is even telling that this discourse on intimacy and miscegenation is now understood as mythic, and that preoccupation with the myth now serves to maintain the same conversation, academically speaking.

2. SOS Racismo drafted a petition for the antidiscrimination bill two days after Monteiro's death, on June 12, 1995. It was finally passed by the National Assembly as Article 3, Number 1 of Law 134 / 99, and put into effect on August 28, 1999.

3. The distinction between urban poor and rural migrants presupposes that rural and urban inhabitants are not connected to each other, a presupposition that has been questioned. See Cordeiro 2001.

TWO: RI(GH)TES OF INTIMACY AT DOCAPESCA

1. Katchupa is considered Cape Verde's national dish. It is a stew composed of meat, various tubers, corn, beans, and kale.

2. Eduardo Melo, "Câmara de Lisboa exige clarificação do Governo no caso MARL/Docapesca," *Público* (Lisbon), March 23, 2001.

3. Eduardo Melo, "Governo pediu visita técnica à Docapesca," *Público* (Lisbon), March 23, 2001.

THREE: BLACK MAGIK WOMEN

The title of this chapter refers to the song "Black Magik Woman" by General D, one of Portugal's first popular rappers. The name and refrain of the song is in English. The music video features Cape Verdean peixeiras as an example of female endurance.

1. I thank Andrea Muehlebach, Jonathan Rosa, and Michael Silverstein for comments on an earlier draft of this chapter that helped me frame my observations in this way.

2. I thank Miguel Vale de Almeida for providing a more textured picture of the social position of the street sweeper in Lisbon.

3. In Cape Verde, rural women middle-aged or above use the pano on the island of Santiago. When wrapped around the waist, it signifies respectability. Dancing or being seen in public without the pano has historically been considered shameless and indecent.

FOUR: BEING IN PLACE

1. Manuela initially chose not to work after selling fish; she stayed at home and watched her young grandchildren for her daughters and sons. Sometimes she did substitute domestic labor for her peixeira colleagues.

FIVE: REGULATING THE CITIZEN, DISCIPLINING THE MIGRANT

1. *Mandiga* is a derogatory term for Africans. The Mandiga ethnic group in West Africa is racialized through this negative referent.

2. Here I would argue that colonial studies criticisms of "new racisms" were not correct because the potential of diasporic community (as it is forged today) as a response to repression is new and thus suggests that the nature and practice of racism is new as well.

REFERENCES

Agamben, Giorgio. 1998. *Homo Sacer: Sovereign Power and Bare Life.* Trans. Daniel Heller-Roazen. Stanford, Calif.: Stanford University Press.

Alexandre, Valentim. 1995. "A África no imaginário político português (seculos XIX e XX)." *Penélope,* no. 15:39–52.

———. 1998. "The Colonial Empire." In *Modern Portugal,* ed. António Costa Pinto, 41–59. Palo Alto, Calif.: Society for the Promotion of Science and Scholarship.

Almeida, Ana Nunes de. 1985. "Trabalho feminino e estrategias familiars." *Análise social* 21 (85): 7–44.

———. 1988. "Relações familiares: Mudança e diversidade." In *Portugal, que modernidade?,* ed. Leite Veigas. Oeiras, 45–78. Portugal: Centro de Investigação e Estudos de Sociologia.

Almeida, Miguel Vale de. 1995. *Senhores de si: Uma interpretação antropólogica da masculinidade.* Oeiras, Portugal: Celta.

———. 2000. *O mar da côr da terra.* Oeiras, Portugal: Celta.

Althusser, Louis, and Étienne Balibar, eds. 1970. *Reading Capital.* Trans. Ben Brewster. London: Verso.

Amaral, Ilidio do. 1964. *Santiago de Cabo Verde: A terra e os homes.* Lisbon: Junta de Invesitgação do Ultramar.

Amselle, Jean-Loup. 2003. *Affirmative Exclusion: Cultural Pluralism and the Rule of Custom in France.* Trans. Jane Marie Todd. Ithaca, N.Y.: Cornell University Press.

Anderson, Benedict. 1991. *Imagined Communities: Reflections on the Origins and Spread of Nationalism.* 2nd rev. ed. London: Verso.

Anderson, Bridget. 2000. *Doing the Dirty Work? The Global Politics of Domestic Labour.* London: Zed.

Appadurai, Arjun. 1996. *Modernity at Large: Cultural Dimensions of Globalization.* Minneapolis: University of Minnesota Press.

Arenas, Fernando. 2003. *Utopias of Otherness: Nationhood and Subjectivity in Portugal and Brazil.* Minneapolis: University of Minnesota Press.

Baganha, Maria Ioannis. 1998. "Portuguese Emigration after World War II." In *Modern Portugal*, ed. António Costa Pinto, 189–205. Palo Alto, Calif.: Society for the Promotion of Science and Scholarship.

Bakan, Abigail, and Daiva Stasiulus. 1995. "Making the Match: Domestic Placement Agencies and the Racialization of Women's Household Work." *Signs* 20 (2): 303–35.

Balibar, Étienne. 2004. *We, the People of Europe? Reflections on Transnational Citizenship*. Trans. James Swenson. Princeton, N.J.: Princeton University Press.

Barreto, António. 1995. *A Situação social em Portugal, 1960–1995*. Lisbon: ICS, Universidade de Lisboa.

Bastos, Cristiana. 1998. "Tristes trópicos e alegres luso-tropicalismos: Das notas de viagem em Lévi-Stauss e Gilberto Freyre." *Análise social* 34 (146–47): 415–32.

Batalha, Luís. 2004. *The Cape Verdean Diaspora in Portugal: Colonial Subjects in a Postcolonial World*. Lanham, Md.: Lexington Books.

Baudrillard, Jean. [1972] 1981. *For a Critique of the Political Economy of the Sign*. Trans. Charles Levin. St. Louis, Mo.: Telos.

Bellier, Irène, and Thomas M. Wilson, eds. 2000. *An Anthropology of the European Union: Building, Imaging, and Experiencing the New Europe*. Oxford: Berg.

Bender, Gerald. 1978. *Angola under the Portuguese: Myth and Reality*. Berkeley: University of California Press.

Berdahl, Daphne. 1999. *Where the World Ended: Re-unification and Identity in the German Borderland*. Berkeley: University of California Press.

Berdahl, Daphne, Matti Bunzl, and Martha Lampland. 2000. *Altering States: Ethnographies of Transition in Eastern Europe and the Former Soviet Union*. Ann Arbor: University of Michigan Press.

Boxer, C. R. 1963. *Race Relations in the Portuguese Colonial Empire, 1415–1825*. Oxford: Oxford University Press.

Brodkin, Karen. 1998. *How Jews Became White Folks and What That Says about Race in America*. New Brunswick, N.J.: Rutgers University Press.

Brown, Jacqueline Nassy. 2005. *Dropping Anchor, Setting Sail: Geographies of Race in Black Liverpool*. Princeton, N.J.: Princeton University Press.

Brown, Wendy. 1995. *States of Injury: Power and Freedom in Late Modernity*. Princeton, N.J.: Princeton University Press.

——. 2003. "Neo-liberalism and the End of Liberal Democracy." *Theory and Event* 7 (1).

——. 2006. *Regulating Aversion: Tolerance in the Age of Identity and Empire*. Princeton, N.J.: Princeton University Press.

Butler, Judith. 1993. *Bodies That Matter: On the Discursive Limits of "Sex."* New York: Routledge.

——. 1997. *Excitable Speech: A Politics of the Performative*. New York: Routledge.

Carreira, Antonio. 1977. *Migrações nas Ilhas de Cabo Verde*. Praia-Santiago: Instituto Caboverdiano do Livro.

———. 1983. *Cabo Verde: Formação e extinção de uma sociedade escravocrata (1460–1878)*. Praia-Santiago: Instituto Caboverdiano do Livro.

Carter, Donald Martin. 1997. *States of Grace: Senegalese in Italy and the New European Immigration*. Minnesota: University of Minnesota Press.

Castelo, Cláudia. 1998. *O modo português de estar no mundo: O luso-tropicalismo e a ideologia colonial portuguesa, 1933–1961*. Porto, Portugal: Edições Afrontamento.

———. 2007. *Passagens para a África portugesa: Povoamento da Angola e Moçambique com naturais da metrópole (1920–1974)*. Porto: Edições Afrontamento.

Certeau, Michel de. 1984. *The Practice of Everyday Life*. Trans. Steven Rendall. Berkeley: University of California.

Chang, Grace. 2000. *Disposable Domestics: Immigrant Women Workers in the Global Economy*. Cambridge, Mass.: South End.

Chatterjee, Partha. 1995. *The Nation and Its Fragments*. Princeton, N.J.: Princeton University Press.

Chaves, Miguel. 1999. *Casal ventoso: Da gandaia ao narcotráfico*. Lisbon: Imprensa de Ciências Socias.

Clarke, Kamari, and Deborah Thomas, eds. 2006. *Globalization and Race: Transformations in the Cultural Production of Blackness*. Durham, N.C.: Duke University Press.

Comaroff, John, and Jean Comaroff. 1992. *Ethnography and the Historical Imagination*. Boulder, Colo.: Westview.

———. 2004. "Criminal Obsessions, after Foucault: Postcoloniality, Policing, and the Metaphysics of Disorder." *Critical Inquiry* 30 (4): 800–824.

Comité Económico e Social das Comunidades Europeias (CES). 1977. document 485, 15.

———. 1979. document 002.

Constable, Nicole. 1997. *Maid to Order in Hong Kong: Stories of Filipina Workers*. Ithaca, N.Y.: Cornell University Press.

Cordeiro, Maria G. Í. 2001. "Trabalho e Profissões no imaginário de uma cidade: sobre os tipos populares de Lisboa." *Etnográfica* 5(1): 7–24.

Corrêa, Mendes. 1943. *Raças do império*. Lisbon: Junta de Investigações do Ultramar.

Dacosta-Holton, Kimberly. 1998. "Dressing for Success: Lisbon as European Cultural Capital." *Journal of American Folklore* 111 (438): 174–96.

De Genova, Nicholas. 2002. "Migrant 'Illegality' and Deportability in Everyday Life." *Annual Review of Anthropology*, no. 31:419–47.

Deranty, Jean-Philippe. 2003. "Rancière and Contemporary Political Ontology." *Theory and Event* 6 (4).

dos Anjos, José Carlos Gomes. 2002. *Intelectuais, literature e poder em Cabo Verde: Lutas de definição da identidade nacional*. Praia: Instituto Nacional de Investigação Promoção e Património Culturais Cabo Verde (NIPC).

Duranti, Alessandro, and Charles Goodwin. 1992. "Rethinking Context: An Introduction." In *Rethinking Context: Language as an Interactive Phenomenon*, ed. Alessandro Duranti and Charles Goodwin, 1–42. Cambridge: Cambridge University Press.

Ebron, Paulla. 1997. "The Traffic in Men." In *Gendered Encounters: Challenging Cultural Boundaries and Social Hierarchies in Africa*, ed. Maria Luise Grosz-Ngaté and Omari H. Kokole, 223–44. New York: Routledge.

Eisfeld, Rainer. 1986. "Portugal and Western Europe." In *Portugal in the 1980s: Dilemmas of Democratic Consolidation*, ed. Kenneth Maxwell, 29–62. Westport, Conn.: Greenwood.

Esteves, Maria do Céu. 1991. *Portugal, país de imigração*. Lisbon: Instituto de Estudos para o Desenvolvimento.

Fanon, Frantz. 1967. *Black Skin, White Masks*. Trans. Charles Lam Markmann. New York: Grove.

Fernandes, Gabriel. 2002. *A diluição da África: Uma interpretação da saga identitária cabo-verdiana no panorama político (pós)colonia*. Florianopolis, Brazil: Da Universidade Federal de Santa Catarina.

Ferreira, Denise da Silva. 1998. "Facts of Blackness." *Social Identities* 4 (2): 201–34.

Ferreira, Virginia. 1994. "Women's Employment in the European Semiperipheral Countries: Analysis of the Portuguese Case." *Women's Studies International Forum* 17 (2–3): 141–55.

——. 1995. "Office Work, Gender, and Technological Change: The Portuguese Case." In *The New Division of Labor: Emerging Forms of Work Organization in International Perspective*, ed. Wolfgang Littek and Tony Charles, 419–36. Berlin: Walter de Gruyter.

——. 1998. "Engendering Portugal: Social Change, State Politics, and Women's Social Mobilization." In *Modern Portugal*, ed. António Costa Pinto, 162–88. Palo Alto, Calif.: Society for the Promotion of Science and Scholarship.

Fikes, Kesha. 2000. "Santiaguense Women's Transnationality in Portugal: Labor Rights, Diasporic Transformation, and Citizenship." PhD diss., University of California, Los Angeles.

——. 2005a. "Ri(gh)tes of Intimacy at Doca Pesca: Race versus Racism at a Fish Market in Portugal." *The DuBois Review* 2 (2): 247–66.

——. 2005b. "The Cape Verdean Woman Worker and Portuguese Civil Society." *Revista: Revista de Estudos Cabo-verdianos*, no. 3.

——. 2007. "Emigration and the Spatial Production of Difference from Cape Verde." In *Cultures of the Lusophone Black Atlantic*, ed. Nancy Priscilla Naro,

Roger Sansi-Roca, and David H. Treece, 159–74. New York: Palgrave
Macmillan.

——. 2008. "Discipline and Diasporic Governmentality: On the Gendered Limits
of Wage-Labor in Portugal." *Feminist Review*, no. 90: 48–67.

——. Forthcoming. *Foreign Privatization, Waning National Remittance: The Predicament of Middle Development Status in Cape Verde*. Manuscript in preparation.

Foucault, Michel. 2003. *Society Must Be Defended: Lectures at the College de France,
1975–1976*. Trans. David Macey. New York: Picador.

——. 2004. *Abnormal: Lectures at the College de France, 1974–1975*. Trans. Graham
Burchell. New York: Picador.

——. 2008. *The Birth of Biopolitics: Lectures at the College de France, 1978–1979*.
Trans. Graham Burchell. New York: Palgrave Macmillan.

França, Luís de. 1992. *A communidade cabo-verdiana em Portugal*. Lisbon:
Instituto de Estudos para o Desenvolvimento.

Freyre, Gilberto. [1933] 1957. *Casa grande e senzala: Formação da família brasileira
sob o regime de economia patriarcal*. Lisbon: Edições Livros do Brasil.

——. 1958. *Integração portuguesa nos trópicos*. Col. ECPS, n.ƒa6. Lisbon: JIU.

——. 1961. *O luso e o trópico. Sugestões em torno dos métodos portugueses de integração de povos autóctones e de culturas diferentes da europeia num complexo
novo de civilização: o luso-tropical*. Lisbon: Comissão Executiva das Com-
emorações do V Centenário da Morte do Infante D. Henrique.

Fullwiley, Duana. 2007. "The Molecularization of Race: Institutionalizing Racial
Difference in Pharmacogenetics Practice." *Science as Culture* 16 (1): 1–30.

Furtado, Cláudio Alves. 1993. *A transformação das estruturas agrárias numa
sociedade de Mudança—Santiago, Cabo Verde*. Praia-Santiago: Instituto
Caboverdiando do Livro.

Gal, Susan. 2002. "A Semiotics of the Public/Private Distinction." *Differences* 13
(1): 77–95.

——. 2005. "Language Ideologies Compared: Metaphors and Circulations of
Public and Private." *Journal of Linguistic Anthropology* 15 (1): 23–37.

Gal, Susan, and Gail Kligman. 2000. *The Politics of Gender after Socialism: A Comparative Historical Essay*. Princeton, N.J.: Princeton University Press.

——, eds. 2000. *Reproducing Gender: Politics, Publics, and Everyday Life after
Socialism*. Princeton, N.J.: Princeton University Press.

Gardner, Martha. 2005. *The Qualities of a Citizen: Women, Immigration, and Citizenship, 1870–1965*. Princeton, N.J.: Princeton University Press.

Geschiere, Peter, and Francis Nyamnjoh. 2000. "Capitalism and Autochthony:
The Seesaw of Mobility and Belonging." *Public Culture* 12 (2): 423–52.

Gilroy, Paul. 1987. *"There Ain't No Black in the Union Jack": The Cultural Politics of
Race and Nation*. Chicago: University of Chicago Press.

———. 2000. *Against Race: Imagining Political Culture beyond the Color Line.* New York: Belknap Press.

———. 2005. *Postcolonial Melacholia.* New York: Columbia University Press.

Glenn, Evelyn Nakano. 1992. "From Servitude to Service Work." *Signs* 18 (1): 1–43.

Goffman, Erving. 1963. *Stigma: Notes on the Management of Spoiled Identity.* New York: Simon and Schuster.

———. 1967. *Interaction Ritual: Essays on Face-to-Face Behavior.* Garden City, N.Y.: Anchor.

———. 1981. *Forms of Talk.* Philadelphia: University of Pennsylvania Press.

Gramsci, Antonio. 1971. *Selections from the Prison Notebooks of Antonio Gramsci.* Ed. and trans. Quintin Hoare and Geoffrey Nowell Smith. New York: International Publishers.

Grewal, Inderpal. 1996. *Home and Harem: Nation, Gender, Empire, and the Cultures of Travel.* Durham, N.C.: Duke University Press.

Habermas, Jürgen. 1992. "Citizenship and National Identity: Some Reflections on Future of Europe." *Praxis International* 12 (1): 1–19.

Hall, Stuart. 1996. "The After-life of Frantz Fanon: Why Fanon? Why Now? Why *Black Skin, White Masks*?" In *The Fact of Blackness: Frantz Fanon and Visual Representation*, ed. Alan Read, 12–37. Seattle: Bay.

Halter, Marilyn. 1993. *Between Race and Ethnicity: Cape Verdean American Immigrants—1860 to 1965.* Urbana-Champagne, Ill.: University of Illinois Press.

Hansen, Randall, and Patrick Weil. 2001. *Towards a European Nationality: Citizenship, Immigration, and Nationality Law in the EU.* New York: Palgrave.

Harvey, David. 2001. *Spaces of Capital: Towards a Critical Geography.* New York: Routledge.

Hegel, G. W. F. [1807] 1977. *Phenomenology of Spirit.* Ed. J. N. Findlay. Trans. A. V. Miller. Oxford: Clarendon.

———. [1807] 2003. *Phenomenology of Mind.* Ed. and trans. J. B. Baillie. Mineola, N.Y.: Dover.

Hertzfeld, Michael. 2005. *Cultural Intimacy: Social Poetics in the Nation-State.* New York: Routledge.

Hesse, Barnor. 2007. "Racialized Modernity: An Analytics of White Mythologies." *Ethnic and Racial Studies* 30 (4): 643–63.

Heyman, Josiah, McC. 1995. "Putting Power in the Anthropology of Bureaucracy: The Immigration and Naturalization Service at the Mexico–US Border." *Current Anthropology* 36 (2): 261–87.

Holmes, Douglas R. 2000. *Integral Europe: Fast Capitalism, Multiculturalism, Neofascism.* Princeton, N.J.: Princeton University Press.

Holston, James. 2008. *Insurgent Citizenship: Disjunctions of Democracy and Modernity in Brazil.* Princeton, N.J.: Princeton University Press.

Hondagneu-Sotelo, Pierrette. 2001. *Doméstica: Immigrant Workers Cleaning and Caring in the Shadows of Affluence*. Berkeley: University of California Press.

Honig, Bonnie. 2001. *Democracy and the Foreigner*. Princeton, N.J.: Princeton University Press.

Humphrey, Caroline. 2002. *The Unmaking of Soviet Life: Everyday Economies after Socialism*. Ithaca, N.Y.: Cornell University Press.

Jackson, John. 2008. *Racial Paranoia: The Unintended Consequences of Political Correctness*. New York: Basic Books.

Kearney, Michael. 1995. "The Local and the Global: The Anthropology of Globalization and Transnationalism." *Annual Review of Anthropology* 24:547–65.

Kondo, Dorinne. 1988. *Crafting Selves: Power, Gender, and Discourses of Identity in a Japanese Workplace*. Chicago: University of Chicago Press.

Lee, Benjamin, and Edward LiPuma. 2002. "Cultures of Circulation: The Imaginations of Modernity." *Public Culture* 14 (1): 191–214.

Lefebvre, Henri. [1940] 1968. *Dialectical Materialism*. Trans. John Sturrock. London: Jonathan Cape.

——. [1974] 1991. *The Production of Space*. Trans. D. Nicholson-Smith. Cambridge, Mass.: Blackwell.

——. 1991. *Critique of Everyday Life*. Vol. 1. Trans. John Moore. New York: Verso.

Lemke, Thomas. 2001. " 'The Birth of Bio-politics': Michel Foucault's Lecture at the Collège de France on Neo-liberal Governmentality." *Economy and Society* 30 (2): 190–207.

Lessa, Almerindo, and Jacques Ruffié. 1960. *Seroantropologia das Ilhas de Cabo Verde: Mesa redonda sobre o homen cabo-verdiano*. Lisbon: Junta de Investigações do Ultramar.

Linke, Uli. 1999a. *Blood and Nation: The European Aesthetics of Race*. Philadelphia: University of Pennsylvania Press.

——. 1999b. *German Bodies: Race and Representation after Hitler*. New York: Routledge.

Lopes, Baltasar. 1956. "Cabo Verde visto por Gilberto Freyre." Transcription of radio broadcast. Praia: Impresna Nacional.

Lopes, Daniel Seabra. 2006. "Mercados encobertos: Os ciganos de Lisboa e a venda ambulante." *Etnográfica* 10(2): 319–35.

Lopes Filho, Joao. 2007. *Imigrantes em Terra de Emigrantes*. Praia, Santiago: Instituto da Biblioteca Nacional e do Livro.

Maciel, Cármen. 2005. "Maio 2004: Mês de África em Lisboa." MA thesis, Universidade Nova de Lisboa.

Magalhães, Maria Jose. 1998. *Movimento feminista e educação: Portugal, décadas de 70 e 80*. Oeiras, Portugal: Celta.

Margarido, Alfredo. 2000. *A lusofonia e os lusófonos: Novos mitos Portugueses*. Lisbon: Edições Universitárias Lusófonas.

Markell, Patchen. 2003. *Bound by Recognition*. Princeton, N.J.: Princeton University Press.

Marx, Karl. [1867] 1977. *Capital: A Critique of Political Economy*. Trans. Ben Fowkes. New York: Vintage.

——. [1859] 1999. *A Contribution to the Critique of Political Economy*. Ed. Maurice Dobb. Trans. S. W. Ryazanskaya. New York: International Publishers.

Mbembe, Achille. 2001. *On the Postcolony*. Berkeley: University of California Press.

McClintock, Anne. 1992. "The Angle of Progress: Pitfalls of the Term 'Postcolonialism.'" *Social Text*, nos. 31–32:84–98.

——. 1995. *Imperial Leather: Race, Gender, and Sexuality in the Colonial Contest*. New York: Routldege.

Meersschaert, Lieve. 1986. "Alguns contributos para o estudo da identidade das empregadas domésticas em Portugal." *Análise social* 22 (92–93): 633–42.

Meintel, Diedre. 1984. *Race, Culture, and Portuguese Colonialism in Cabo Verde*. Syracuse, N.Y.: Syracuse University Press.

Memmi, Albert. 1965. *The Colonizer and the Colonized*. Trans. Howard Greenfeld. New York: Orion.

Merleau-Ponty, Maurice. [1945] 1958. *Phenomenology of Perception*. Trans. Colin Smith. New York: Routledge.

Mongia, Radhika Viyas. 1999. "Race, Nationality, Mobility: A History of the Passport." *Public Culture* 11 (3): 527–55.

Monteiro, Vladimir Nobre. 1994. *Portugal/Crioulo*. Praia-Santiago: Instituto Caboverdiano do Livro.

Morgan, Marcyliena. 1996. "Conversational Signifying: Grammar and Indirectness among African American Women." In *Interaction and Grammar*, ed. Elinor Ochs, Emanuel A. Schegloff, and Sandra A. Thompson, 405–34. Cambridge: Cambridge University Press.

Moutinho, Mario. 2000. *O indígena no pensamento colonial português: 1895–1961*. Lisbon: Edições Universitárias Lusófonas.

Nataf, Daniel. 1995. *Democratization and Social Settlements: The Politics of Change in Contemporary Portugal*. Albany: State University of New York Press.

Ngai, Mae M. 2004. *Impossible Subjects: Illegal Aliens and the Making of Modern America*. Princeton, N.J.: Princeton University Press.

Nietzsche, Friedrich. [1887] 2003. *The Genealogy of Morals*. Trans. Horace B. Samuel. Mineola: Dover.

Ong, Aihwa. 1999. *Flexible Citizenship: The Cultural Logics of Transnationality*. Durham, N.C.: Duke University Press.

———. 2003. *Buddha Is Hiding: Refugees, Citizenship, and the New America.* Berkeley: University of California Press.

Paiva, Amadeu. 1985. *Portugal e a Europa: O fim de um ciclo migratório.* Lisbon: Instituto DE Estudos para o Desenvolvimento.

Pandolfo, Stefania. 1997. *Impasse of the Angels: Scenes from a Moroccan Space of Memory.* Chicago: University of Chicago Press.

Parrenas, Rhacel. 2001. *Servants of Globalization: Women Migration and Domestic Work.* Stanford, Calif.: Stanford University Press.

Passavant, Paul. 2005. "The Strong Neo-liberal State: Crime, Consumption, Governance." *Theory and Event* 8 (3).

Pina-Cabral, João de. 2003. *O homen na família: Cinco ensaios de antropologia.* Lisbon: Impensa de Ciêcias Sociais.

Pinto, António Costa, and Nuno Severiano Teixeira. 1998. *Portugal e a unificação europeia.* Lisbon: Edições Cosmos.

Pinto, António Costa, ed. 1998. *Modern Portugal.* Palo Alto, Calif.: Society for the Promotion of Science and Scholarship.

Pires, Rui Pena. 1984. *Os retornados: Um estudo sociográfico.* Lisbon: Imprensa de Estudos Para o Desenvolvimento.

Povinelli, Elizabeth A. 2002. *The Cunning of Recognition: Indigenous Alterities and the Making of Australian Multiculturalism.* Durham, N.C.: Duke University Press.

———. 2006. *The Empire of Love: Toward a Theory of Intimacy, Genealogy, and Carnality.* Durham, N.C.: Duke University Press.

Programa de Informação para o Cidadão Europeu. 1997. "Igualdade de direitos e oportunidades entre mulheres e homens." Luxembourg: Serviço das Publicações Oficias das Comunidades Europeias.

Rancière, Jacques. 1995. *On the Shores of Politics.* Trans. Liz Heron. London: Verso.

———. 1999. *Disagreement: Politics and Philosophy.* Trans. Julie Rose. Minneapolis: University of Minnesota Press.

———. 2004. "Who Is the Subject of the Rights of Man?" *South Atlantic Quarterly,* no. 103:297–310.

———. 2006. *Hatred of Democracy.* Trans. Steve Corcoran. London: Verso.

Rich, Adrienne. 1986. *Blood, Bread, and Poetry.* New York: Norton Paperback.

Rocha-Trindade, Maria Beatriz. 1992. *Sociologia das migrações.* Lisbon: Universidade Aberta.

Rollins, Judith. 1985. *Between Women: Domestics and Their Employers.* Philadelphia: Temple University Press.

Romero, Mary. 1992. *Maid in the U.S.A.* New York: Routledge.

Roque, Ricardo. 2001. *Antropologia e império: Fonseca Cardoso e a expedição à Índia em 1895.* Lisbon: Imprensa de Ciências Socias.

Saint-Maurice, Ana de. 1996. *Identidades reconstuídas: Cabo-verdianos em Portugal*: Oeiras, Portugal: Centro de Investigação e Estudos de Sociologia.

Sacks, Karen. 1987. *Caring by the Hour: Women, Work, and Organizing at Duke Medical Center*. Chicago: University of Illinois Press.

Schegloff, Emanuel A. 1988. "Goffman and the Analysis of Conversation," In *Erving Goffman: Exploring the Interaction Order*, ed. P. Drew and T. Wootton, 9–135. Cambridge: Polity Press.

Schumann, William. 2005. "Producing Democracy: The Construction of Institutional Legitimacy in the Nation Assembly of Wales." PhD diss., University of Florida, Gainesville.

Scott, David. 1999. *Refashioning Futures: Criticism after Postcoloniality*. Princeton, N.J.: Princeton University Press.

———. 2004. *Conscripts of Modernity: The Tragedy of Colonial Enlightenment*. Durham, N.C.: Duke University Press.

Seshadri-Crooks, Kalpana. 2000. *Desiring Whiteness: A Lacanian Analysis of Race*. New York: Routledge.

Shore, Chris. 2000. *Building Europe: The Cultural Politics of European Integration*. New York: Routledge.

———. 2004. "Whither European Citizenship? Eros and Civilization Revisited." *European Journal of Social Theory* 7 (1): 27–44.

Silva, J. M. da. 1953. *O sistema português de política indígena*. Coimbra, Portugal: Coimbra Editora Lda.

Silverman, Maxim. 1992. *Deconstructing the Nation: Immigration, Racism, and Citizenship in Modern France*. New York: Routledge.

Silverstein, Michael. 2003. "Indexical Order and the Dialectics of Sociolinguistic Life." *Language and Communication* 23 (3–4): 194–229.

———. 2004. " 'Cultural' Concepts and the Language-Culture Nexus." *Current Anthropology* 45 (5): 621–52.

Silverstein, Paul. 2004. *Algeria in France: Transpolitics, Race, and Nation*. Bloomington: Indiana University Press.

Smith, Adam. 1982. *The Wealth of Nations*. New York: Penguin Classics.

SOS Racismo. 1998. *Colectânea de direito de estrangeiros: Inclui normas anti-discriminatórias*. Lisbon: SOS Racismo.

———. 2002. *A Imigração em Portugal: Os movimentos humanos e culturais em Portugal*. Lisbon: SOS Racismo.

Sousa, Nardi Abraão Dias de. 2003. *Imigração e cidadania local: Associativismo imigrante e políticas públicas de Portugal*. Praia, Cabo Verde: Instituto da Biblioteca Nacional e do Livro.

Sousa Santos, Boaventura. 1990. *O estado e a sociedade em Portugal (1974–1988)*. Porto: Edições Afrontamento.

Stoler, Ann Laura. 1995a. " 'Mixed-Blood' and the Cultural Politics of European Identity in Colonial Southeast Asia." In *The Decolonization of the Imagination: Culture, Knowledge and Power*, ed. Jans Nederveen Pieterse and Bhikhu Parekh, 128–48. London: Zed Books.

———. 1995b. *Race and the Education of Desire: Foucault's "History of Sexuality" and the Colonial Order of Things*. Durham, N.C.: Duke University Press.

———. 2002. *Carnal Knowledge and Imperial Power: Race and the Intimate in Colonial Rule*. Berkeley: University of California Press.

Stolke, Verena. 1995. "Europe: New Boundaries, New Rhetorics of Exclusion." *Current Anthropology* 36 (1): 1–24.

Tamagnini, Eusebio. 1934. "Os problemas da mestiçagem." Paper presented at the I Congresso Nacional de Anthropologia Colonial, Porto, Portugal.

Taylor, Charles. 1994. "The Politics of Recognition." In *Multiculturalism: Examining the Politics of Recognition*, ed. Amy Gutman, 25–73. Princeton, N.J.: Princeton University Press.

Teixeira, Nuno Severiano. 1998. "Between Africa and Europe." In *Modern Portugal*, ed. António Costa Pinto, 60–87. Palo Alto, Calif.: Society for the Promotion of Science and Scholarship.

Thomas, Deborah A. 2004. *Modern Blackness: Nationalism, Globalization, and the Politics of Culture in Jamaica*. Durham, N.C.: Duke University Press.

Thomaz, Omar Ribeiro. 2002. "Tigres do papel: Gilberto Freyre, Portugal e os países africanos de língua oficial portuguesa." In *Trânsitos colonias: Diálogos críticos luso-brasileiros*. Lisbon: Imprensa de Ciêcias Sociais.

Ticktin, Miriam. 2007. "Where Ethics and Politics Meet: The Violence of Humanitarianism in France." *American Ethnologist* 33 (1): 33–49.

Tinhorão, José Ramos. 1988. *Os negros em Portugal: Uma presença silenciosa*. Lisbon: Editorial Caminho.

Tomás, António. 2007. *O fazedor de utopias: Uma biografia de Amílcar Cabral*. Lisbon: Tinta da China.

Trouillot, Michel-Rolph. 1995. *Silencing the Past: Power and the Production of History*. Boston: Beacon.

Vane, Frances Ann. 1843. *A Journal of a Three Months' Tour in Portugal, Spain, Africa*. London: Mitchell and Company.

Vasconcelos, Luís Almeida. 2003. *Heroína e agência: Lisboa como território psicotrópico nos anos noventa*. Lisbon: Imprensa de Ciências Socias.

Verdery, Katherine. 1996. *What Was Socialism, What Comes Next?* Princeton, N.J.: Princeton University Press.

Vergès, Françoise. 1999. *Monsters and Revolutionaries: Colonial Family Romance and Métissage*. Durham, N.C.: Duke University Press.

Weiner, Antje. 1998. *European Citizenship Practice: Building Institutions of a Non-state*. Boulder, Colo.: Westview.

Williams, Brackette. 1989. "A Class Act: Anthropology and the Race to Nation across the Ethnic Terrain." *Annual Review of Anthropology*, no. 18:401–44.

———. 1991. *Stains on My Name, War in My Veins: Guyana and the Politics of Cultural Struggle*. Durham, N.C.: Duke University Press.

———. 2007. "Mitigated Forms." Paper presented at the University of Chicago, November 29.

Yankah, Kwesi. 1995. *Speaking for the Chief: Okyeame and the Politics of Akan Royal Oratory*. Indianapolis, Ind.: Indiana University Press.

Yurchak, Alexei. 2006. *Everything Was Forever, Until It Was No More: The Last Soviet Generation*. Princeton, N.J.: Princeton University Press.

Žižek, Slavoj. 1989. *The Sublime Object of Ideology*. London: Verso.

INDEX

Page numbers in italics refer to illustrations.

Catholicism, 132; charity and, 38

CATU. *See* Centro de Apoio de Trabalhador do Ultramar

CCB. *See* Centro Cultural de Belém

Centro Cultural de Belém, 4

Centro de Apoio de Trabalhador do Ultramar (Support Center for the Overseas Worker), 25, 147. *See also* Nucleo de Apoio aos Trabalhadores Migrantes Caboverdianos

Chaves, Miguel, 102

China, xvii, 54

Citizen-administrator, xi

Citizen-Migrant Relation, xiv–xvii, 14, 46, 58–59, 62, 126, 138, 143–44; antiracism and, 156; distance within, 16, 154, 156; income equality and, 142; within the neoliberal state, 9–10, 163–64; physiological traces of, 145; policing and, 120; research on, 11–12; sociality of, 12–13

Citizen-officials, 12

Citizens: Cape Verdeans as, ix–xi, 21; colonial subjects as, 149; EU citizens, 7; Portuguese citizens as middle class, 7–8; as social managers, 144

Citizenship, 109; antidemocratic core of, 154; colonial determination of, xi; consumer practice and, 9–10, 153; criminality and denial of, 103; defined, 9; EEC accession and, xiv; EU integration and, ix, xvi, 11, 112; European citizenship, 149, 152, 155; as exclusionary, 155–56; inhabitance of, xiv–xv, 149; limits on, 43–44; managerial/regulatory capacity of, 13–16, 144; mo-

dernity and, 112, 155, 163; Portuguese citizenship, 149; race and, 122; research on, 11–12; social engagement as component of, 155

Civility, xviii, 16, 21; bourgeois civility, 152; in domestic work relationships, 130–31

Civilizados, 31–32

Cleanliness: of Lisbon, 59; as rationale for treatment of peixeiras, 99; of seafood, 85

Colonialism, xii, 45, 117, 149; classification of African immigrants, 31; Lusotropicalism as justification for, 38

Colonial past, ix, xii; irrelevancy of, 130; references to, xiii, xvii–xviii, 35, 62, 78, 118, 120

Colonial studies, 155

Colonizer–colonized dichotomy, xiv

Comaroff, Jean, 103

Comaroff, John, 103

Compassion: in antiracism campaign, 38–39; in domestic labor relationships, 127; in liberalism, 164

Compliance: in domestic labor relationships, 127; in liberalism, 164

Comunidade dos Países de Língua Portuguesa (Community of Portuguese Language Countries), 48–49

Consent: as basis for citizenship, 13–14

Constitution of 1975, 44

Consumer practices, 153; citizenship and, 9–10, 155; EC membership and, 6–7, 17–20; fish purchases and, 112, 121; leisure consumption, 7, 18; modernization and, 7–8, 155; nonsubsistence consumption, 40;

Greece, 17

Guinea-Bissau, x, 2; Cape Verde and, 117; civil war, 47, 113; as colony of Portugal, ix; independence of, xii; labor recruitment and, 21; men, 113; men, as peixeiras' drivers, 66, 88, 90; peixeiras' interaction with emigrants from, 116–17; women, as janitors, 139–40

Hérman, 19

Hotel Ofir, 147–48

Housing projects, 87, 144

ILO. See International Labor Organization

Immigrants. See Migrants

Immigration and nationality laws, 43–46; amnesty periods, 45

Inclusion. See Belonging

India, 37; Indians in Portugal, 5, 54

Indígenas (indigenous subjects), ix, xi; Cabo-indígenas, xi, 148; "indigenous continental subjects," 148; outlawing of legal status as, 149

Instituto do Trabalho, Previdência e Acção Social (Institute for Labor, Support, and Social Action), 22–23, 147–49. See also Nucleo de Apoio aos Trabalhadores Migrantes Caboverdianos

International Labor Organization, 40

Intimacy, 59; in business negotiations, 68, 71–72; in domestic work relationships, 131; inter-racial, 168n1; Lusotropicalism and, 1, 35, 37–41, 83; racial-cultural, 150; in supervisor/custodian relationships, 142

ITPAS. See Instituto do Trabalho, Previdência e Acção Social

Janitors, 26, 30, 56; peixeiras as, 125, 128–29, 135, 137–39

Katchupa, 72–74

Kriolu, 123; in Cape Verdean/Guinean relations, 66, 116–17, 140; kunhadu, 116–17; patrisiu, 116–17; Portuguese vs., in custodial worker interactions, 140; Portuguese vs., in peixeira/African interactions, 115–18; Portuguese vs., in peixeira/vendor negotiations, 71, 75. See also Language

Labor contracts, 55, 67, 88, 126, 151, 156; termination of, 141

Labor recruitment: bureaucratic management of, 22–23; family-reunification policies, 23–24; islands of origin, 21; reasons for, 20. See also Work

Language: among custodial workers, 135–36; in domestic labor relationships, 127, 131–32; forms of address, 77, 79, 140; honorifics, 110; nasal accents, as elite, 77–78; nasal accents, as form of mockery, 78, 120; in peixeira/African interactions, 115–18; in peixeira/middle-class women interactions, 110–11; in peixeira/vendor negotiations, 71, 75. See also Kriolu

Laws: abortion referendum of 2007, 159; amnesty, for undocumented migrants, 45; anti-clandestine vending law (Decreto-lei 122), 5; antidiscrimination law (Article 3, Number 1, Law 134/99), 50; citizenship law of 1975, 44; Decreto-lei 305A/1975, 44–45; Decreto-lei

4/2001, 133–34; immigration and nationality laws, 43–46, 156; indigenous labor codes, 149; legal definition of citizen-migrant relation, 143; Lei 37/81, 44–45; non-national labor laws, 126, 144; US immigration law, xi; vending laws, 28

Leftists, 31–32, 63

Leisure, 60; eco-friendly leisure, 85; leisure consumption, 7, 18; subsistence vs., 29, 96, 134

Likeness, ix, 20

Lip: flipping of, 119–20

Lisbon, xii, 28; Alentejo region vs., 19; Bairro Alto neighborhood, 49–50; Baixa, 112; as City of European Culture, 4, 96; Departamento de Higiene Urbana, 59–60; domestic migration to, 22; EEC accession and, 4–5; historic descriptions of, 167n1; multicultural events, 46; port facility, 6; racialized discourse of, 51–52; Rossio, 113; urban development of, 49, 59, 62, 96. *See also* Docapesca de Lisboa; Train stations stops

Loures, 6, 84

Lusofonia, 48–49, 56, 161

Lusophone studies, 150

Lusotropicalism, 46, 56, 68, 75, 161; adoption by Salazar regime, 38–39; challenges to, xi; defined, 1; Lusofonia vs., 48; miscegenation as component of, 38, 58–59; political correctness vs., 88–89; same-sex labor arrangements' effect on, 57; sexism and, 82. *See also* Freyre, Gilberto

Macau, 54

Madeira, x, 37

MAN. *See* Movimento de Acçao Nacional

Mandingas, 148–49, 169n1 (chap. 5)

Margarido, Alfredo, 48

Market: EEC entry and, 2, 41–42; EU integration and, 6; market intervention, 97; peixeiras' niche in, 126; post-coup changes in, 41; EFTA and, 22

MARL. *See* Mercado Abastecedor da Região de Lisboa

Marx, Karl, 13

Masters and Slaves (Casa Grande e Senzala), 37, 168n1

Media: consumer behavior reports, 17; economy of Portugal in, 42; immigrant lives in, 105; Monteiro death in, 51; reporting on racism, 50–52, 105; representations of race, xvii, 53; representations of women, 57, 81; stereotypes of Cape Verdeans, 26

Mercado Abastecedor da Região de Lisboa (Market Provider for the Region of Lisbon), 84, 86, 89; effect on subsistence entrepreneurs, 90

Mestiçagem. *See* Miscegenation

Mestiço/a, 20, 31; disappearance of mestiça, 59, 159; mestiça as central to Lusotropicalism, 58. *See also* Mulato/a

Middle class, 7–8, 93; middle classness as means for defining citizenship, 155; middle-class white women, 109–12, 122; rise of, 18

Migrancy, 138

Migrants, x, 7, 153; amnesty for non-

Migrants (*cont.*)
documented migrants, 45; criminalization of, 45, 120; migrant crisis in Europe, xiii–xiv, 5, 11; NA monitoring of, 22–23; recent migrants to Portugal, xvii; tradition and, 19–20; working poor and, 7. *See also* Citizen–migrant relation; Lusofonia

Ministério de Ultramar (Overseas Ministry), 22–23

Ministry of Agriculture and Fisheries, 28, 84–85, 96

Minoria étnica, 52–53

Miscegenation (mestiçagem), 57; in Brazil, 58; Freyre on, 37; hybridity of Portuguese population and, 167–168n1; Lusofonia's avoidance of, 48; rhetoric of, 7

Modernity/modernization, 162; citizenship and, 112, 155, 163; consumer practices and, 7, 112, 155; EU and, xvi–xviii, 17; racism as sign of, 19–20; women and, 7, 57

Monteiro, Alcino, 50–51, 151

Moors, 167n1

Movimento de Acçao Nacional (Movement for National Action), 49. *See also* Skinheads

Mozambique, 2, 47, 54; as colony of Portugal, ix, 37; labor recruitment and, 21; Mozambican immigrant/peixeira interaction, 117–18; reference to, as failed sign of familiarity, 78–79

Mulato/a, 31, 83; concerns of artists, 33–35; disappearance of, 36. *See also* Mestiço/a

Multiculturalism, 8, 32–33, 35, 46–55,

151; campaign, in Lisbon, 52. *See also* Antiracism

NA. *See* Nucleo de Apoio aos Trabalhadores Migrantes Caboverdianos

Nataf, Daniel, 41

National Assembly, 168n2

Nationalism, xiv

Negro/a, 20, 52; history of usage, 53

Neoliberal state: interplay of market intervention and crime, 97; management of citizenship, 9–10, 163–64

"Neves mil em abril," 52

Normalcy, xvii, 12; appearance of, 138, 150; enactment of, xviii

Nucleo de Apoio aos Trabalhadores Migrantes Caboverdianos (Nucleus of Support for the Cape Verdean Migrant Worker), 22–23. *See also* Centro de Apoio de Trabalhador do Ultramar

Obama, Barack, xvii

Ondjaki, 48

Ong, Aihwa, 12, 165n3

O público, 58; *Público*, 85

Order: citizen–migrant relation as, 62; in colonial settings, 99; as rationale for treatment of peixeiras, 99

Ovambo, 2

PAIGC. *See* Partido Africano da Independência da Guiné e Cabo Verde

Paisana (state police), 97, 105

Países Africanos de Língua Oficial Portuguesa (African Countries Whose Official Language is Portuguese), 19; musicians, 46

Pakistan, 54

Race: categories, 31–32; citizenship and, 122; concerns of mulato artists, 33–35; disappearance of mestiça, 59, 159; emergence of binarism, 36, 59, 63; ethnographic analysis of, 165n2; gender and, 159–60; mestiço/a, 20, 31; mestiça as central to Lusotropicalism, 58; mulato/a, 31, 36, 83; in peixeira/customer interactions, 95, 106; in peixeira/vendor interactions, 74, 79; political discussion of, xviii, 51; preto, 51–53; purity of, 37; race-racism distinction, 54, 84, 157–62; terminology, 53. *See also* Blackness; Whiteness

Racialization: advertising and, 18; of African emigrants to Portugal, 20, 31; anthropological justification for, 37; artistic expression and, 32–36; of Cape Verdean emigrants to Portugal, 21; criminality and, 103; diasporic/racial consciousness among African immigrants, 115, 118, 144; discourse of, 51–52; multiracialism, 36, 58; racial knowledge, 144; racial profiling, 112, 122, 142; of righteousness, 99; self-identification, 165n2. *See also* Africanity; Blackness; Whiteness

Racism, xi, 82, 108, 113, 154–55, 163, 166n5; acknowledgement of, 53; attributed to individuals rather than society, 39–40; historical understanding of, 168n1; Lusotropicalism and, 1, 38–39; media coverage, 50–51; modernization and, 7–8, 19–20; peixeira/vendor negotiation and, 75, 78–79; policing of peixeira market

and, 5, 99; race-racism distinction, 54, 84, 157–62; sexism and, 81; speech acts of, 99, 102. *See also* Racialization

Radiodifusão Portuguesa, 46

Rancière, Jacques, 13–14, 152

RDP Africa, 46–48

Research methods, 26–27, 29–30, 61–62, 93

Residency, 126; domestic employer's control of, 134; establishment of legal residency, 27, 44, 133; nondocumented, criminalization of, 45; visas, 125

Respect, 16, 78, 127; for Africanity, 63

Retornados, 4, 41

Righteousness: peixeiras' casting of fish purchase as, 106; police clarification of righteous practice, 95; racialization of, 99; righteous practice defined, 103

Rights, xv, 39; of Cape Verdeans as citizens, ix, xi; citizenship's relation to, 15; consent to norms as basis of, 13–14; laws affecting rights of citizens and noncitizens, 44; political rights equated with whiteness, 114

Right-wing political activity: xiv, 49

Roma, 5, 61, 87

Salazar, António de Oliveira, xi, 3

Salazar–Caetano dictatorship, xii, 3, 41; adoption of Lusotropicalism, 38–39, 168n1; nonregulation of street fish vending, 126; racialization efforts, 37

Santiago, 47, 125–26, 139, 169n3 (chap. 3); Badius as synonym for Santiaguense, 120; inhabitants and forced labor, 24–25; reference to as sign of familiarity, 72

Santo Antão, 21, 47, 138, 148

São Nicolau, 21, 47

São Tomé e Príncipe, 2, 47; Cape Verdeans workers in, xi, 21, 24, 148; as colony of Portugal, ix; emigrants to Portugal/peixeira interactions, 117–18

São Vicente, 21, 47

Schegloff, Emmanuel, 29

Schengen states, 18

Scott, David, 155

Sephardic Jews, 167n1

Sétima Coluna (Seventh Hill Project), 96

Setúbal, 25

Sex and sexuality, 38, 58, 154; black women as desexualized, 56–57; sexual overtures in peixeira/vendor interactions, 83–84

Sexism: acceptability of, 82; sexual harassment, 81

Shanty communities, 67, 124, 135, 139; bulldozing of, 86–87; Casal Ventoso, 102; Guinean, 93; nation-based, 47, 112, 144

Shellfish, 85, 87.

Silva, Denise Ferreira da: "Facts of Blackness," 58

Skinheads, xviii, 49–50; graffiti by, 2, 5

Slavery, 20

Sociality: "African," 87; citizen-migrant relation, 12–13; democracy in Portugal and, xiii; *djunta mon*, 125, 132; fish vending as source of, 125–26; of food purchases, 60

Social security, 125

SOS Racismo, 45, 49–50, 168n2

South Africa: as destination for Portuguese emigrants, x, 4; Mozambican workers in, 21

Spain, xiv, 2, 17

State: as space between law and action, 152

State Secretary for Youth, 50

State Secretary of Fisheries, 85

Stoler, Ann Laura, 15, 152, 155

Street sweepers. *See* Garbage sweepers

Subsistence, 90; of agrarian work force, 42; defense of, 109; leisure vs., 29, 96, 134; as "play" work, 60; righteousness of, 106

Tagus River, 1, 3, 6, 28, 65

Tamagnini, Eusebio, 37

Ticktin, Miriam, 11

Tolerance, 166n5; discourse of, 53

Train stations/stops: as sites for fish sales by Cape Verdean peixeiras, 2, 5, 28, 93. *See also individual stations*

Tropicalism. *See* Lusotropicalism

"Uma Pátria, Dois Países," 117

United States of America, xvii; immigration law, xi; Portuguese worker visas, 18–19

Urban hygiene. *See* Public health

Urban poor, 25, 60, 62

Urban space: regulation of activities in, 59, 139, 151; as site of leisure, 96

Vagrancy, 23; anti-vagrancy policies, 24

Vale de Almeida, Miguel, 169n2 (chap. 3)

Vane, Frances Anne, Marchioness of

teraction, 153; competition with immigrants, 7; concerns about EEC accession, 2, 43; men, 88; mothers, 140–41; right to subsistence, 106; settlement program, 38; white Portuguese women, 107–9, 128

Youth: African youth in Portugal, 48; participation in Lisbon projects, 49

Zona ribeirinha, 3–4

Kesha Fikes

is an anthropologist and independent scholar. She has taught in the departments of anthropology at the University of Florida and the University of Chicago.

Library of Congress Cataloging-in-Publication Data
Fikes, Kesha, 1969–
Managing African Portugal : the citizen-migrant distinction / Kesha Fikes.
p. cm.
Includes bibliographical references and index.
ISBN 978-0-8223-4498-8 (cloth : alk. paper)
ISBN 978-0-8223-4512-1 (pbk. : alk. paper)
1. Cape Verdeans—Portugal—Social conditions.
2. Immigrants—Government policy—Portugal.
3. Portugal—Race relations.
4. Citizenship—Portugal.
I. Title.
DP534.C36F55 2009
305.896'6580469—dc22
2009022401